New Frontiers in Regional Science: Asian Perspectives

Volume 26

New Frontiers in Regional Science: Asian Perspectives

This series is a constellation of works by scholars in the field of regional science and in related disciplines specifically focusing on dynamism in Asia.

Asia is the most dynamic part of the world. Japan, Korea, Taiwan, and Singapore experienced rapid and miracle economic growth in the 1970s. Malaysia, Indonesia, and Thailand followed in the 1980s. China, India, and Vietnam are now rising countries in Asia and are even leading the world economy. Due to their rapid economic development and growth, Asian countries continue to face a variety of urgent issues including regional and institutional unbalanced growth, environmental problems, poverty amidst prosperity, an ageing society, the collapse of the bubble economy, and deflation, among others.

Asian countries are diversified as they have their own cultural, historical, and geographical as well as political conditions. Due to this fact, scholars specializing in regional science as an inter- and multi-discipline have taken leading roles in providing mitigating policy proposals based on robust interdisciplinary analysis of multifaceted regional issues and subjects in Asia. This series not only will present unique research results from Asia that are unfamiliar in other parts of the world because of language barriers, but also will publish advanced research results from those regions that have focused on regional and urban issues in Asia from different perspectives.

The series aims to expand the frontiers of regional science through diffusion of intrinsically developed and advanced modern regional science methodologies in Asia and other areas of the world. Readers will be inspired to realize that regional and urban issues in the world are so vast that their established methodologies still have space for development and refinement, and to understand the importance of the interdisciplinary and multidisciplinary approach that is inherent in regional science for analyzing and resolving urgent regional and urban issues in Asia.

Topics under consideration in this series include the theory of social cost and benefit analysis and criteria of public investments, socio-economic vulnerability against disasters, food security and policy, agro-food systems in China, industrial clustering in Asia, comprehensive management of water environment and resources in a river basin, the international trade bloc and food security, migration and labor market in Asia, land policy and local property tax, Information and Communication Technology planning, consumer "shop-around" movements, and regeneration of downtowns, among others.

More information about this series at http://www.springer.com/series/13039

Binh Tran-Nam • Makoto Tawada
Masayuki Okawa

Editors

Recent Developments in Normative Trade Theory and Welfare Economics

 Springer

Editors
Binh Tran-Nam
School of Taxation and Business Law
The University of New South Wales
Sydney
Kensington, NSW, Australia

School of Business and Management
RMIT University Vietnam
Ho Chi Minh City, Vietnam

Masayuki Okawa
Faculty of Economics
Ritsumeikan University
Kusatsu, Shiga, Japan

Makoto Tawada
Faculty of Economics
Aichi Gakuin University
Nagoya, Aichi, Japan

ISSN 2199-5974   ISSN 2199-5982   (electronic)
New Frontiers in Regional Science: Asian Perspectives
ISBN 978-981-10-8614-4   ISBN 978-981-10-8615-1   (eBook)
https://doi.org/10.1007/978-981-10-8615-1

Library of Congress Control Number: 2018935908

Printed on acid-free paper

This Springer imprint is published by the registered company Springer Nature Singapore Pte Ltd.
The registered company address is: 152 Beach Road, #21-01/04 Gateway East, Singapore 189721, Singapore

Foreword: Emeritus Professor Murray Chilvers Kemp AO

This book, a *festschrift* containing essays by Emeritus Professor Murray Kemp's former students and colleagues, as well as several papers by Murray himself and with a former student, is dedicated to him in celebration of his 90th birthday. It follows the celebration of his 65th, 70th and 80th birthdays and the books associated with those occasions. Apart from the scholarship of the *festschrift*, it is a testimony of the affection, admiration and regard for Murray by his colleagues and former students.

Prof. Murray is a direct descendant of Captain Anthony Fenn Kemp, a colorful and forceful leader after the First Fleet arrived at the new British colony in Australia. Born in Melbourne in 1926, the son of a bank manager, his last few years at school were at Wesley College. He was dux of the school and he commenced his studies at the University of Melbourne in 1944. He had contemplated doing Medicine or Law but lacked the necessary prerequisite subjects. And so, he decided to do Commerce and Economics. No doubt a loss to those disciplines but what a tremendous gain to Economics! He was also a keen sportsman and played tennis, cricket and golf. Graduating B.Com., B.A. (1st class Honours) in 1947 and an MA in 1949, he had intended to work in the Commonwealth Treasury in Canberra. But the stern intervention of Ben Higgins, who was then Professor at Melbourne University, led him to undertake graduate studies at Johns Hopkins instead, completing his Ph.D. in 1955 under the supervision of Evsey Domar. In the meantime, from 1951 to 1959, he taught at McGill and MIT, with a short stint as Nuffield Fellow in Cambridge, England. Since taking up his appointment as Professor of Economics in 1961, he has spent most of his academic career at the University of New South Wales, where he is now Emeritus Professor.

Murray's international reputation as an outstanding and wide-ranging economic theorist is widely recognised – having moved from Keynesian to post-Keynesian economics and finally to an attachment to neo-classical economics. His list of publications is prodigious – some 50 books and close to 300 papers in leading journals. It has been said that no Australian economist has been more cited since 1980. He could not be accused of being prolix in his writings. He wrote incisively, relying on mathematics to tell his story. The large number of students, many having travelled from other countries to work with him, testify to his dedication and an inspiration as a supervisor. Blessed with a friendly and warm disposition and a smile permanently etched on his face, he was accessible to all.

His international reputation is also reflected in the invitations to spend time in many universities including MIT, LSE, University of Minnesota, University of Southampton, University of Stockholm, University of California at Berkeley, University Paris-Dauphine, University of Mannheim, University of Western Ontario, Hebrew University of Jerusalem, Columbia University, Kobe University, University of Kiel, University of Munich, Nagoya City University, Copenhagen Business School, Chukyo University, Australian Graduate School of Management, Ritsumeikan University, Nanyang Technological University, Macquarie University and City University of Hong Kong.

His contributions have been recognised by various prestigious appointments and awards – Fellow of the Econometric Society in 1971, Member of Council of Econometric Society from 1995 to1998, Distinguished Fellow of the Economic Society of Australia in 1989, President, International Economics and Finance Society from 1997 to 1998, award of the Alexander von Humboldt Prize in 1987, and honorary doctorates conferred on him by many universities including the Universities of Melbourne, New South Wales, Kiel, Kobe and Laval.

He was made Officer in the Order of Australia in 2014 for 'distinguished service to education as an economic theorist and academic, to international trade, through contributions to leading professional publications, and as a mentor'.

I had the good fortune to be Murray's tutor when he took up residence at Queen's College in 1945, his second year at the University of Melbourne. The *General Theory* was still novel in the curriculum of the University and a source of lively academic and public debate. As was Pigou's *Welfare Economics*, Murray stood out in the tutorial group at Queen's and I had no doubt about his potential. For me, as a teacher, one of the more satisfying rewards has been to have students who show the potential to outclass the teacher in academic ability and achievement. Murray was one such student who within a few years after graduating realised this potential. I confess that much of his writings are beyond my reach but our relationship is sustained by a longstanding warm friendship. It has been a source of great pleasure for me to have been allowed to share from time to time in his family setting, with his late wife Therese, and his children Fenn and Nadia.

As Murray approaches 92, he continues to publish. We look forward to the next *festschrift* when he turns 95.

Emeritus Professor (Monash   Joe Isaac
University), Melbourne, Australia

Contents

Contributors

Geoffrey Fishburn Independent Researcher, Sydney, Australia

Masayuki Hayashibara Faculty of Economics, Otemon Gakuin University, Ibaraki, Japan

Tatsuya Iguchi Faculty of Economics, Ritsumeikan University, Kusatsu, Japan

Murray C. Kemp School of Economics, UNSW Sydney, Sydney, NSW, Australia

Kenji Kondoh School of Economics, Chukyo University, Nagoya, Japan

Cuong Le-Van IPAG Business School, Paris School of Economics and Centre National de la Recherche Scientifique, Paris, France

Thi-Do-Hanh Nguyen Center d'Economie de la Sorbonne, University of Paris I Panthon-Sorbonne, Paris, France

Ryoichi Nomura Faculty of Economics, Ritsumeikan University, Kusatsu, Japan

Takeshi Ogawa Faculty of Economics, Senshu University, Kawasaki-shi, Kanagawa-ken, Japan

Takao Ohkawa Faculty of Economics, Ritsumeikan University, Kusatsu, Japan

Makoto Okamura Faculty of Economics, Gakushuin University, Tokyo, Japan

Masayuki Okawa Faculty of Economics, Ritsumeikan University, Kusatsu, Japan

Ngoc-Sang Pham Montpellier Business School, Montpellier Research in Management, Montpellier, France

Ling Qi China Institute for Actuarial Science, Central University of Finance and Economics, Beijing, China

Makoto Tawada Faculty of Economics, Aichi Gakuin University, Nagoya, Japan

Binh Tran-Nam School of Taxation and Business Law, The University of New South Wales Sydney, Kensington, NSW, Australia

School of Business and Management, RMIT University Vietnam, Ho Chi Minh City, Vietnam

Ngo Van Long Department of Economics, McGill University, Montreal, Quebec, Canada

Henry Wan, Jr. Department of Economics, Cornell University, Ithaca, NY, USA

Shigemi Yabuuchi Aichi University, Nagoya, Aichi, Japan

Acronyms and Abbreviations

CUs	Customs Unions
EU	European Union
FDI	Foreign Direct Investment
FOCs	First-Order Conditions
FTA	Free Trade Agreement
GATT	General Agreement on Tariffs and Trade
GATS	General Agreement on Trade in Services
GE	General Equilibrium
GNP	Gross National Product
HOS	Heckscher–Ohlin–Samuelson
OLGs	Overlapping Generations
PPF	Production Possibility Frontier
RTA	Regional Trade Agreement
SOCs	Second-Order Conditions
UNCTAD	United Nations Conference on Trade and Development
UNESCO	United Nations Educational, Scientific and Cultural Organization
WADM	Walras–Arrow–Debreu or McKenzie

List of Figures

List of Tables

Chapter 1
Introduction

Binh Tran-Nam, Makoto Tawada, and Masayuki Okawa

Abstract This introductory chapter explains the origin of this edited volume. Many of the chapters in this book are derived from a conference in honour of Professor Murray Kemp's 90th birthday held at University of New South Wales Sydney in August 2016. In addition, this chapter also describes the nature and structure of the book, and provides a brief overview of each of the remaining chapters. Finally, there is an appendix that lists Kemp's publications from 2001 to 2018.

Keywords Trade theory · Economic theory · Murray Kemp

This edited volume has its origin in a conference entitled "Recent Developments in Trade and Economic Theory". Held at the Kensington Campus of the University of New South Wales (UNSW) Sydney on 19 August 2016, this conference brought together a small group of economic theorists from Australia, Japan and the USA to celebrate the 90th birthday of Professor Emeritus Murray C. Kemp. Conference participants and presenters included Professor Emeritus Murray C. Kemp AO (UNSW Sydney), Professor Emeritus Joseph Isaac AO (Kemp's former teacher at the University of Melbourne), Professor Emeritus Geoff Harcourt AO (Kemp's fellow student at Wesley College and the University of Melbourne), Professor Henry Wan Jr. (Kemp's sit-in student at MIT and

B. Tran-Nam (✉)
School of Taxation and Business Law, The University of New South Wales Sydney, Kensington, NSW 2052, Australia

School of Business and Management, RMIT University Vietnam, Ho Chi Minh City, Vietnam
e-mail: b.tran-nam@unsw.edu.au; binh.trannam@rmit.edu.vn

M. Tawada
Faculty of Economics, Aichi Gakuin University, Nagoya, Aichi, Japan
e-mail: mtawada2@dpc.agu.ac.jp

M. Okawa
Faculty of Economics, Ritsumeikan University, Kusatsu, Japan
e-mail: mokawa@ec.ritsumei.ac.jp

colleague at the UNSW), Professor Martin Richardson (Australian National University), Professor Daniel Leonard (Flinders University), Professor John Lodewijks (SP Jain School of Global Management) and many of his former PhD students, including Professors Hiroshi Ohta, Hideo Suzuki, Makoto Tawada, Binh Tran-Nam, Masayuki Okawa and Partha Gangopadhyay. The event was organized by the School of Taxation and Business Law of the UNSW Sydney and jointly sponsored by the Research School of Economics at ANU and the School of Taxation and Business Law.

Murray Kemp is certainly one of the world's outstanding and prolific economic theorists. In a career that spans almost seven decades, he has made fundamental contributions to different fields of economics which include exhaustible resources, welfare economics and international trade. He is perhaps best known for his path-breaking trade textbook (1964, 1969)[1] and pioneering work in the normative theory of international trade. Focusing on international trade and welfare economics, this volume pays tribute to Murray's longevity and importance as an economic theorist. For a more complete account of his achievements as a scholar, discipliner builder and teacher, the interested reader is referred to Tran-Nam (2008).

The present volume is edited by three of Murray Kemp's former PhD graduates. It belongs to a series of edited volumes dedicated to him, including *Trade, welfare, and economic policies: Essays in honor of Murray C. Kemp* (edited by Horst Herberg and Ngo Van Long on the occasion of his 65th birthday, published by the University of Michigan Press), *Economic theory and international trade: Essays in honour of Murray C. Kemp* (edited by Alan Woodland on the occasion of his 70th birthday; published by Edward Elgar) and *Globalization and emerging issues in trade theory and policy* (edited by Binh Tran-Nam, Ngo Van Long and Makoto Tawada on the occasion of his 80th birthday; published by Emerald). In particular, Woodland (2002, pp. xiv−xvii) offered a list of Murray Kemp's publications from 1992 to 2000. For completeness, a list of his publications from 2001 to date is provided as an appendix to this introduction.

The chapters of this edited book are derived from selected papers presented at the conference and invited papers authored by Murray Kemp's co-authors and colleagues around the world. They represent some of the most recent findings in the field of welfare economic and international trade, particularly normative trade theory. Further, virtually all chapters are related to Murray Kemp's research interest, as evident in their list of references.

Consistent with the book's positivistic research framework, the chapters basically utilize mathematical methods in their analyses. Although these chapters are all motivated by real-world problems, they are abstract studies in the sense that there is no analysis of empirical data. Moreover, despite the common research framework and method, the chapters vary considerably in terms of topics under study, degree of generality, methods of proof and level of detail of analysis.

---

[1]Samuelson (1993, p. vii) suggested that Kemp's textbook has provided international trade with secure foundations, clear definitions and distinct boundaries.

The generally diverse chapters are grouped into five parts. Except Part V, each part consists of three chapters. Part I, comprising Chaps. 2, 3 and 4, focuses on the gains from trade under what may be termed as non-standard assumptions. Chapters 5, 6 and 7 constitute Part II of the book, which examines welfare and trade theory under the Gossenian assumption that consumption itself takes time. Part III, containing Chaps. 8, 9 and 10, deals with selected trade policy issues which are both current and relevant. In Part IV of the book, Chaps. 11, 12 and 13 consider the important but often neglected issue of income transfer policy. Finally, Part V, consisting solely of Chap. 14, presents a theoretical study of positive trade theory.

It is well known that some deviations from standard assumptions of the Walras–Arrow–Debreu–McKenzie (WADM) economy may render cherished theorems on the potential gainfulness of free trade invalid. Chapters 2, 3 and 4 seek to examine normative trade theory in the presence of overlapping generations (OLSs), externalities and international oligopoly, respectively. In Chap. 2, Kemp and Fishburn commence by stating the three core normative trade propositions, namely, potential gainfulness of trade for (i) any country, (ii) a customs union (CU)[2] and (iii) a free trade association. Extending the finite WADM model to an overlapping generations (OLGs) economy of mortal individuals, the authors demonstrate that, in the absence of intergenerational bequests, the three core propositions remain valid. Sadly, in the presence of unregulated bequests from parents and parents-in-law, none of these propositions survive. However, if the government of each trading country requires its parents and parents-in-law to maintain under free trade their autarkic vectors of bequests, then the three core propositions remain intact, although inefficiency will be found under free trade.

In Chap. 3, Wan Jr. conducts a novel re-examination of Graham's paradox. The paradox asserts that, under the assumption of Marshallian production externalities, trade gains can become negative. Starting with the Helpman and Krugman (1985) model, he shows that the key of Graham's paradox rests on the relative sizes of labour endowment of countries under study. Using the parametric map approach for global analysis, he demonstrates that externality causes multiple equilibria and that there always exists another more intuitive alternative equilibrium, with both countries enjoying equal gain. Graham's demonstration against free trade relies on the counter-intuitive alternative, and the tariff he promoted is dominated by a simple interstate bargaining. Wan's chapter appears to be thus another milestone of his many contributions to normative trade theory commencing with his famous joint paper with Murray Kemp in 1972 (see Kemp and Wan Jr. 1972).

Chapter 4 considers the welfare effects of gradual trade liberalization accompanied by coordinated sales tax reform in the presence of international oligopoly. Authors Okawa and Iguchi argue that welfare implications of trade liberalization based on static analyses could be misleading. They set up a simple partial equilibrium model in which three groups of oligopoly firms, namely, domestic firms,

---

[2]It is not difficult to see (ii) or (iii) implies (i). When a CU or free trade association approaches the whole world, we obtain (i).

foreign exporting firms and fully foreign-owned subsidiary firms, face linear domestic demands. Using the game theoretic approach, two types of sales tax reform are studied: (i) welfare-maximizing and (ii) revenue-neutral. Under scenario (i), depending on the initial conditions, complete liberalization (tariff = zero) may or may not raise the initial level of welfare. Under scenario (ii) and the assumption of symmetrical oligopoly, many welfare outcomes are possible. In particular, there are phases in which the reduction of import tariff raises both welfare and government revenue, but the government must raise the sales tax by a greater amount than that necessary for welfare maximization, as the import tariff approaches zero.

Part II contains a set of three theoretical papers that study the effects on the economy of the Gossenian assumption that consumption is itself time consuming. This often neglected topic has been a great research interest of Murray Kemp in recent years. He demonstrates in Chap. 5 that, in the context of a WADM economy, all key propositions in normative trade theory remain valid in the presence of a Gossenian time constraint. It is argued that the admission of Gossenian time constraints has almost no bearing on the existence of free-trade equilibrium or on the gainfulness of free trade; however, it does help determine the extent of the trade gains. In his analysis, Kemp pays careful attention to the possibility that members of each household pool their time in joint consumption within their household and with members of other households.

In Chap. 6, Tran-Nam incorporates a Gossenian–Beckerian consumption time constraint into a two-by-two model with representative agents. In this simple economy, he introduces the generalized transformation curve which captures information about the resource endowment and production and consumption technologies. In the case of an open economy, the pattern of trade continues to be dictated by the principle of comparative advantage. However, unlike the standard trade model, an increase in the relative price of a good may not necessarily lead to an increase in the supply of that good. Further, while conventional exchange and specialization gains vanish, there are positive gains from time reallocation (away from production toward consumption) and specialization associated with this time reallocation.

In Chap. 7, Le-Van et al. incorporates a Gossenian consumption time constraint into a two-factor, many-good model with heterogeneous households. Unlike Chap. 6 which derives the autarkic equilibrium as a solution to the central planner's problem, this chapter demonstrates the existence of an autarkic equilibrium as a solution to the decentralized Walrasian problem. To this end, the dividend approach proposed by Le-Van and Nguyen (2007) is utilized. Various sufficient conditions for uniqueness of the equilibrium are then explored. An example with specific functional forms is provided to illustrate the working of the model, including some comparative static results. It is further argued that the closed-economy results carry over to the open economy in a straightforward manner.

Moving on, Part III of the book contains three chapters on selected topical trade policy issues, namely, (i) tourism, (un)employment and environment, (ii) international migration via midstream countries and (iii) trade policy decision-making. In Chap. 8, Yabuuchi constructs a small open economy model with the agricultural sector (in the rural area), manufacturing sector (in the urban area) and tourism sector (in the rural area). The tourism sector generates harmful effects on the rural sector's environment so that a pollution tax is imposed on tourism and a subsidy is provided to agriculture. The author then shows that tourism promotion has complex effects on pollution, unemployment, output and welfare. These effects depend crucially on the relationship between the model parameters, particularly the tax rate, the subsidy rate, elasticity of the negative externality of the tourism sector on the agricultural sector and elasticity of factor substitution in the agricultural sectors. However, it is apparent that tourism promotion, accompanied by an agricultural subsidy, is likely to reduce unemployment, raise agriculture output and improve welfare. This has an important implication for policymakers in labour-surplus, developing countries that rely heavily on tourism.

In Chap. 9, Kondoh studies the recent trends of illegal migrants in Europe. In his model, illegal migrants (from country S) initially cross the border of gateway countries (called countries I and G), which are part of a large economic bloc, with the intention of moving within the bloc to settle in more developed countries (called country D). Country G is a purely transit country as its wage rate is lower than both of countries I and D. There are two available options for controlling illegal migrants by country D: (i) internal enforcement (costs financed by penalties levied on firms hiring illegal workers) and (ii) border restriction by countries I and G (which requires cooperation and public expenditure). Kondoh's analysis reveals that, supposing countries D and I cooperate, encouraging border control by country I is not a sustainable policy. However, under reasonable conditions, to enhance the wage rate of domestic workers and national welfare, country D should introduce border control to restrict labour inflow from the transit country G. To satisfy revenue neutrality condition, this policy should be partially substituted for the previous internal enforcement policy.

In Chap. 10, Hayashibara et al. consider a trading economy in which there are home and foreign firms. Trade policy is implemented by two departments: the subsidy department (which subsidizes the home firm) and the tariff department (which imposes a tariff on the foreign firm). The subsidy department is interested in producer surplus maximization while the subsidy department in tariff revenue maximization, i.e. both of them are self-interested. The authors then formulate a three-stage game. In the first stage, each department independently adopts welfare maximization or self-interest maximization as its surface objective. In the second stage, each department independently sets its subsidy/tariff level in view of its surface objective. In the third stage, the home and foreign firms compete in the home market in a Cournot fashion. Solving this three-stage game by backward induction, the authors show that when the cost difference between home and foreign firms is at the intermediate level, the subsidy department does not disguise itself as a benevolent policymaker, whereas the tariff department may do so. In addition, the welfare level in the partial disguise case is lower than that in the no disguise case.

Part IV of the book is primarily concerned with transfer policy from both domestic and international perspectives. This is undoubtedly an important but often neglected topic in economic theory. To prepare for the discussions that follow, Kemp and Fishburn in Chap. 11 explore the concept of self in economic theory, particularly in trade theory. They argue that the concept of self has evolved over time and attempt to trace out one line of evolution of the concept starting with Adam Smith. In their historical analysis, the authors sketch out the contributions of Walras, Pareto, Arrow, Debreu and Gossen in extending and refining Adam Smith's concept of self. In particular, the authors show how, with the application of the most extended concept to date of the self, the three core propositions in normative trade theory must now be abandoned.

In Chap. 12, Tawada and Qi investigate the welfare effects of an income transfer from urban manufacturing workers to rural agricultural workers in a Harris–Todaro, small open economy where the urban manufacturing wage is fixed under the minimum wage legislation. They find capital mobility matters. In the sector-specific capital case, they show that the utility of a rural worker may be reduced by the transfer although such a paradox can never arise in the mobile capital case. The authors then derive the result that, in the sector-specific capital case, the transfer increases labour employment in the agricultural sector and reduces the urban unemployment. In the mobile capital case, the introduction of the transfer is likely to increase the labour and capital employment in the agricultural industry and decrease the labour and capital employment in the manufacturing industry.

In Chap. 13, Long innovatively incorporates insights from behavioural economics into the traditional theory of foreign aid. He considers in particular a foreign aid model in which donor countries belong to two different behavioural types: Kantian (moral) or Nashian (rational). His game theoretic model is quite general in the sense that there is no need to specify the utility function of donor countries. Both pure and mixed strategies are examined, utilizing the Kant–Nash equilibrium proposed by Long (2016). He finds that, under certain conditions, Kantian donors may randomize between low and high level of foreign aid, while Nashian donors will choose to free ride. Further, if there is a decline (increase) in the number of Kantian donors because some Kantian (Nashian) countries become Nashian (Kantian), the aggregate foreign aid may fall (rise) more than proportionately.

The final part of the book contains a single chapter. In Chap. 14, Tawada and Ogawa provide a three-country, three-good geometrical proof of the Shiozawa's (2015) generalization of Jones' (1961) well-known theorem on complete specialization in a n-factor, n–country Ricardian model. While the graphical approach does not reveal anything particularly novel, its intuition paves the way for extending the Ricardian theory of comparative advantage to incorporate the case in which tradable produced commodities can be used as intermediate goods in production.

Appendix: Murray Kemp's Publications from 2001 to 2018

Books

Kemp, M. C. (2001). *International trade and national welfare*. London: Routledge.
Kemp, M. C. (2003). *International trade and economic welfare*. Kobe: Editorial Board of Kobe University.

Kemp, M. C. (2008). *International trade theory: A critical review*. London: Routledge.

Kemp, M. C., Nakagawa, H., & Uchida, T. (Eds.) (2012). *Positive and normative analysis of international economics: Essays in honour of Hiroshi Ohta*. Basingstoke/New Hampshire: Palgrave Macmillan.

Articles

Kemp, M. C., Shimomura, K. & Wan H. Y. Jr. (2001). Trade gains when the opportunity to trade changes the state of information. *Review of International Economics 9*, 24−28. Reprinted in M. C. Kemp (2001). *International trade and national welfare* (pp. 36−41), London: Routledge.

Kemp, M. C., & Shimomura, K. (2001). A second elementary proposition concerning the formation of customs unions.*Japanese Economic Review, 52*, 64−69. Reprinted in M. C. Kemp (2001). *International trade and national welfare*(pp. 51−57). London: Routledge, and M. C. Kemp (2003). *International trade and economic welfare*(pp. 57−66). Kobe: Editorial Board of Kobe University.

Kemp. M. C. (2001). Factor price equalization when the world equilibrium is not unique. *Review of Development Economics, 5*, 205−210. Reprinted in M. C. Kemp (2008). *International trade theory: A critical review* (pp. 145−150). London: Routledge.

Kemp, M .C., Long, N. V, & Shimomura, K. (2001). A differential game model of tariff war. *Japan and the World Economy, 13*, 279−298.

Kemp, M. C., & Yamada, M. (2001). Factor market distortions, dynamic stability, and paradoxical comparative statics. *Review of International Economics, 9*, 383−400.

Kemp, M. C., & Shimomura, K. (2001). Gains from trade in a Cournot−Nash general equilibrium. *Japanese Economic Review, 52*, 284−302. Reprinted in M. C. Kemp (2001). *International trade and national welfare* (pp. 134−157). London: Routledge.

Kemp, M. C. (2001). Economic theory: Past and future. *Kobe Economic and Business Review, 46*, 1−3.

Kemp, M. C., & Shimomura, K. (2002). A new approach to the theory of International trade under increasing returns: The two-commodities case. In A. D. Woodland (Ed.), *Economic theory and international trade. Essays in honour of Murray C. Kemp* (pp. 3−21). Aldershot: Hants Edward Elgar. Reprinted in M. C. Kemp (2002). *International trade and national welfare* (pp. 111−127). London: Routledge.

Kemp, M. C., Kimura Y., & Shimomura, K. (2002). A second correspondence principle. In A. D. Woodland (Ed.), *Economic theory and international trade. Essays in honour of Murray C. Kemp* (pp. 37−56). Aldershot: Hants Edward

Elgar. Reprinted in M. C. Kemp (2008). *International trade theory: A critical review* (pp. 88–104). London: Routledge.

Kemp, M. C., & Shimomura, K. (2002). A theory of voluntary unrequited international transfers. *Japanese Economic Review, 53*, 290–300. Reprinted in M. C. Kemp (2008). *International trade theory: A critical review* (pp. 105–110). London: Routledge.

Kemp, M. C. (2002). Heckscher-Ohlin theory: Has it a future? *Singapore Economic Review, 47*, 193–198. Reprinted in M. C. Kemp (2008). *International trade theory: A critical review* (pp. 153–156). London: Routledge.

Kemp, M. C., & Shimomura, K. (2002). The Sonnenschein–Debreu–Mantel proposition and the theory of international trade. *Review of International Economics, 10*, 671–679.

Kemp, M. C., & Shimomura, K. (2002). Recent challenges to the classical gains-from-trade proposition. *German Economic Review, 3*, 485–489. Reprinted in M. C. Kemp (2008). *International trade theory: A critical review* (pp 161–164). London: Routledge.

Kemp, M. C., & Yamada, M. (2003). Dynamic stability, paradoxical comparative statics and factor-market distortions in an economy with three production sectors. *Review of International Economics, 11*, 28–37.

Kemp, M. C. (2003). On a misconception concerning the classical gains-from-trade propositions. In R. Pethig, & M. Rauscher (Eds.), *Challenges to the world economy. festschrift for Horst Siebert* (pp. 277–279). Berlin/Heidelberg: Springer. Reprinted in M. C. Kemp (2008). *International trade theory: A critical review* (pp. 159–160). London: Routledge.

Kemp, M. C., & Shimomura, K. (2003). A theory of involuntary unrequited international transfers. *Journal of Political Economy, 111*, 686–692. Reprinted in M. C. Kemp (2008). *International trade theory: A critical review* (pp. 105–110). London: Routledge.

Kemp, M. C., & Shimomura, K. (2003). A dynamic Heckscher–Ohlin model: The case of costly factor reallocation. *Japanese Economic Review, 54*, 237–252. Reprinted in M. C. Kemp (2008). *International trade theory: A critical review* (pp 71–87). London: Routledge.

Kemp, M. C. (2003). International trade without Autarkic Equilibria. *Japanese Economic Review, 54*, 353–360.

Kemp, M. C., & Wan, H. Y. Jr. (2003). Lumpsum versus non-lumpsum redistribution: A second glance. In M. Oda (Ed.), *International trade and factor mobility* (pp. 1–9). Osaka: Institute of Legal Studies, Kansai University.

Kemp, M. C., Hu, Y., & Shimomura, K. (2003). A factor endowment theory of endogenous growth and international trade. In M. Oda (Ed.), *International trade and factor mobility* (pp. 315–331). Osaka: Institute of Legal Studies, Kansai University.

Kemp, M. C. (2004). Ben Higgins in Melbourne. *History of Economics Review, 40*, 118–120.

Kemp, M. C. (2005). Aid tied to the donor's exports. *Pacific Economic Review, 25*, 317–322. Reprinted in M. C. Kemp (2008). *International trade theory: A critical review* (pp. 128–134). London: Routledge.

Kemp, M. C. (2005). International trade without Autarkic Equilibria. *India macroeconomics annual 2004–2005* (pp. 115–129). Reprinted in M. C. Kemp (2008). *International trade theory: A critical review* (pp. 49–61). London: Routledge.

Kemp, M. C. (2005). Economic development and the gains from international trade and investment. In M. Chatterji, & P. Gangopadhay (Eds.), *Globalization and economic reform* (pp. 7–11). Aldershot: Ashgate.

Kemp, M. C., Hu, Y., & Shimomura, K. (2005). A factor endowment theory of endogenous growth and international trade. *Review of Development Economics, 9*, 467–481.

Kemp, M. C., & Shimomura, K. (2005). Price taking in general equilibrium. *American Journal of Applied Sciences*, Special Issue, 78–80. Reprinted in M. C. Kemp (2008). *International trade theory: A critical review* (pp. 199–201). London: Routledge.

Kemp, M. C., & Wan, H. Y. Jr. (2005). On the existence of equivalent tariff vectors: When the status quo matters. *Singapore Economic Review, 50*, 345–360. Reprinted in M. C. Kemp (2008). *International trade theory: A critical review* (pp. 181–194). London: Routledge.

Kemp, M. C. (2005). Trade gains: The end of the road? *Singapore Economic Review, 50*, 361–368. Reprinted in M. C. Kemp (2008). *International trade theory: A critical review* (pp. 165–171). London: Routledge.

Kemp, M. C., & Shimomura, K. (2005). Trade between countries with radically different preferences. *Economics Bulletin, 6*, 1–9. Reprinted in M. C. Kemp (2008). *International trade theory: A critical review* (pp. 25–31). London: Routledge.

Kemp, M. C. (2005). A case for subsidizing child-rearing? *Keio Economic Studies, 42*, 99–101.

Kemp, M. C., Hu, Y., & Shimomura, K. (2006). Endogenous growth: Fragile foundations? *Review of Development Economics, 10*, 113–116.

Kemp, M. C., & Okawa, M. (2006). The Torrens-Ricardo principle of comparative advantage: An extension. *Review of International Economics, 14*, 466–477. Reprinted in M. C. Kemp (2008). *International trade theory: A critical review* (pp. 3–15). London: Routledge.

Kemp, M. C., & Okawa, M. (2006). Gottfried Haberler's principle of comparative advantage. *Asia-Pacific Journal of Accounting and Economics, 13*, 1–10. Reprinted in M. C. Kemp (2008). *International trade theory: A critical review* (pp. 16–24). London: Routledge.

Kemp, M. C. (2006). Factor price equalization in a world of many trading countries. *Review of International Economics, 14*, 675–677. Reprinted in M. C. Kemp, *International trade theory: A critical review* (pp. 151–152). London: Routledge.

Kemp, M. C., & Shimomura, K. (2007). Optimal commodity taxation with a representative agent. *Review of Development Economics, 11*, 385–389.

Kemp, M. C., & Fishburn, G. (2007). Impoverishing technical and preferential improvements. *Pacific Economic Review, 12*, 205–212. Reprinted in M. C. Kemp, *International trade theory: A critical review* (pp. 62–70). London: Routledge.

Kemp, M. C. (2007). Normative comparisons of customs unions and other types of free trade association. *European Journal of Political Economy, 23*, 416–422. Reprinted in B. Tran-Nam, N. V. Long, & M. Tawada (Eds.), *Globalization and emerging issues in trade theory and policy* (pp. 77–86). Bingley: Emerald.

Kemp, M. C., & Wan, H. Y. Jr. (2008). Tariff reform: Some pre-strategic considerations. In M. C. Kemp (Ed.), *International trade theory: A critical review* (pp. 172–181). London: Routledge.

Kemp, M. C. (2008). The representative agent in economic theory. In M. C. Kemp (Ed.), *International trade theory: A critical review* (pp. 197–198). London: Routledge.

Kemp, M. C. (2008). Generality versus tractability. In M. C. Kemp (Ed.), *International trade theory: A critical review* (pp. 202–203). London: Routledge.

Kemp, M. C. (2008). How normal is normality in consumption? *Economics Letters, 101*, 44–47.

Kemp, M. C. (2008). Non-competing factor groups and the normative propositions of trade theory. *International Review of Economics and Finance, 17*, 388–390.

Kemp, M. C. (2009). Koji Shimomura: Emerging trade theorist. In T. Kamihigashi, & L. Zhao (Eds.), *International trade and economic dynamics – essays in memory of Koji Shimomura* (pp. 5–6). Berlin/Heidelberg: Springer.

Kemp, M. C., & Tran-Nam, B. (2009). On trade gains and international disparities in factor proportions. In T. Kamihigashi, & L. Zhao (Eds.), *International trade and economic dynamics – essays in memory of Koji Shimomura* (pp. 13–18). Berlin–Heidelberg: Springer.

Kemp, M. C. (2009). Vilfredo Pareto's principle of compensation. In T. Kamihigashi, & L. Zhao (Eds.), *International trade and economic dynamics – essays in memory of Koji Shimomura* (pp. 525–532). Berlin/Heidelberg: Springer.

Kemp, M. C., & Long, N. V. (2009). Foreign aid in the presence of corruption: Differential games among donors. *Review of International Economics, 17*, 230–243.

Kemp, M. C. (2009). An inaugural conjecture. *Oxford Economic Papers, 61*, 823–826.

Kemp, M. C., Hu, Y., & Shimomura, K. (2009). A two-country dynamic Heckscher–Ohlin model with physical and human capital accumulation. *Economic Theory, 41*, 67–84.

Kemp, M. C., & Long, N. V. (2009). Extracting resource deposits of unknown size: Optimal order. *German Economic Review, 10*, 401–421.

Kemp, M. C. (2009). Normative trade theory under gossenian assumptions. In J. Vint, S. Metcalfe, H. D. Kurz, N. Salvadori, & P. A. Samuelson (Eds.), *Economic theory and economic thought. Essays in honour of Ian Steedman* (pp. 98–105). London: Routledge).

Kemp, M. C. (2010). The gains from trade in a Cournot–Nash Trading equilibrium. *Review of International Economics, 18*, 832–834.

Kemp, M. C. (2010). The offer curve. In P. J. Lloyd, & M. Blaug (Eds.), *Famous figures and diagrams in economics* (pp. 295–299). Cheltenham: Edward Elgar.

Kemp, M. C. (2010). The optimal tariff. In P. J. Lloyd, & M. Blaug (Eds.), *Famous figures and diagrams in economics* (pp. 328–334). Cheltenham: Edward Elgar.

Kemp, M. C. (2011). A unified analysis of trade gains in the presence of public goods. *Japanese Economic Review, 62*, 425–429.

Kemp, M. C. (2012). Normative trade theory. In M. C. Kemp, H. Nakagawa, & T. Uchida, (Eds.), *Positive and normative analysis of international economics: Essays in honour of Hiroshi Ohta* (pp. 7–16). Basingstoke/New Hampshire: Palgrave Macmillan.

Kemp, M. C. (2018). Normative trade theory under Gossenian assumptions. In B. Tran-Nam, M. Tawada, & M. Okawa (Eds.), *Recent developments in normative trade theory and welfare economics* (pp. 65–75) Singapore: Spinger. (This is a corrected and expanded version of a book chapter with the same title published in 2009 in an edited volume in honour of Ian Steedman).

Kemp, M. C., & Tran-Nam, B. (2012). The gains from international trade and international aid in the presence of public goods. *Global Journal of Economics, 1*, http://www.worldscientific.com/doi/pdf/10.1142/S2251361212500085.

Kemp, M. C., & Fishburn, G. (2013). Normative trade theory in a context of overlapping generations and inter-generational bequests. *Global Journal of Economics, 2*, http://www.worldscientific.com/doi/abs/10.1142/S2251361213500043.

Kemp, M. C., & Fishburn, G. (2014). The gains from international trade in pool goods and private goods. *Review of International Economics, 22*, 167–169.

Kemp, M. C., & Fishburn, G. (2018a). The rise and fall of normative trade theory. In B. Tran-Nam, M. Tawada, & M. Okawa (Eds.), *Recent developments in normative trade theory and welfare economics* (pp. 15–22). Singapore: Spinger.

Kemp, M. C., & Fishburn, G. (2018b). The rise and fall of political economy. In B. Tran-Nam, M. Tawada, & M. Okawa (Eds.), *Recent developments in normative trade theory and welfare economics* (pp. 171–176). Singapore: Springer.

References

Helpman, E., & Krugman, P. R. (1985). *Market structure and foreign trade: Increasing returns, imperfect competition and the international economy.* Cambridge, MA: MIT Press.

Jones, R. W. (1961). Comparative advantage and the theory of tariffs: A multi-country, multi-commodity model. *Review of Economic Studies, 28*, 161–175.

Kemp, M. C. (1964). *The pure theory of international trade.* Englewood Cliffs: Prentice-Hall.

Kemp, M. C. (1969). *The pure theory of international trade and investment.* Englewood Cliffs: Prentice-Hall.

Kemp, M. C., & Wan, H. Y., Jr. (1972). The gains from free trade. *International Economic Review, 13*, 509–522.

Le-Van, C., & Nguyen, B. M. (2007). No-arbitrage condition and existence of equilibrium with dividends. *Journal of Mathematical Economics, 43*, 135–152.

Long, N. V. (2016). Kant–Nash equilibrium in a quantity setting oligopoly. In P. von Mouch & F. Quartieri (Eds.), *Equilibrium theory for Cournot oligopolies and related games: Essays in honour of Koji Okuguchi* (pp. 199–202). Berlin: Springer.

Samuelson, P. A. (1993). Foreword. In H. Herberg & N. V. Long (Eds.), *Trade, welfare, and economic policies: Essays in honour of Murray C. Kemp*. Ann Arbor: Michigan University Press.

Shiozawa, Y. (2015). International trade theory and exotic algebras. *Evolutionary and Institutional Economics Review, 12*, 177–212.

Tran-Nam, B. (2008). The contribution of Murray Kemp to the discipline of international trade and welfare economics. In B. Tran-Nam, N. V. Long, & M. Tawada (Eds.), *Globalization and emerging issues in trade theory and policy* (pp. 165–191). Bingley: Emerald.

Part I
The Gains from Trade Under Non-standard Assumptions

Chapter 2
The Rise and Fall of Normative Trade Theory

Murray C. Kemp and Geoffrey Fishburn

Abstract Three core normative propositions of the theory of international trade have been established in the context of finite competitive economies of the Walras−Arrow−Debreu or McKenzie (WADM) type. Whether the propositions survive the recognition that economies might last forever, with overlapping generations (OLGs) of mortal individuals and intergenerational bequests, is still unknown. In the present chapter, it is shown that none of the core propositions survives the recognition of intergenerational bequests. It is also noted that, if a particular tailor-made assumption is introduced, all three propositions survive.

Keywords International trade · Normative propositions · Finite economies · Overlapping generations · Bequests

2.1 Introduction

The normative theory of international trade now contains three core propositions, none of which was known to trade theorists 60 years ago when Kemp (1964) and Chipman (1965) published their well-known surveys of the subject:

(a) Each country, whether large or small, is potentially (after Paretian compensation) better off under free trade than in autarky; see Grandmont and McFadden (1972), and Kemp and Wan Jr. (1972).
(b) Any two or more countries, all part of an initial tariff-distorted world trading equilibrium, can form a mutually advantageous customs union without harming any excluded country; see Kemp (1964: 176), Kemp and Wan Jr. (1976, 1986a), and Kemp and Shimomura (2001).

M. C. Kemp (✉)
School of Economics, UNSW Sydney, Sydney, NSW 2052, Australia

G. Fishburn
Independent Researcher, Sydney, Australia

© Springer Nature Singapore Pte Ltd. 2018
B. Tran-Nam et al. (eds.), *Recent Developments in Normative Trade Theory and Welfare Economics*, New Frontiers in Regional Science: Asian Perspectives 26, https://doi.org/10.1007/978-981-10-8615-1_2

15

(c) Any two or more countries, all part of an initial tariff-distorted world trading equilibrium, can form a mutually advantageous free trade association without harming any excluded country. Corresponding to each free trade association, whether or not it is Pareto preferred to the initial tariff-distorted trading equilibrium, there is a Pareto-preferred Kemp–Wan customs union; see Kemp (2007).[1]

These are core propositions in that they are valid for any country or for any subset of countries. Of course the normative theory of international trade contains many noncore propositions dealing, for example, with the optimal tariff vector of a single perfectly or imperfectly competitive country.[2]

Each of the core propositions has been established in the context of finite competitive economies of the Walras (1874), Arrow and Debreu (1954), and McKenzie (1954) type but extended to accommodate a finite number of countries; economies of this type will be referred to as Walras–Arrow–Debreu or McKenzie (WADM) economies. Among these distinguishing features of WADM economies:

(i) all inputs and outputs are defined in terms of their countries of origin and the time zones of those countries;
(ii) everything (the population, the number of primary factors, the number of products, the time horizon) is finite;
(iii) all households and firms are price-takers.

As Kemp (2012) has shown, these features of WADM economies are mutually compatible if (α) all households are unaware of the finiteness of their numbers and/or (β) all households are incompletely rational in that they cannot appreciate that the finiteness of everything implies that they possess market power. However, neither (α) nor (β) fits comfortably in the static WADM framework. Moreover, in WADM economies, there is no role for intergenerational bequests.

In the present chapter, therefore, we draw on the findings of Kemp and Wong (1995) to reconsider the core propositions in a dynamic framework, recognizing that economies might last forever, with populations composed of overlapping generations (OLGs) of mortal individuals. We know, of course, that models of *closed* economies with OLGs may have Pareto-suboptimal competitive equilibria; see Allais (1947) and Samuelson (1958). Moreover, we now have several examples of competitive *world* economies with OLGs for which, in the absence of government-sponsored compensatory schemes, autarky is Pareto preferred to free trade; see

---

[1]Ohyama (2002) and Panagariya and Krishna (2002) produced a result not unlike Proposition (c). However, their finding was based on the assumption that each country chooses its new tariff vector so that its vector of imports remains at its initial level, whereas Proposition (c) was established under the weaker Kemp–Wan assumption that only the aggregate import vector of the free trade association need be kept at its initial level.

[2]After reading Kemp and Fishburn (2013), several distinguished theorists wondered why we had confined our attention to just three of the much larger set of normative trade propositions. In this brief chapter, we outline the reasoning of our earlier paper. We focussed with core proofs because only they are always valid under the core assumptions.

Kemp and Long (1979), Tran-Nam (1985), and Serra (1991). These examples evidently raise questions about the robustness of each of the core propositions in a dynamic world with OLGs.[3]

It will be shown that none of the core propositions survives the recognition of OLGs and intergenerational bequests. Only by introducing a very special (tailor-made) additional assumption might a qualified validity be restored. Such an assumption will be examined in Sect. 2.3.

2.2 No Bequests

For a particular category of economies with OLGs and for the types of disturbance considered in Propositions (a)–(c), there can always be found systems of lump-sum transfers which compensate those households that would have been harmed by the disturbance; moreover, this is true even when, in the absence of compensatory transfers, free trade is Pareto inferior to autarky.

That much has been established by Kemp and Wolik (1995) for Propositions (a) and (b) on the basis of assumptions all of which were, at the time of writing, quite conventional.[4]

  (i) Time is discrete. At the beginning of each period, a new generation appears. The new generation may be more or less numerous than its predecessor. Each member of the new generation lives for two periods, after an infancy of one period spent with his/her parents.

 (ii) During each of the two periods of adulthood, a member of the new generation receives a vector of natural resources, including land and the skills associated with several types of labor.

(iii) Entering the first period of adulthood, members of the new generation collaborate to establish a finite set of firms each capable of producing a given set of commodities. For the time being, it will be assumed that all commodities are perishable; that is, they last for only one period and are sold on spot markets in each period. The firms do not necessarily share a common technology.

---

[3]The core propositions have been based on the additional assumption that lump-sum compensatory payments can be made by governments without distorting the worldwide allocation of resources. That assumption has been examined in the companion papers of Kemp and Wan (1986b, 1999). This feature of our analysis contrasts sharply with the analysis of Aiyagari (1989) and that of his predecessors, who work with single-parent families and endow some individuals with perfect knowledge of the preferences of all their descendants.

[4]Indeed, assumptions (ii) and (iii), allowing household preferences and endowments to differ within and across generations are weaker than is customary in models incorporating OLGs. Moreover, not all of these assumptions were needed by Kemp and Wolik. The assumption that all commodities are perishable was not needed; nor was the assumption of two-parent families – Kemp and Wolik might have relied on the alternative Platonic assumption of one-parent families or on a blend of the two assumptions.

However, the set of production possibilities available to a firm is closed and convex, includes the origin, and does not admit free production. Members of the new generation agree on the manner in which the profits of each firm are to be shared. Each firm survives for two periods (the adult lifetime of a generation).

(iv) All households and all firms are price-takers.

(v) In the first period of adulthood, each member of the new generation works, marries, and raises a family. The household's income in that period includes rent derived from its vector of natural resources and also includes the household's share of the firms' profits. The household's preferences are continuous and convex, without satiation. The preferences of households may differ, whether or not they are members of the same generation.

(vi) At the end of the first period of adulthood, each member of the generation retires from work and lives thereafter on rents and profits.

(vii) During each of the two periods of an adult lifetime, each individual enjoys certainty about present and future prices and has no fear of divorce or premature death.

(viii) Each economy is irreducible in the sense of McKenzie (1959).

On the basis of assumptions (i)–(viii), Kemp and Wolik established[5] that *in a dynamic world with OLGs*:

1. There exists a competitive world equilibrium [Kemp and Wolik (1995, Theorem 2)].
2. For each trading country, there can be found a scheme of Paretian lump-sum compensation such that each household in that country benefits from free trade [Kemp and Wolik (1995, Theorem 3)].
3. Given any initial tariff-ridden world equilibrium, any proper subset of the trading countries can form a customs union with a common tariff vector and a system of compensatory lump-sum payments which ensures that all households, whether or not they are members of the union, are better off than before the formation of the union [Kemp and Wolik (1995, Theorem 4)].

Proposition (c) emerged only in 2007 and therefore could not have been considered by Kemp and Wolik in 1995. However, had Proposition (c) been available in 1995, they would have had no difficulty in deducing from assumptions (i)–(viii) that:

4. Given any initial tariff-ridden world equilibrium, any proper subset of the trading countries can form a free trade association with a system of compensatory lump-sum payments such that all households, whether or not they are members of the association, are better off than they were before the formation of the association; moreover, corresponding to each free trade association (whether or not it is Pareto

---

[5]The proofs provided by Kemp and Wolik (1995) were correct in intent but marred by several notational misprints.

preferred to the initial tariff-distorted world equilibrium) is a Pareto-preferred customs union.

However, Kemp and Wolik neglected bequests, dowries, and other types of intergenerational transfer. This was a serious oversight for, in advanced economies, a considerable proportion of private property that has been obtained by means of bequests from parents and parents-in-law; in a path-breaking paper, Kotlikoff and Summers (1981) suggested that, in the United States and at the time of writing, two-thirds of private wealth had been obtained by bequests or by gifts inter vivos from parents and parents-in-law.[6] Moreover, pairs of parents and parents-in-law can hardly fail to realize that they are in a strategic relationship with each other. Indeed, they may find themselves playing a many-person noncooperative game in bequests the inevitable outcome of which is a loss of efficiency, a loss that may be greater under free trade than in autarky and may be incompatible with the three core propositions.[7] In short, bequests are incompatible with perfect competition and, therefore, may be incompatible with each of the core propositions.

2.3 Modified Bequests

The above bleak finding will disappoint many economists, especially those who had placed their faith in Proposition (a). However, perfect competition and each of the core propositions do survive in a context of OLGs and intergenerational bequests if the government of each trading country requires its parents and parents-in-law to maintain under free trade their autarkic vectors of bequests.[8] Given that requirement and assume that the resources needed for the administration and enforcement of the requirement are zero, *inefficiency will be found both in autarky and under free trade, but Propositions (a)–(c) will remain intact.*

Consider Proposition (a). If the vectors of bequests are the same under free trade and in autarky, we can include them in the resource or endowment vectors of both parents and children and then appeal to Theorem 3 of Kemp and Wolik to establish that free trade benefits each country even in the context of bequests.

Let us turn next to Proposition (b). We can again include the vectors of bequests in the resource vectors of both parents and children and then appeal to Theorem

---

[6]The appearance of Kotlikoff and Summers (1981) gave rise to a lively debate concerning the statistical data employed; see Modigliani (1988), Kessler and Masson (1989), Zhang (1994), and Gale and Scholz (1994).

[7]Each pair of parents knows its own children and their partners in marriage, but they cannot know their adult grandchildren. Parents will therefore play the "bequest game" with only their own children and children-in-law in mind.

[8]Under autarky, the games played in any particular country are played only by the parents and parents-in-law of that country. Hence, the proposed intervention of the government under free trade rules out all international bequests.

(4) of Kemp and Wolik to confirm that, when the trading countries are in an initial tariff-distorted world equilibrium, it is always possible for a subset of those countries to establish a customs union which leaves each country (whether or not it is a member of the union) at least as well-off as in the initial world equilibrium.

Finally, we turn to Proposition (c). The world economy is again in an initial tariff-distorted equilibrium. That equilibrium is disturbed when a subset of countries forms a customs union in which at least one country is strictly better off than in the initial world equilibrium, all other member countries remaining at least as well-off as in the initial equilibrium.[9] If the excess demand functions of the member countries are differentiable, then the tariff vectors of these countries can be marginally manipulated to leave the aggregate import vector (and therefore the world price vector) unchanged at its initial value. A member country that has already benefited (non-marginally) from the union can now compensate the other member countries for the second-order losses suffered when their tariffs were manipulated. The customs union has at this stage become a free trade association. Both enjoy the same aggregate import vector from the rest of the world and both are better off than in the initial world equilibrium. However, the free trade association cannot be Pareto superior to the customs union for, while the free trade association is based on a complex mixture of tariff vectors (and therefore has a complex mixture of domestic price vectors), the customs union is based on a single tariff vector.

Thus, we have established, on the basis of a unique sufficient condition, that each of the three core propositions survives under OLGs and intergenerational bequests. However, to impose the condition, governing bodies would need accurate and up-to-date knowledge of all bequests by parents and parents-in-law. It is clear that the cost of administering the condition could never be zero or even minimal. Hence, the core propositions cannot be expected to reappear under OLGs and intergenerational bequests, even on the basis of the unique sufficient condition.

2.4 Looking Back

In the present chapter, we have questioned what have long been accepted as the core normative propositions of the theory of international trade. In particular, it has been shown that if WADM economies are more realistically defined to embrace two-parent families and intergenerational transfers, then the core propositions may be abandoned.

We are not the first to have challenged the core propositions. Earlier challenges have been directed mainly at Proposition (a) and were penned by Thurow (1980),

---

[9]For this outcome, it suffices that, after the formation of the customs union, at least one household in a member country engages in consumption substitution or is a shareholder in a firm that engages in production substitution; see Kemp and Wolik (1995: Theorem 4).

Newbery and Stiglitz (1984), Cordella and Ventura (1992), and Tompkinson (1999). Kemp and Shimomura (2002) have rejected *all* of these challenges, sometimes because of logical slips and sometimes because of hidden changes in basic assumptions.

References

Aiyagari, S. R. (1989). Equilibrium existence in an overlapping generations model with altruistic preferences. *Journal of Economic Theory, 47*, 130–152.

Allais, M. (1947). *Economie et intérêt*. Paris: Librairie des Publications Officielles.

Arrow, K. J., & Debreu, G. (1954). Existence of an equilibrium for a competitive economy. *Econometrica, 32*, 265–290.

Chipman, J. S. (1965). A survey of the theory of international trade: Part 2. *Econometrica, 33*, 685–760.

Cordella, T., & Ventura, L. (1992). A note on redistributions and gains from trade. *Economics Letters, 39*, 449–453.

Gale, W. G., & Scholz, J. K. (1994). Intergenerational transfers and the accumulation of wealth. *Journal of Economic Perspectives, 8*, 145–160.

Grandmont, J. M., & McFadden, D. (1972). A technical note on classical gains from trade. *Journal of International Economics, 2*, 109–125.

Kemp, M. C. (1964). *The pure theory of international trade*. Englewood Cliffs: Prentice-Hall.

Kemp, M. C. (2007). Normative comparisons of customs unions and other types of free trade association. *European Journal of Political Economy, 23*, 416–422.

Kemp, M. C. (2012). Normative trade theory. In M. C. Kemp, H. Nakagawa, & T. Uchida (Eds.), *Positive and normative analysis in international economics. Essays in Honour of Hiroshi Ohta* (pp. 7–16). London: Palgrave Macmillan.

Kemp, M. C., & Fishburn, G. (2013). Normative trade in the context of overlapping generations and inter-generational bequests. *Global Journal of Economics, 2*., https://doi.org/10.1142/S2251361213500043, 1350004.

Kemp, M. C., & Long, N. V. (1979). The under-exploitation of natural resources: A model with overlapping generations. *Economic Record, 53*, 214–221.

Kemp, M. C., & Shimomura, K. (2001). A second elementary proposition concerning the formation of customs unions. *Japanese Economic Review, 52*, 64–69.

Kemp, M. C., & Shimomura, K. (2002). Recent challenges to the classic gains from trade proposition. *German Economic Review, 2*, 183–193. Reprinted in Kemp, M. C. (2008). *International trade theory. A critical review* (pp.161–164). London: Routledge.

Kemp, M. C., & Wan, H. Y., Jr. (1972). The gains from free trade. *International Economic Review, 13*, 509–522.

Kemp, M. C., & Wan, H. Y., Jr. (1976). An elementary proposition concerning the formation of customs unions. *Journal of International Economics, 6*, 95–97.

Kemp, M. C., & Wan, H. Y., Jr. (1986a). The comparison of second-best equilibria: The case of customs unions. In D. Bös & C. Seidl (Eds.), *The welfare economics of the second best, Supplementum 5 to the Zeitschift für Nationalökonomie* (pp. 161–167). Wein/New York: Springer.

Kemp, M. C., & Wan, H. Y., Jr. (1986b). Gains from trade with and without lump-sum compensation. *Journal of International Economics, 21*, 99–110.

Kemp, M. C., & Wan, H. Y., Jr. (1999). On Lump sum compensation. In J. C. Moore, R. Riezman, & J. R. Melvin (Eds.), *Trade, theory and econometrics. Essays in Honor of John S. Chipman* (pp. 27–34). London: Routledge.

Kemp, M. C., & Wolik, N. (1995). The gains from trade in a context of overlapping generations. In M. C. Kemp (Ed.), (`995), The gains from trade and the gains from aid (pp. 129–146). London: Routledge.

Kemp, M. C., & Wong, K.-Y. (1995). Gains from trade with overlapping generations. Economic Theory, 6, 283–303.

Kessler, D., & Masson, A. (1989). Bequest and wealth accumulation: Are some pieces of the puzzle missing? Journal of International Economics, 3, 141–152.

Kotlikoff, L. J., & Summers, L. H. (1981). The role of intergenerational transfers in aggregate capital accumulation. Journal of Political Economy, 89, 706–732.

McKenzie, L. W. (1954). On equilibrium in Graham's model of world trade and other competitive systems. Econometrica, 22, 147–161.

McKenzie, L. W. (1959). On the existence of general equilibrium for a competitive market. Econometrica, 27, 54–71.

Modigliani, F. (1988). The role of intergenerational transfers and life cycle saving in the accumulation of wealth. Journal of Economic Perspectives, 2, 15–40.

Newbery, D. M. G., & Stiglitz, J. E. (1984). Pareto inferior trade. Review of Economic Studies, 51(1), 12.

Ohyama, M. (2002). The economic significance of the GATT/WTO rules. In A. D. Woodland (Ed.), Economic theory and international trade (pp. 71–85). Cheltenham: Edward Elgar.

Panagariya, A., & Krishna, P. (2002). On necessarily welfare-enhancing free trade areas. Journal of International Economics, 57, 353–367.

Samuelson, P. A. (1958). An exact consumption-loan model of interest with or without the social contrivance of money. Journal of Political Economy, 66, 467–482.

Serra, P. (1991). Short-run and long-run welfare implications of free trade. Canadian Journal of Economics, 24, 21–33.

Thurow, L. C. (1980). Psychic income: A market failure. Journal of Post Keynesian Economics, 3, 183–193.

Tompkinson, P. (1999). The gains from trade in a Ricardian model when workers have preferences among occupations. Journal of Post Keynesian Economics, 21, 611–620.

Tran-Nam, B. (1985). A neo-Ricardian world with overlapping generations. Economic Record, 61, 707–718.

Walras, L. (1874). Eléments d'économie politique pure, ou théorie de la richesse sociale. Lausanne: L Corbaz.

Zhang, J. (1994). Bequest as a public good within marriage: A note. Journal of Political Economy, 102, 187–193.

Chapter 3
Deconstruct the Graham's Paradox

Henry Wan, Jr.

Abstract In the normative theory of trade, much mainstream attention focuses on trading gains under conditions that are *sufficient* (Samuelson PA, Am Econ Rev 28:261–266, 1938; Kemp MC, Econ J 87:803–819, 1962; Grandmont J-M, McFadden, D, J Int Econ 2:109–125, 1972; Kemp MC, Wan H Jr. *The welfare economics of international trade*, Harwood Academic, London, 1993), but *not necessary* (Kemp MC, Negishi T, Swed J Econ 72:1–11, 1970; Wan H Jr., Int Econ 2:173–180, 1972). Sometimes trade gain reduces to none, say for economies with solely miniscule partners, but never negative. But in justifying tariffs, Graham (Q J Econ 37:199–227, 1923) asserted intriguingly trade might cause countries *actual loss*, not *zero gain*. He assumed externalities in terms of Marshallian increasing returns in a country's production. After many challenges and debates, Chipman (Q J Econ 84:347–385, 1970) affirmed Graham's counter example with parametrized externalities, where a country's production set depends increasingly on aggregate industry, country, or world output. One can gain further insight, relying upon a convenient example (Helpman E, Krugman PR, *Market structure and foreign trade: Increasing returns, imperfect competition and the international economy*. MIT Press, Cambridge, MA, 1985) and the tractable, parametric map approach for global analysis. It turns out apparently unknown in the literature, here the externality causes multiple equilibria. There always exists another more intuitive alternative equilibrium, with both countries enjoy equal gain. Graham's demonstration against free trade rests on the counterintuitive alternative in country-industry matching. The tariff he promoted is dominated by a simple interstate bargaining. His case merits reconsideration but not simple acceptance.

Keywords Graham's paradox · Externalities · Multiple equilibria · Global analysis

H. Wan, Jr. (✉)
Department of Economics, Cornell University, Ithaca, NY, USA
e-mail: hyw1@cornell.edu

© Springer Nature Singapore Pte Ltd. 2018
B. Tran-Nam et al. (eds.), *Recent Developments in Normative Trade Theory and Welfare Economics*, New Frontiers in Regional Science: Asian Perspectives 26, https://doi.org/10.1007/978-981-10-8615-1_3

3.1 Introduction

For his first paper on international trade, Samuelson (1938) noted in his *epigram* that "International trade theory was developed by practical men interested in normative welfare problems." In arguing for or against free trade, participants in policy debates reasoned rigorously from abstract assumptions, contributing to the rise of economic theory. In this tradition, the mainstream normative theory of trade seeks to prove gains from trade under successively more general *sufficient* conditions (Samuelson 1938; Kemp 1962; Grandmont and MacFadden 1972) and show previous versions are not always *necessary* (Kemp and Negishi 1970; Wan 1972). In such framework, it is known that under certain circumstances, like Mill's paradox, trading gain declines to zero if a country trades only with miniscule partners, but is *never* negative. Imagine the trade gain of a Switzerland in WWII, with Liechtenstein as its only trading partner.

In contrast, as Bobulescu (2002, 2007) showed, Graham (1923) advocated tariffs, following a long train of papers since Sidgwick (1887), and argued trade could bring *actual loss*, in the presence of *externalities*. It took decade-long argument and debates, before Chipman (1970) affirmed Graham's viewpoint by example, employing the simplifying assumption of parametrized externality, where increasing returns depend functionally on aggregate outputs over industries, countries, or the entire world. This introduces novel perspectives relative to the familiar world of Jones (1961).

What is intriguing is that the argument from Sidgwick to Graham does not involve any exotic cross-border externalities like global warming, where trade-induced growth causes the ocean to flood a totally hapless Kiribati, whatever the latter does. Their argument is based upon externalities of a garden variety, the external increasing returns in production of Marshall: the same type behind the industrial districts of Manchester and Sheffield in his day and later made Kansai, Japan, and Pearl River Delta, China, such central links in global supply chains.

Leaving aside for now Graham's case of tariff protection as remedy, it is still difficult to explain why the worst outcome for trading should be *actual loss* with externalities, but *zero gain* without. *Natura non facit saltum.* It is best to first disentangle the interacting forces in a simple model, like the elegant example in Helpman and Krugman (1985). One may then learn the true nature of this trade-damning example and the efficacy of tariff as remedy.

3.1.1 Why Graham's Paradox Matters

Externalities are part of real life. Graham's paradox has been regarded as a curiosum in the normative theory of international trade. Some rethinking may well be due.

First, the possibility of *loss from trade* highlights the *exceptional* nature of trade equilibrium with externalities. Exceptions may imply deep regularities worthy of study.

Second, discussions of tariff are motivated by the central role of the state in policy studies, even though tariff may be neither the only, nor the best, available option.

Third, to disentangle the complexities from externalities, one might employ the parametric map, with structural parameters for supply and demand playing fundamental roles. In such a global analysis, one considers all possibilities, not any coincidental parameter choices. Both regions and borders in the map deserve attention. Properties prevailing over entire regions signify robustness in a model; changes in the nature of equilibrium at borders in between reveal deep structural issues.

3.2 The Helpman-Krugman Example Revisited

In Helpman and Krugman (1985), the Graham model is in the two-country, two-good model of Ricardo. The novelty is an increasing returns sector under the Marshallian externality.

The universal input, labor, is distributed over the countries, Home and Foreign, as endowments, L and L^*.

Assumption 3.1 *(Supply parameter β for relative size of country endowment)*
Without losing generality, the Home Country is not the more populous:

$$L/L^* = \beta \in (0, 1]. \tag{3.1}$$

Labor is assigned over two sectors in both countries:

$$L = L_1 + L_2,$$
$$L^* = L_1^* + L_2^*.$$

Each sector 1 firm uses L_1 or L^*_1 to produce goods 1 (*watches*), at levels x_1 or x^*_1 with scale economy under Marshallian externality. Each sector 2 firm uses L_2 or L^*_2 to produce good 2 (*wheat*), at levels x_2 and x^*_2, under constant returns.

There is a continuum of infinitesimal firms with a mass of unity in each sector, each country, as in Aumann (1964).

The vector of externality is in terms of aggregate outputs of each sector and each country, as in Ethier (1982):

$$\xi = \begin{bmatrix} X_1 \\ X_2 \\ X_1^* \\ X_2^* \end{bmatrix}. \tag{3.2}$$

This vector is perceived by all firms, as independent of their own individual actions.

Assumption 3.2 *(Marshallian production possibilities)*
First, form now a matrix of the unit labor requirements:

$$A(\xi) = \begin{bmatrix} a_1(\xi) & a_2(\xi) & 0 & 0 \\ 0 & 0 & a_1{}^*(\xi) & a_2{}^*(\xi) \end{bmatrix}, \tag{3.3}$$

where externalities are assumed to arise through the aggregate outputs in the same sector.

Second, externalities supposedly exist in sector 1 (for watches) in the form:

$$a_1(\xi) = (X_1)^{-1/2}, a_1{}^*(\xi) = (X_1{}^*)^{-1/2.}$$

but not in sector 2 (for wheat):

$$a_2(\xi) = 1 = a_2{}^*(\xi)$$

Therefore, (3.3) now becomes:

$$A(\xi) = \begin{bmatrix} (X_1)^{-1/2} & 1 & 0 & 0 \\ 0 & 0 & (X_1^*)^{-1/2} & 1 \end{bmatrix}, \tag{3.4}$$

and is equivalent to some more intuitive form in (3.6).

Proposition 3.1 *(The supply side: full employment condition)*
The relation of cross-country proportionality in input quantities takes the form:

$$A(\xi)\xi = \begin{pmatrix} (X_1)^{1/2} + X_2 \\ (X_1^*)^{1/2} + X_2^* \end{pmatrix}$$

$$= \begin{pmatrix} L_1 + L_2 \\ L_1{}^* + L_2{}^* \end{pmatrix}$$

$$= \begin{pmatrix} 1 \\ 1/\beta \end{pmatrix} L. \tag{3.5}$$

Note this is equivalent to the simple, intuitive results below:

$$X_1 = (L_1)^2, X_2 = L_2; X_1{}^* = (L_1{}^*)^2, X_2{}^* = L_2{}^*. \tag{3.6}$$

Thus, one obtains:

$$(X_1)^{1/2} + X_2 = L; \ (X_1{}^*)^{1/2} + X_2{}^* = L^*. \tag{3.7}$$

(The *parabolic* production possibility frontiers)
Also, one now has Table 3.1:
Going from quantities to prices, one obtains by redefinition and normalization:

Table 3.1 Marginal value product of labor (Home Country)

	Sectors	
	1	2
Marginal physical *private* product of labor	$(X_1)^{1/2}$	1
Marginal value of labor	$p_1(X_1)^{1/2}$	p_2

$$p_1 = p, \quad p_2 = 1,$$

for the output prices and by introducing the wage, w, for the labor input. One then has for the Home Country at equilibrium:

Proposition 3.2 *(The Karush–Kuhn–Tucker conditions of complementary slackness)*

$$w - (X_1)^{1/2}p \geq 0, \quad L_1 \geq 0, \quad L_1\left[w - (X_1)^{1/2}p\right] = 0;$$
$$w\text{-}1 \geq 0, \quad L_2 \geq 0, \quad L_2(w\text{-}1) = 0. \tag{3.8}$$

(The competitive profit condition)

Thus, no labor input is assigned to any sector if the marginal *private* value product of labor cannot cover the wage; if there is any labor input assigned, producing output, then the marginal *private* value product of labor must be equal to the wage rate.

Corollary 3.1

At any ordinary (rather than corner) equilibrium on the production frontier, $X = (X_1, X_2)$,*with both outputs being positive,*

$$X_1 > 0, X_2 > 0,$$

the slope of the actual production frontier is:

$$-1/2X_1^{1/2} > -1/X_1^{1/2} = -p, \tag{3.9}$$

the latter being the slope of the perceived production frontier of firms in sector 1, in (3.8).

See Fig. 3.1 where sector 1 employers hire workers by their marginal private product of labor, q, irrespective of their marginal social product of labor, r ($p = q/s$, with the workers' marginal product, sector 2, being s). As expected, the market equilibrium is not Pareto optimal in the presence of externalities: Good 1 is undersupplied in production and underutilized in consumption. Similar results can be derived for the Foreign Country.

To complete the model, more is postulated.

Assumption 3.3 *(Demand parameter α for relative spending shares)*

All individuals share the same Mill-Graham utility index:

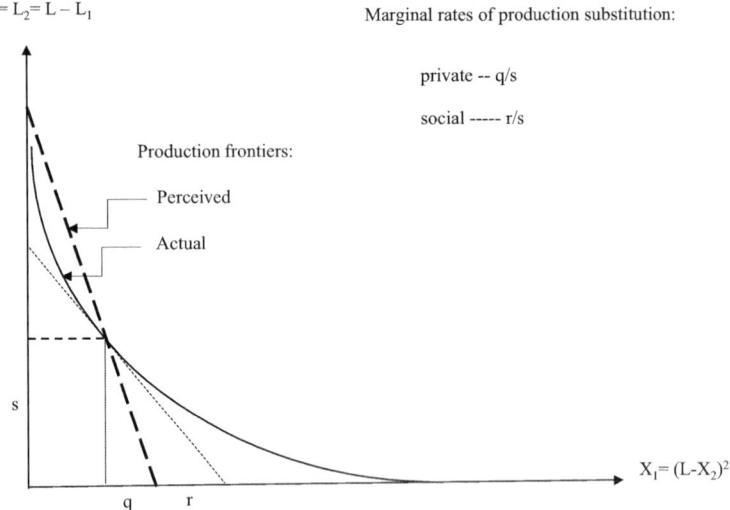

$X_2 = L_2 = L - L_1$

Marginal rates of production substitution:

private -- q/s

social ----- r/s

Production frontiers:

Perceived

Actual

s

$X_1 = (L-X_2)^2$

q   r

Fig. 3.1 Production frontiers and marginal rate of production substitution

$$U(C_1, C_2) = C_1{}^\alpha C_2{}^{1-\alpha}, \quad \alpha \in (0, 1/2) \tag{3.10}$$

with its first order homogenous form. Individuals consume both goods to survive.

Next, to close in on the truth of the debate, consider sequentially three cases below:

Case (i) Any country in autarky
Case (ii) Two countries with equal sizes of labor endowment trade
Case (iii) Two countries with unequal sizes of labor endowment trade

To examine Graham's claim that trade can harm a country, one must first study that country in autarky for comparison. Next, it is not enough to know *whether*, in some scenario, a trading country can end up worse than in autarky. Four more questions need be answered: *why* is that so? In that same scenario, *whether* and *how* can a country also end up better, somehow? And finally *what* control, if any, a country can deploy to master its own fate under that scenario? It turns out that the key rests in the relative sizes of labor endowment. These ultimately decide *how* successful was Graham in promoting tariffs.

3.2.1   Any Country Under Autarky

It is easy to show that the autarkic equilibrium $E = (X_1, X_2) = (C_1, C_2)$ *must* satisfy a pair of conditions:

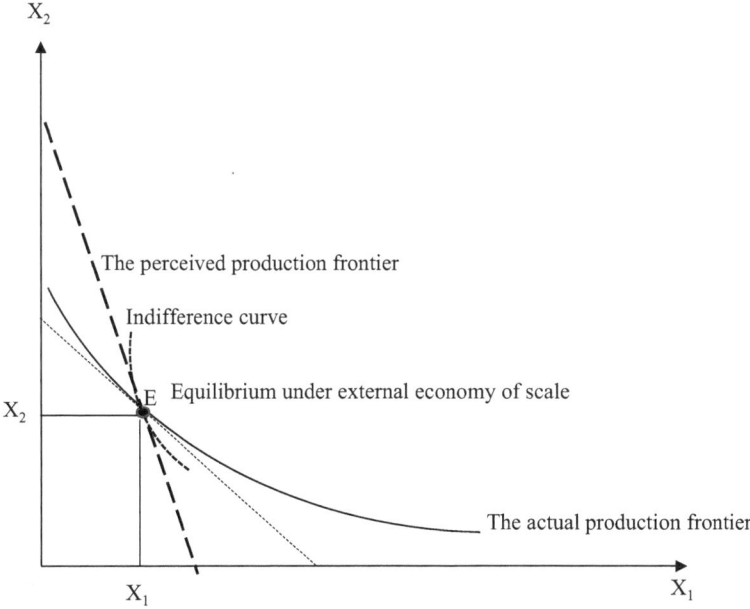

Fig. 3.2 Equilibrium under external economy of scale

$$(X_1)^{1/2} + X_2 = L, \quad (E \text{ is on the } \textit{actual} \text{ production frontier in } (3.7))$$
$$\frac{(1-\alpha)}{X_2} = \frac{\alpha}{pX_1} = \frac{\alpha}{(X_1)^{1/2}} \quad (E \text{ maximizes } U \text{ on that } \textit{perceived} \text{ production frontier}).$$

$$(3.11)$$

See Fig. 3.2 where the indifference locus at E is shown as a dotted curve.

The results for the outputs in the Home Country are:

$$X_1 = (\alpha L)^2, \quad X_2 = (1-\alpha)L \qquad (3.12)$$

One can also derive the Foreign outputs $(X_1{}^*, X_2{}^*)$ and the associated labor allocations.

Proposition 3.3 (*Autarkic equilibrium patterns*)

Tabulated below are the autarkic patterns for prices and quantities of inputs and outputs (Table 3.2).

3.2.2   Two Equally Endowed Trading Countries

Here this example would yield four results of interest.

Table 3.2 Patterns of price, quantity, input-output, and utility: two autarkic countries

Any input endowment		Countries	
L, L^*		Home	Foreign
Prices	Input	$w = 1$	$w* = 1$
	Output	$p = 1/\alpha L$	$p^* = 1/\alpha L^*$
Quantities	Input	$\binom{L_1}{L_2} = \binom{\alpha}{1-\alpha}L$	$\binom{L_1^*}{L_2^*} = \binom{\alpha}{1-\alpha}L^*$
	Output	$\binom{X_1}{X_2} = \binom{(\alpha L)^2}{(1-\alpha)L}$	$\binom{X_1^*}{X_2^*} = \binom{(\alpha L^*)^2}{(1-\alpha)L^*}$
Utility per worker		$\frac{U(C_1,C_2)}{L} = \mu(L)^\alpha \begin{cases} < \\ = \\ > \end{cases} \frac{U(C_1^*,C_2^*)}{L^*} = \mu(L^*)^\alpha$ iff $L \begin{cases} < \\ = \\ > \end{cases} L^*,$	
		for	
		$\mu = \alpha^{2\alpha}(1-\alpha)^{1-\alpha}$	

First, for any output exhibiting scale economy, rational resource allocation calls to concentrate its production in one country only.

Second, the gain from trade does not immediately disappear in the presence of *any* external increasing returns.

Third, in fact, when two trading countries hold *equal comparative advantage*, trade brings *equal* positive gain to both traders, under *increasing*, but not *constant* returns.

Fourth, countries identical in input endowment may differ in output assignments, yet *factor price equalization* remains preserved.

These sharpen one's insight for Graham's case, regarding *how* trade can bring actual harm to any of the countries joining trade with each other.

For two countries with equal amounts of input, one can derive constructively the trade equilibrium in Fig. 3.3, starting from the results about autarky. At an equilibrium with equal gain, both countries presumably consume both goods in equal amounts:

$$C_1 = C_1^*, C_2 = C_2^*, \tag{3.13}$$

at the same bundle:

$$C = (C_1, C_2) = (C_1^*, C_2^*) = C^*, \tag{3.14}$$

But to enjoy the scale economy, production is concentrated for the increasing returns good, say, in one location, the Home Country (by Helpman and Krugman):

$$X_1 = C_1 + C_1^*, X_1^* = 0, \tag{3.15}$$
$$X_2 + X_2^* = C_2 + C_2^*. \tag{3.16}$$

This implies the production bundles of both countries share the same production frontier:

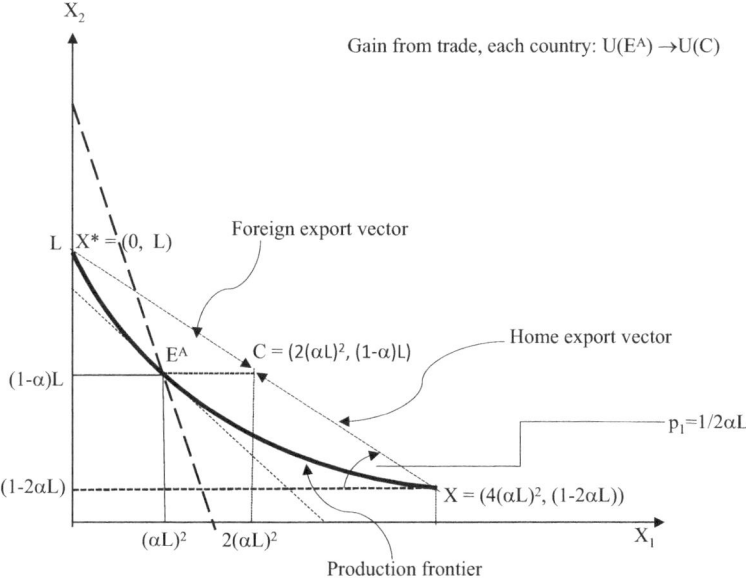

Fig. 3.3 Production and consumption in a world of two countries with equal size

$$X = (X_1, X_2); X^* = (0, X_2{}^*) = (0, L^*) = (0, L), \qquad (3.17)$$

with the common consumption bundle: $C = C^*$ is the middle point of the straight line linking these two production bundles and a slope, $-p = -1/L_1$.

One can now compare with (3.6) and derive the twin conditions in this trading case. First, to be at the middle point along the actual production frontier means:

$$(C_1, C_2) = (X_1/2, \quad (X_2 + X_2{}^*)/2) = \left(L_1{}^2/2, \quad (2L - L_1)/2\right) \qquad (3.18)$$

Next, to achieve the constrained optimum, a condition analogous to (3.11) is:

$$\frac{2\alpha}{L_1} = \frac{\alpha}{pC_1} = \frac{(1-\alpha)}{C_2} = \frac{2(1-\alpha)}{2L - L_1}.$$

which satisfies the solution:

$$L_1 = 2\alpha L; \quad p = 1/2\alpha L. \qquad (3.19)$$

Thus, one has:

Proposition 3.4 *(Trade equilibrium patterns – two countries with equal size)*
Tabulated below are the patterns for prices and quantities of inputs and outputs:

In this special example, Fig. 3.3 shows trade doubles the consumption of good 1 and keeps the same consumption amount of good 2 for everyone. Given the model structure, factor price equalization ensures uniform gains from trade.

3.2.3   Two Unequally Endowed Trading Countries

Next, one shall observe that differences in input endowment *may* (or *may not*) prevent *factor price equalization*. Under some conditions, factor price inequality may cause trade harmful to one country. As an analytic tour de force, this elegant demonstration of the claim of Graham work has been completed by the time of Helpman and Krugman (1985) and was repeated in Krugman (2011).

This example is revisited now because much more can still be learned from a new perspective, both about the true nature of that confirmation of Graham's claim and that policy position *for tariff protection and against trade* by Graham.

Return now to Table 3.3 and focus on the property of *factor price equalization*. This property depends on the *proportions* of input quantities, but not the *equality* in input quantities. Adopt the Helpman–Krugman *convention* on input endowment sizes in (3.1):

$$\beta = L/L^* \leq 1; \tag{3.20}$$

also, the Helpman-Krugman *assumption* for output assignment in (3.15) means:

$$(C_1 + C_1{}^*) = (X_1 + X_1{}^*) = X_1 = L_1{}^2 \tag{3.21}$$

(All good 1 will be produced in the Home Country)

Table 3.3 Patterns of price, quantity, input-output, and utility: two symmetric countries

Equal input endowment		Countries	
$L = L^*$		Home	Foreign
Prices (*factor price equalization*)	Input	$w = 1$	
	Output	$p = 1/2\alpha L$	
Quantities (diversity in production, uniformity in consumption)	Input	$\binom{L_1}{L_2} = \binom{\frac{2\alpha}{1-2\alpha}}{}L$	$\binom{L_1{}^*}{L_2{}^*} = \binom{0}{1}L^*$
	Output	$\binom{X_1}{X_2} = \binom{4(\alpha L)^2}{(1-2\alpha)L}$	$\binom{X_1{}^*}{X_2{}^*} = \binom{0}{L^*}$
	Consumption	$\binom{C_1}{C_2} = \frac{1}{2}\left[\binom{X_1}{X_2} + \binom{X_1{}^*}{X_2{}^*}\right] = \binom{C_1{}^*}{C_2{}^*}$	
Utility (uniform gains from trade)	Autarky	$U(E^A) = \alpha^{2\alpha}(1-\alpha)^{1-\alpha}L^{1+\alpha}$	
	Trade	$U(C) = 2^{\alpha}(\alpha)^{2\alpha}(1-\alpha)^{1-\alpha}L^{1+\alpha} = 2^{\alpha}U$ (E^A)	

$$(C_2 + C_2^*) = (X_2 + X_2^*) = (L - L_1) + L^* = (L - L_1) + L/\beta \qquad (3.22)$$

(All leftover Home Country labor and all Foreign Country labor produce good 2)
Under *factor price equalization*, with $w = w^* = 1$ (by normalization):

$$\text{``World Income''} = w\,(L + L^*) = L + L^* = (1 + 1/\beta)L.$$

The constrained maximization of the Mill-Graham utility index assures that:

$$p(C_1 + C_1^*)/\alpha = L + L^* = (1 + 1/\beta)L = (C_2 + C_2^*)/(1 - \alpha). \qquad (3.23)$$

Substituting (3.21) and (3.22) into (3.23), one gets the "terms of trade" condition:

$$p = [\alpha/(1 - \alpha)]\,[(L - L_1) + L/\beta]/L_1{}^2 \qquad (3.24)$$

At lower β, this assignment has a limit, $L_1 = L$:*complete specialization* in both countries.

To repeat, start from the solution for two countries of equal size. A smaller Home Country relative to the Foreign Country (a lower β) may be offset by a higher portion of Home Country labor assigned to sector 1 (a higher value L_1/L). Equal wages persist in both countries, as long as both countries produce good 2 under constant returns.

At the point of *complete specialization*, with all Home Country labor goes to good 1, produced under increasing returns, one then has for input and output allocations:

$$L_1 = L, \ \ X_1 = L_1{}^2 = L^2, L_2 = 0 = X_2;$$
$$L_1{}^* = 0 = X_1{}^*, L_2{}^* = L^* = L/\beta, X_2{}^* = L/\beta;$$
$$C_1 + C_1{}^* = L^2,$$
$$C_2 + C_2{}^* = L/\beta.$$

The spending shares of income, under the Mill-Graham utility function, imply:

$$p(C_1 + C_1^*) = pL^2 = \alpha\left[pL^2 + L/\beta\right]; \qquad (3.25)$$
$$C_2 + C_2^* = L/\beta = (1 - \alpha)\left[pL^2 + L/\beta\right]. \qquad (3.26)$$

From both the world spending on the two goods, and the output-value and national income identity of the Home Country, one gets the two (non-normalized) price parameters for the system: the unit price for good 1 and wage rate for the Home Country:

$$p = [\alpha/(1 - \alpha)]/\beta L. \qquad (3.27)$$

(from (3.25) and (3.26))

$$w = pX_1/L = pL. \tag{3.28}$$

One can further derive a general formula for wages from the last two expressions:

$$w = max\ \{[\alpha/(1-\alpha)]/\beta, 1\} \geq 1 \equiv\ w^* \tag{3.29}$$

Whether *factor price equalization* ($w = w^*$) happens depends on whether there is proportionately enough Home Country labor to produce the constant returns product, good 2, along with Foreign Country labor. If not, the Home Country wage rises in scarcity. Scarcity is decided by the relative labor proportion, β,not the absolute level, L.

The relevant information of the case of complete specialization can now be tabulated (Table 3.4).

There *may* be *terms of trade* effect in *p for* the Home Country and *against* the Foreign Country, eroding trade gain of the latter, occasionally offsetting it so that trade is harmful. How has this happened is further seen in Fig. 3.4 through the changes in the budget triangles for individuals in the Home Country and the Foreign Country.

3.3 The Approach of the Parametric Map as Global Analysis

To clinch the critical issues, one can now focus attention to the pair of parameters (α, β) underlying the various cases studied so far.
Set:

$$S = \{(\alpha, \beta) : \alpha \in (0, 1/2); \beta \in (0, \infty)\}$$

Next introduce functions:

$$\varphi_1(\alpha) = \alpha/(1-\alpha), \varphi_2(\alpha) = (1-\alpha)^{1/2}\varphi_1(\alpha) < \varphi_1(\alpha).$$

Now partition S into three subsets:

$$S_1 = \{(\alpha, \beta) : \alpha \in (0, 1/2); \varphi_1(\alpha) \leq \beta\},$$
$$S_2 = \{(\alpha, \beta) : \alpha \in (0, 1/2);\ \varphi_2(\alpha) \leq \beta < \varphi_1(\alpha)\}$$
$$S_3 = \{(\alpha, \beta) : \alpha \in (0, 1/2);\ \beta \leq \varphi_2(\alpha)\}.$$

First, by the Foreign Country's budget lines in Fig. 3.4, trade causes loss only if:

$$[\beta(1-\alpha)/\alpha]L < (\alpha/\beta)L,$$

or,

Table 3.4 Patterns of price, quantity, input-output, and utility: two specialized countries

Unequal input endowment		Countries	
$L < L^* = L/\beta,\ \beta < 1$		Home	Foreign
Price	Input	$w = [\alpha/(1-\alpha)]/\beta \geq 1 = w^*$	
	Output	$p_1 = p = [\alpha/(1-\alpha)]/\beta L$	
Quantity	Input	$\binom{L_1}{L_2} = \binom{1}{0}L$	$\binom{L_1^*}{L_2^*} = \binom{0}{1/\beta}L$
	Output	$\binom{X_1}{X_2} = \binom{L^2}{0}$	$\binom{X_1^*}{X_2^*} = \binom{0}{L/\beta}$
	Consumption	$\binom{C_1}{C_2} = \alpha\left(pL + \frac{1}{\beta}\right)L\binom{\alpha/p}{1-\alpha}$	$\binom{C^*_1}{C^*_2} = (1-\alpha)\left(pL + \frac{1}{\beta}\right)L\binom{\alpha/p}{1-\alpha}$
Income		$Y = [\alpha/(1-\alpha)](L/\beta)$	$Y^* = (L/\beta)$
Utility	Autarky	$U^A = \alpha^{2\alpha}(1-\alpha)^{1-\alpha}L^{1+\alpha}$	$U^{A*} = \alpha^{2\alpha}(1-\alpha)^{1-\alpha}(L/\beta)^{1+\alpha}$
	Trade	$U = \{[\alpha/(1-\alpha)\beta]^{1-\alpha}/\alpha^\alpha\}U^A$	$U^* = \{\beta/[(1-\alpha)^{(1/2)}\alpha/(1-\alpha)]\}^{2\alpha}U^{A*}$
	Comparison	$\beta < \alpha/(1-\alpha) \Rightarrow U > U^A$	$\beta < [(1-\alpha)^{(1/2)}\alpha/(1-\alpha)] \Rightarrow U^* < U^{A*}$

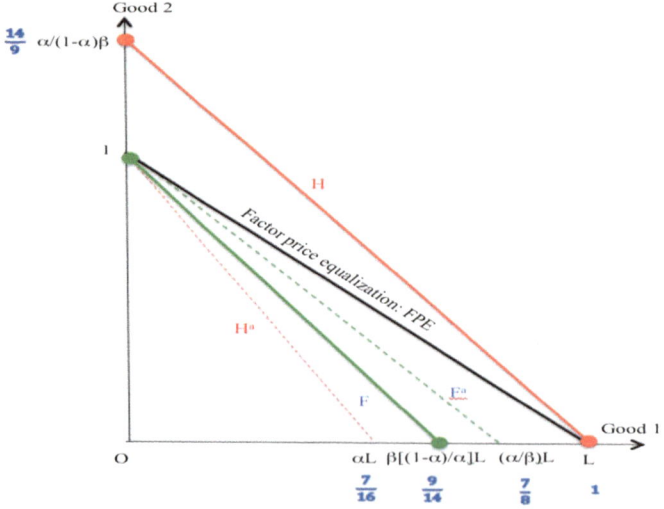

Fig. 3.4 The Graham case with individual budget lines: Home Country gains, Foreign Country loses

	Decomposition of Effects		
	Opening to trade	Terms of trade	Total
	Pivoting toward FPE counter-clockwise	Pivoting from FPE clockwise	
Home country	H^a to FPZ	FPZ to H	Gaining: H^a to H
Foreign country	F^a to FPZ	FPZ to F	Losing: F^a to F
Illustrative values	a = 7/16, b = 1/2, L = 1		

$$\beta < (1-\alpha)^{1/2}\varphi_1(\alpha) = \varphi_2(\alpha)$$

or,

$$(\alpha, \beta) \in S_3.$$

Second, factor prices equalize across countries, if and only if, $w = w^* = 1$. By (3.25), a critical point is reached, with:

$\beta = \alpha/(1 - \alpha) = \varphi_1(\alpha)$, the locus separating the regions S_1 and S_2, in Fig. 3.5. One can thus summarize the analysis so far and tabulate the findings on trade patterns so far:

Proposition 3.5 *A summary of results from the parametric map* (Table 3.5).

It is now clear *what* attracts attention to the Graham case is its anomaly: *trade brings loss. What* makes this happen: a *necessary* but *insufficient* condition is *unequal factor prices*.

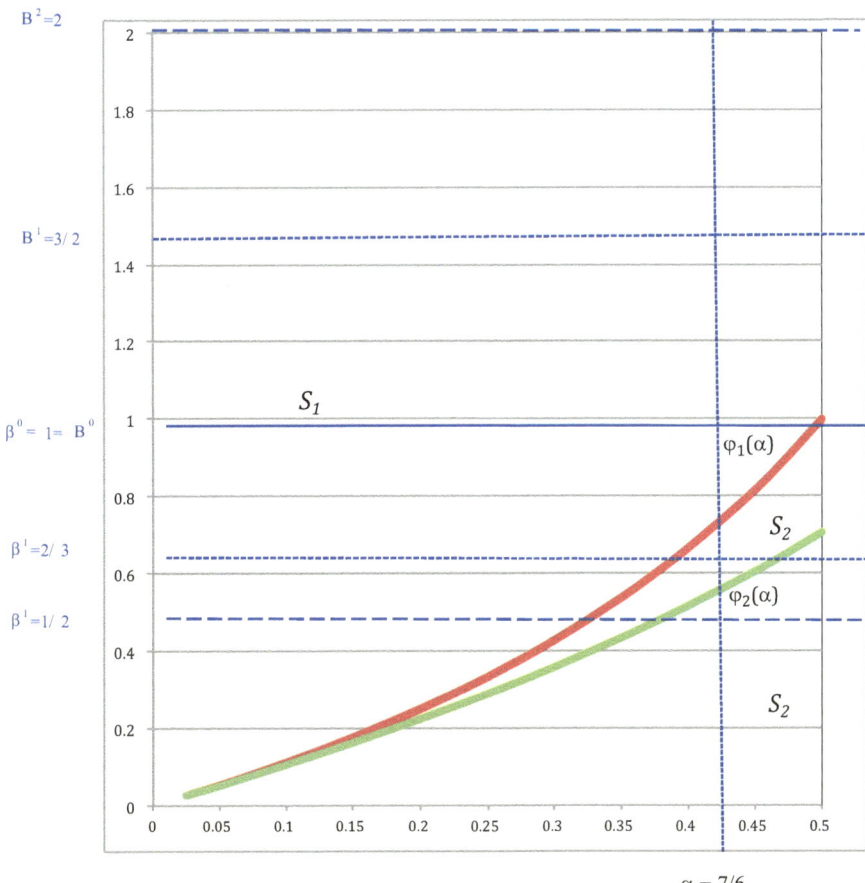

Fig. 3.5 A parametric map for global analysis

Table 3.5 Equilibrium patterns under trade in the parametric map: typology in trichotomy

Zones	Output production	Input prices	Gain from trade
S_1	HOME diversified	Factor prices equalized	Equal positive gains
	FOREIGN specialized		
S_2	BOTH specialized	Factor prices unequal	Unequal positive gains:
			Home, more; foreign, less
S_3	BOTH specialized	Factor prices unequal	HOME: gain
			Foreign: loss

And *what* is the economic cause behind this? That the country (Home) hosting the increasing returns sector lacks labor for a diversified economy: not that the world is labor scarce but that labor is distributed too *unequally*, so neither country can share a constant returns good (good 2) in production – the basis of equal wage between the countries.

3.4   The Alternative Equilibrium Pattern

This study takes advantage of the previous contributions on the production sets under the externalities (Herberg and Kemp 1969; Panagariya 1981; Ethier 1982; Kemp and Tawada 1986) and studies of the Graham model (Chipman 1970), in particular, the elegant example of Helpman and Krugman (1985).

This includes the following conceptual elements, which have to be carefully considered:

(i) The principle, *taking full advantage* of *the scale economy* in trading, implying
(ii) The main result, *producing the increasing returns product in one country* only

This latter implies the presence of multiplicity of equilibrium matching, specifically:

(iii) There are always exactly *two* alternative country-industry assignments:
(iv) The increasing returns sector in the country with no more labor than the other
 (v) The increasing returns sector in the country with no less labor than the other

and the two overlap only in the exceptional case of two countries of equal size

Helpman and Krugman then made a pair of assumptions about the Home Country:

(vi) It is no larger than the Foreign Country, ($\beta \leq 1$).
(vii) It alone hosts the increasing returns industry ($L_1^* = 0$).

The above two are both separately innocuous, without losing generality; together they imply (iv) instead of (v), which is a corollary of (i) along with (ii).

Having worked through the complex and interesting consequences under (iv) in the previous sections, one might now follow (vi).

Actually, this mirror-image model can be easily studied, if in all the formulae under (iv), replacing every symbol β by its reciprocal, $B = 1/\beta$. The result is stated below as:

Proposition 3.6 *When the increasing returns good is always produced in, and only in, the economy with a labor force no less than (instead of no more than) the other country, $\beta \geq 1$. That means,*

$$(\alpha, \beta) \in S_1$$

Thus, factor price equalization obtains; both countries have equal, *positive* trading gain.

A numerical example

Consider:

$$\alpha = 7/16; \ \varphi_1 = \alpha/(1-\alpha) = 7/9; \varphi_2 = (1-\alpha)^{1/2}\varphi_1 = 7/12; L = 1.$$

Next, set:

$$\beta^0 = 1; \ \beta^1 = 2/3; \beta^2 = 1/2;$$
$$B^0 = 1, \ B^1 = 3/2; B^2 = 2.$$

and one immediately finds that:

$$B^2 > B^1 > B^0 = \beta^0 > \varphi_1 > \beta^1 > \varphi_2 > \beta^2 > 0,$$

This implies:

$$(\alpha, B^2), (\alpha, B^1), (\alpha, B^0) \in S_1,$$

that illustrates the above **Proposition 3.6**.

It is time to return to what motivated Graham, arguing for tariff protection. How does Graham's case stand up, in real life? Here, interpreted literally, the story of "trade bringing loss" appears artificial, difficult to defend. Ultimately, in this model, the country smaller in size, less suitable for an increasing returns industry, would insist on hosting that sector, *beggaring thy neighbor* in the process. In contrast, the country enjoying the advantages of a larger population, with higher efficiency in the increasing returns sector in autarky, should consider the self-damaging mode of trade and select tariffs as defense. If it has the sovereignty to impose tariffs as assumed,[1] it ought to engage in interstate bargaining instead and demand *either* no trade at all for both countries *or* trading under factor price equalization, equal gains from trade for both, under that alternative matching between industries and countries. By logic, and the perspective of Samuelson mentioned earlier, the latter is an offer nobody can ever refuse. From the viewpoint of multi-agent decision process (aka game theory), the Graham case for tariff is just unsupportable.

3.5 Concluding Remarks

Economics evolves with time, so does the field of international trade, as one of the component parts. Literature on past issues may not be all directly applicable to issues of the present. Yet they serve as points for reference. Like in chess, serious players follow avidly the record of past matches.

---

[1]In (Asian) history, after geopolitical debacles, debilitated states may lack the sovereignty either to refuse trade or to charge tariff. But that is a different story.

The current study serves notice to the fact that in the context of multiple equilibria, one ought to question the mechanism deciding which of the possible outcomes will prevail in global interactions.

What is excluded for tractability is the element of time in the discussion. Entry to trade by willing parties should not bring immediate harm. But an economy can be easily trapped by the Qwerty effect as shown by David (1985). One might argue that what economists like Graham and his predecessors had in mind (but not analyzed) is compatible with the global view discussed in the present study. The presence of hysteresis prevents infant industries of better-endowed economies to change the world economy from one country product matching to another, and tariff protection may serve to trigger the switch. That story seems to explain how Britain displaced the Netherlands and America displaced Britain. But there have been also too many failures in import substitution industrialization like Argentina under Peron. A full-fledged study would have to proceed rigorously from abstract assumptions, in a global scope.

Nowadays with waves of creative destruction, speed is the essence, and logistics is a tradable service for the rise or fall of countries like firms. New research is needed.

Acknowledgment While retaining responsibilities for all errors and omissions, the author thanks for comments from Professors Roxana Bobulescu, Winston Chang, Nancy Chau, Murray Kemp, Assaf Razin, An-Chi Tung and an anonymous reviewer.

References

Aumann, R. J. (1964). Markets with a continuum of traders. *Econometrica, 32*, 39–50.

Bobulescu, R. (2002). The 'Paradox' of F. Graham (1890–1949): A study in the theory of international trade. *European Journal of the History of Economic Thought, 9*, 402–429.

Bobulescu, R. (2007). Parametric externalities and the Cambridge controversy on returns. *European Journal of the History of Economic Thought, 14*, 349–372.

Chipman, J. S. (1970). External economy of scale and competitive equilibrium. *Quarterly Journal of Economics, 84*, 347–385.

David, P. A. (1985). Clio and the economics of QWERTY. *American Economic Review* (Papers and Proceedings), *75*, 332–337.

Ethier, W. J. (1982). National and international returns to scale in the modern theory of international trade. *American Economic Review, 72*, 389–405.

Graham, F. D. (1923). Some aspects of protection further considered. *Quarterly Journal of Economics, 37*, 199–227.

Grandmont, J.-M. & McFadden, D. (1972). A technical note on classical gains from trade. *Journal of International Economics, 2*, 109–125.

Helpman, E., & Krugman, P. R. (1985). *Market structure and foreign trade: Increasing returns, imperfect competition and the international economy*. Cambridge, MA: MIT Press.

Herberg, H., & Kemp, M. C. (1969). Some Implications of Variable Returns to Scale. *Canadian Journal of Economics, 2*, 403–415.

Jones, R. W. (1961). Comparative Advantage and the Theory of Tariffs: A Multi-country, Multi-commodity Model. *Review of Economic Studies, 28*, 161–175.

Kemp, M. C. (1962). The Gain from International Trade. *Economic Journal, 87*, 803–819.

Kemp, M. C., & Negishi, T. (1970). Variable return to scale, commodity taxes, factor market distortions and their implications for gains from trade. *Swedish Journal of Economics, 72*, 1–11.

Kemp, M. C., & Tawada, M. (1986). The world production frontier under variable returns to scale. *Journal of International Economics, 21*, 251–268.

Kemp, M. C., & Wan, H., Jr. (1993). *The welfare economics of international trade.* London: Harwood Academic.

Krugman, P. (2011). Increasing Returns in a Comparative Advantage World. In R. M. Stern (Ed.), *Comparative advantage, growth, and the gains from trade and globalization, A festschrift in Honor of Alan V. Deardorff* (pp. 43–51). Singapore: World Scientific.

Panagariya, A. (1981). Variable returns to scale in production and patterns of specialization. *American Economic Review, 71*, 221–230.

Samuelson, P. A. (1938). Welfare economics and international trade. *American Economic Review, 28*, 261–266.

Sidgwick, H. (1887). *The principles of political economy.* London: MacMillan.

Wan, H., Jr. (1972). A note on trading gain and externalities. *Journal of International Economics, 2*, 173–180.

Chapter 4
Welfare Effects of Trade Liberalization and Coordinated Domestic Sales Tax Reforms Under International Oligopoly

Masayuki Okawa and Tatsuya Iguchi

Abstract This chapter studies the effects of welfare-maximizing and revenue-neutral tariff reduction and coordinated domestic tax reforms carried out until the market is completely liberalized. The setting is an international oligopoly model in which domestic firms, fully foreign-owned subsidiaries, and foreign exporting firms compete in the home market. We show how welfare varies in the process of trade liberalization starting from an initial level to that attained under complete market liberalization. We find that the results on the welfare effects of a one-time infinitesimal tariff–tax reform obtained in earlier studies may not hold when the reform is completed. We next examine the welfare implications of a revenue-neutral tariff–tax reform under a *symmetric* oligopoly setting. We show that, though there are phases in which the reduction of import tariff and domestic sales tax reform raises both welfare and government revenue, the government must raise the sales tax by a greater amount than that necessary for welfare maximization, as the import tariff approaches zero.

Keywords Trade liberalization · International oligopoly · Sales tax reform

4.1 Introduction

In the last two decades of globalization, a number of developing and emerging countries as well as developed countries have liberalized their goods and service markets unilaterally or multilaterally by forming regional trade agreements (RTAs) such as customs unions (CUs) and free trade agreements (FTAs). The countries also have opened up markets for inward foreign direct investment (FDI). Those liberalization policies have led countries to reform their domestic tax systems in order to make domestic markets more efficient in the new economic environments.

M. Okawa (✉) · T. Iguchi
Faculty of Economics, Ritsumeikan University, Kusatsu, Japan
e-mail: mokawa@ec.ritsumei.ac.jp

© Springer Nature Singapore Pte Ltd. 2018
B. Tran-Nam et al. (eds.), *Recent Developments in Normative Trade Theory and Welfare Economics*, New Frontiers in Regional Science: Asian Perspectives 26, https://doi.org/10.1007/978-981-10-8615-1_4

The questions relating to the gainfulness of free trade and/or trade liberalization have attracted much interest of trade theorists. In particular, in a fairly general formal setting, Kemp and Wan (1972) showed that if a perfectly competitive autarkic country liberalizes to a free trading country, there exists a scheme of lump-sum compensation in the country such that no individual is worse off than autarky.[1] Kemp and Wan (1976) extended the above result to the gainfulness of formation of a CU and established Kemp–Wan proposition concerning CUs that, if two or more countries form a CU by adjusting their common external tariff so as to leave their net external trade at the level prior to their formation and eliminating internal trade barriers, the union as a whole and the rest of the world will not worse off than before. Further Ohyama (2002), Panagariya and Krishna (2002), and Kemp (2007) extended the Kemp–Wan proposition concerning CUs to the gainfulness of formation of FTAs.

Turning to the series of theoretical studies on the welfare effects of tariff reduction combined with domestic consumption tax reform in a small open economy, Michael, Hatzipanayotou, and Miller (1993); Hatzipanayatou, Michael, and Miller (1994); and Keen and Ligthart (2002), among others, examined the welfare and revenue effects of tariff reduction and coordinated consumption tax reforms. Overall, the main result reported in the literature is that the reduction of tariffs combined with the increase in consumption tax raises welfare and government revenue. The intuition behind this is that tariff–tax reforms in a small open economy can realize more efficient allocation of domestic resources.

On the other hand, in an *imperfectly* competitive framework, Keen and Ligthart (2005) studied the welfare effects of the following two types of tariff–consumption tax reform: (i) the consumption tax is raised by the same absolute size as the reduction of the import tariff (point-for-point reform), and (ii) the consumption tax is reformed so that the consumer surplus is kept unchanged at the pre-reform level (consumer surplus neutral reform). They showed that both types of reform unambiguously *decrease* domestic welfare. Karakosta and Tsakiris (2014) extended Keen and Ligthart (2005) to a differentiated goods duopoly setting and incorporated the provision of public goods. The analyses of both studies focused only on the two special types of tariff–tax reforms.[2] Okawa and Iguchi (2016) extended Keen and Ligthart (2005) to a setting of an arbitrary number of home and foreign asymmetric oligopoly firms and showed that there are welfare-improving tariff–sales tax reforms and there exist sets of the initial combination of import tariff and sales tax in which both point-for-point and constant price reforms can raise social welfare.[3]

---

[1]For a concise review, see Kemp and Wan (1993).

[2]Fujiwara (2015) and Haufler, Schjelderup, and Stähler (2005) studied welfare effects of tariff reduction and domestic tax reform in two distinct tax bases: destination and origin principles.

[3]We use the term "sales tax" rather than "consumption tax," because the tax is imposed only on the products of oligopolists and not on the numeraire good. In that sense, the sales tax can be regarded as a "selective commodity tax" (see, e.g., Haufler et al., 2005).

In a general number of oligopolists setting, Naito and Abe (2008) introduced trade of both an intermediate good and a final good and derived the conditions under which the government could increase both welfare and government revenue, while McCorriston and Sheldon (2011) focused on the effects on market access and profits of both upstream and downstream firms.

A common feature of the above research is that the analyses are restricted to the effects of a one-time infinitesimal tariff reduction and coordinated domestic tax changes. Thus the analyses are local in scope. However, the liberalization process of the countries consists of gradual and successive steps toward partial and/or complete liberalization of markets rather than a simple one-time reduction type.[4] Thus the results on the effects on welfare and government revenue of a one-time infinitesimal tariff–tax reform may not hold, if the governments continue to eliminate trade barriers and reform domestic taxes until the market is completely liberalized. Thus the derived policy implications based on the static analyses could be misleading.

Second, all the abovementioned studies have not considered the existence and significant role of foreign subsidiary firms operating in the host country. According to the United Nations Conference on Trade and Development (UNCTAD), the shares of stock of inward FDI in the GDP of developed, transitional, and developing countries increased gradually from around 20% in 2000 to more than 30% in 2014 (except in the financial crisis year of 2008).[5]

The purpose of this chapter is to examine how welfare of the country varies in the process of trade liberalization in which the government continues to reduce import tariff *unilaterally* and adjust sales tax until the market is completely liberalized. To that end and to make our results comparable with earlier studies, we set up a simple partial equilibrium international oligopoly model in which three groups of oligopoly firms with different numbers of firms, domestic firms, foreign exporting firms, and fully foreign-owned subsidiary firms, compete in the domestic market. We focus on the following two analyses: (i) the welfare effects of a continuous tariff reduction and sales tax reform in which, starting from a given initial level of import tariff and sales tax, the sales tax is adjusted optimally to each level of a reduced tariff until the tariff is eliminated completely and (ii) the welfare effects of a revenue-neutral trade liberalization in which sales tax is adjusted to keep initial government revenue unchanged for each level of reduced import tariff until the import tariff is eliminated.

We show that, provided that the initial sales tax is *not* optimal for a given initial import tariff that is lower than the optimal level, a welfare-improving one-time infinitesimal tariff reduction and coordinated sales tax reform always exist. If, however, the government were to continue liberalizing the market and reforming the sales tax, then the economy could be worse off when the market is completely liberalized.

---

[4]In forming a RTA, member countries should follow the Article XXIV of the GATT for goods trade and Article V of GATS for service trade. According to paragraph 5(c) of Article XXIV, a reasonable length of time to complete an RTA should exceed 10 years only in exceptional cases. The theoretical explanations and justifications for gradualism in free trade agreements are provided, among others, by Bond and Park (2002) and Chisik (2003).

[5]www.unctad.org/fdistatistics

We next examine the welfare implications of a revenue-neutral tariff–sales tax reform under a *symmetric* oligopoly setting. We show, among other things, that there are phases in which the reduction of import tariff and sales tax reform raise both welfare and government revenue. However, as the import tariff approaches zero, the government must raise the sales tax by an increasing amount than that necessary for welfare maximization.

The remainder of this chapter is organized as follows. Section 4.2 sets up the model. In Sect. 4.3, we study the welfare effects of coordinated trade liberalization and sales tax reforms. Section 4.4 considers the welfare effects of revenue-neutral coordinated trade liberalization and sales tax reform. Section 4.5 presents our concluding remarks.

4.2   The Model

We set up a simple partial equilibrium oligopoly trading model, in which good x is produced by domestic and foreign oligopoly firms and good y is produced in a perfectly competitive market. We take good y as the numeraire and normalize its price to unity. Good x is consumed in the home market only, and the government imposes a specific tariff (τ) on the imports of good x and a specific sales tax (t) on good x. Good x in the home market is served by a fixed number of oligopoly firms, that is, n^d domestic firms (firm d), n^e foreign exporting firms (firm e), and n^f foreign subsidiary firms that are invested directly in and serve the home market (firm f). There are no trade costs.

To accomplish our analysis, we have to derive explicit formulas for the welfare-maximizing and revenue-maximizing combinations of import tariff and sales tax and examine the global changes in welfare caused by the finite changes in those policy measures. As earlier authors did, we also have to pay for simplifying the preference of consumers to assume that the utility function of home consumers is of a quasi-linear and quadratic type: $U(X, y) = aX - (1/2)bX^2 + y$, where $a > 0$ and $b > 0$. In addition, $X = \sum_{j=d,e,f} \sum_{i=1}^{n^j} x_i^j$ is the consumption of good x, where $x_i^j (j = d, e, f)$ is the output of firm i of group j. The derived inverse demand function for good x can be written as $p(X) = a - bX$, where p is the consumers' price of good x.

The production technologies of the firms are identical in each group of domestic and foreign firms but are different between the three groups and are of a constant marginal cost type. Let $c^j (j = d, e, f)$ be the marginal cost of a firm in group j.[6] The fixed costs of the firms are assumed not to exist. The government

---

[6]At this stage, we do not make any assumption about the relationship between marginal costs of the firms, but, in many cases later, we may assume that $c^f \leq c^e \leq c^d$.

imposes a specific import tariff on imports from foreign exporters e, and it imposes a specific sales tax on the outputs of all firms.

Thus our model consists of a simple two-stage game: in stage 1 the government sets τ and t, and in stage 2 the firms compete in Cournot–Nash fashion in the home market. The equilibrium concept of the game is a subgame perfect Cournot-Nash equilibrium, and we solve it backwardly.

In stage 2, for a given initial import tariff (τ^0) and sales tax (t^0), firms compete in Cournot–Nash fashion in the home market. We assume that both the initial pre-reform specific tariff and sales tax are strictly positive and are *not* necessarily optimal. The profits of oligopoly firms can be written as $\pi_i^j = [p(X) - t - c^j]x_i^j$ for firm $j(j = d,f)$ and $\pi_i^e = [p(X) - \tau - t - c^e]x_i^e$, where π_i^j is the profit of firm i in group $j(j = d, e, f)$. The optimal output and profit of each firm in the three groups, total output of good x, consumer price, and consumer's surplus (CS) in the symmetric Cournot–Nash equilibrium in stage 2 are

$$x^d = [a - t + n^e\tau - (N + 1)c^d + C]/b(N + 1), \tag{4.1}$$
$$x^e = [a - t - (n^d + n^f + 1)\tau - (N + 1)c^e + C]/b(N + 1), \tag{4.2}$$
$$x^f = [a - t + n^e\tau - (N + 1)c^f + C]/b(N + 1), \tag{4.3}$$
$$\pi^d = [a - t + n^e\tau - (N + 1)c^d + C]^2/b(N + 1)^2, \tag{4.4}$$
$$\pi^e = [a - t - (n^d + n^f + 1)\tau - (N + 1)c^e + C]^2/b(N + 1)^2, \tag{4.5}$$
$$\pi^f = [a - t + n^e\tau - (N + 1)c^f + C]^2/b(N + 1)^2, \tag{4.6}$$
$$X = [N(a - t) - n^e\tau - C)]/b(N + 1), \tag{4.7}$$
$$p = (a + Nt + n^e\tau + C)/(N + 1), \tag{4.8}$$
$$CS = [N(a - t) - n^e\tau - C]^2/2b(N + 1)^2, \tag{4.9}$$

respectively, where $N \equiv n^d + n^e + n^f$ and $C \equiv \sum\limits_{j=d,e,f} n^j c^j$ is the sum of the marginal costs of all firms.

We assume that all firms produce positive outputs in the Cournot–Nash equilibrium; $x^j > 0$, $\forall j = d, e, f$.[7] The total revenue of the government can be written as $G \equiv tX + \tau n^e x^e$, and we find that

$$G = \{[N(a - t) - n^e\tau - C]t + [a - t - (n^d + n^f + 1)\tau - (N + 1)c^e + C]n^e\tau\}$$
$$/b(N + 1).$$

$$\tag{4.10}$$

We observe that (i) a reduction of an import tariff reduces the profits of firms d and f and increases the profits of firm e as well as the consumer surplus and (ii) an increase in the sales tax reduces the profits of all firms and consumer surplus.

---

[7]We observe that each output under free trade is also positive. That is, $x^j = a - (N + 1)c^j + C > 0$ ($j = d, e, f$).

4.3   Welfare-Maximizing Coordinated Sales Tax Reform Under Trade Liberalization

4.3.1   Welfare-Maximizing Import Tariff and Sales Tax

We first derive the welfare-maximizing import tariff and sales tax formula as the benchmark for the analysis in the next subsections. The welfare of the country consists of the consumer's surplus (CS), the total profits of domestic firms, and the government revenues. It can be written as $W(\tau, t) \equiv CS(\tau, t) + n^d \pi^d(\tau, t) + G(\tau, t)$. The first-order conditions (FOCs) for the welfare maximization are

$$W_\tau \equiv \partial W / \partial \tau = (n^e/b)(N+1)^{-2}(-A_\tau \tau - Bt + \phi_\tau) = 0, \qquad (4.11)$$
$$W_t \equiv \partial W / \partial t = -(1/b)(N+1)^{-2}(n^e B\tau + A_t t + \phi_t) = 0, \qquad (4.12)$$

where $B \equiv N + 2n^d + 2 > 0$, $A_\tau \equiv 2(n^d + n^f + 1)^2 + n^e(2n^f + 1) > 0$, $A_t \equiv 2(n^e + n^f) + N^2 > 0$, and

$$\phi_\tau \equiv (n^d + 1)[a - (N+1)c^e + C] + n^d[a - (N+1)c^d + C]$$
$$- (N+1)n^f(c^e - c^f) \gtrless 0, \qquad (4.13)$$
$$\phi_t \equiv -\{[n^f(a - c^f) - n^d(a - c^d)] + n^e[a - (N+1)c^e + C]$$
$$+ n^d n^e(c^d - c^e) + 2n^d n^f(c^d - c^f) + n^e n^f(c^e - c^f)\} \gtrless 0. \qquad (4.14)$$

We observe that the social welfare function, $W(\tau, t)$, is strictly concave in τ and t, and the second-order condition (SOC) is satisfied (see Appendix 4.1). Solving (4.11) and (4.12), we obtain the unique pair of welfare-maximizing import tariff and sales tax:

$$\tau^W$$
$$= \{(n^d - 1)[a - (N+1)c^e + C] + n^d[a - (N+1)c^d + C] + (a - c^e) - (3+N)(c^e - c^f)n^f\}$$
$$/\widetilde{\Phi},$$

$$(4.15)$$

$$t^W$$
$$= \{2[n^f(a - c^f) - n^d(a - c^d)] + n^d[4n^f(c^d - c^f) + n^e(c^d - c^e)] + n^e n^f(c^e - c^f)\}$$
$$/\widetilde{\Phi}.$$

$$(4.16)$$

where $\widetilde{\Phi} \equiv 2\left[(n^d + n^f)^2 + n^f(n^e + 2)\right] > 0$. We immediately obtain Lemma 4.1.

Lemma 4.1 *The welfare-maximizing import tariff is positive ($\tau^W > 0$) if (i) the consumer's maximum willingness to pay for the good is large enough, (ii) c^e and c^f are close enough, and/or (iii) n^f is small enough. If $n^d = 0$, then $\tau^W \lessgtr 0$ iff $c^e \gtrless c^f$.[8] The* *sign of the welfare-maximizing sales tax (t^W) is in general ambiguous, but (i) if there is no foreign firm in the domestic market ($n^f = 0$), $t^W < 0$; (ii) if there is no domestic firm ($n^d = 0$), $t^W > 0$; (iii) if all firms have identical marginal costs ($c^j = c$, ($j = d, e,$ f)), then $t^W \gtrless 0$ iff $n^f \gtrless n^d$; and finally, (iv) if the number of firms in each group is identical ($n^j = n$), then $t^W \gtrless 0$ iff $c^d \gtrless c^f$.*

4.3.2 One-Time Infinitesimal Tariff Reduction and Coordinated Sales Tax Reform

In the following subsections, we focus on the environment in which $\tau^W > 0$ and examine both cases in which t^W is positive and negative. We define a constraint set of (τ, t), Ω, which ensures that all firms produce positive outputs in the Cournot–Nash equilibrium in stage 2, that is, $\Omega \equiv \{(\tau, t) : x^j(\tau, t) \geq 0, \forall j = d, e, f\}$. In addition, we assume that both the initial import tariff and the sales tax are strictly positive, and we define the set of possible initial combinations: $\Omega^0 \equiv \{(\tau^0, t^0) : x^j(\tau^0, t^0) \geq 0, \forall j = d, e,$ $f\}$. In Fig. 4.1, the set Ω is illustrated as the area surrounded by $x^d = 0$ and $x^e = 0$ lines, and the set $\Omega^0 \subset \Omega$ is the positive quadrant of Ω.[9]

From the welfare function, we find that

$$dW(\tau^0, t^0)/d\tau = W_t(\tau^0, t^0)\left[dt/d\tau - MRS_{\tau t}^W(\tau^0, t^0)\right], \tag{4.17}$$

where $MRS_{\tau t}^W(\tau^0, t^0) \equiv dt/d\tau|_{W(\tau^0, t^0)=const} = -W_\tau(\tau^0, t^0)/W_t(\tau^0, t^0)$ is the marginal rate of substitution between two policies to keep the initial level of welfare unchanged,[10] where $W_\tau(\tau^0, t^0) = (n^e/b)(N+1)^{-2}(-A_\tau\tau^0 - Bt^0 + \phi_\tau)\gtrless 0$, and $W_t(\tau^0, t^0) = -(1/b)(N+1)^{-2}(n^eB\tau^0 + A_t t^0 + \phi_t)\gtrless 0$. The sign of $W_\tau(\tau^0, t^0)$ and $W_t(\tau^0, t^0)$ depends on (τ^0, t^0), and the relationship between them is illustrated in Fig. 4.1. The first-order conditions (FOCs) in (4.11) and (4.12) can be rewritten as

$$t_{\partial W/\partial \tau = 0} = B^{-1}(-A_\tau \tau + \phi_\tau) \tag{4.18}$$

$$t_{\partial W/\partial t = 0} = -A_t^{-1}(n^e B\tau + \phi_t). \tag{4.19}$$

We find from (4.19) that there exists a substitutability between the sales tax and import tariff. The combination of τ and t in (4.18) and (4.19) is drawn as line $W_\tau = 0$

---

[8]Larue and Gervais (2002) showed that there is possibility that the welfare-maximizing tariff can be negative in a different setting.

[9]In Fig. 4.1, the case in which $c^f < c^d$ is illustrated. This assumption is immaterial for the figure.

[10]We note, from the definition of $MRS_{\tau t}^W$, that the slope of the iso-welfare contour at the intersection points with line $W_\tau = 0$ is equal to 0 and ∞ at those with line $W_t = 0$.

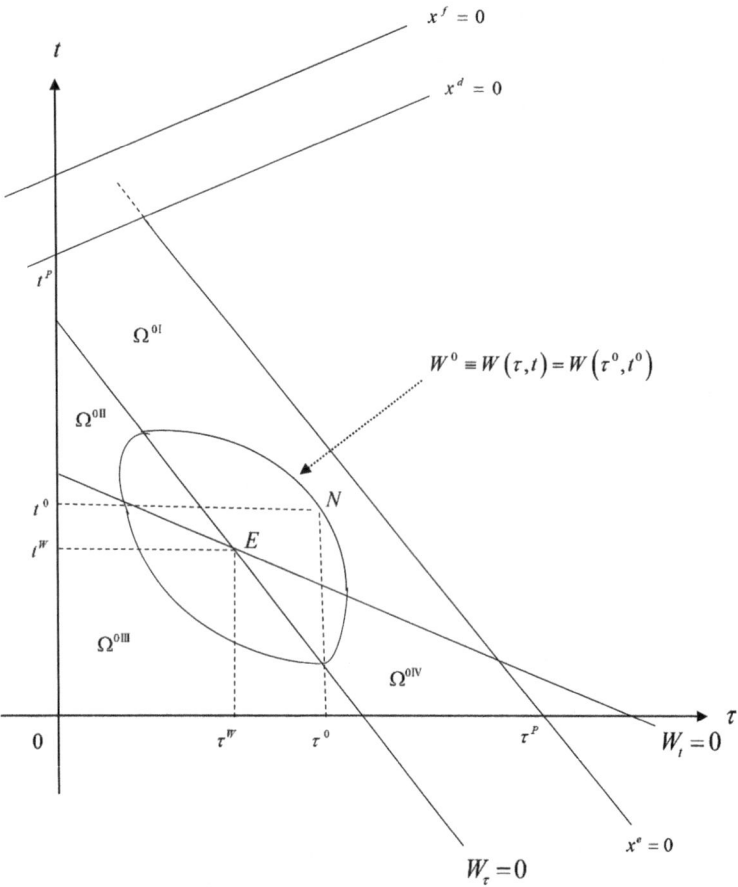

Fig. 4.1 Convex set $W_+^0 \equiv \{(\tau,t) : W(\tau,t) \geq W(\tau^0,t^0)\}$ and the case in which $(\tau^0,t^0) \in \Omega^{0I}$

and line $W_t = 0$, respectively, and (τ^W, t^W) is at intersection point E in Fig. 4.1.[11] τ^P is a prohibitive tariff such that $x^e(\tau^P, 0) = 0$, and t^P is such that $x^d(0, t^P) = 0$. The set Ω^0 is divided into four subsets:

$$\Omega^{0I} \equiv \left\{ (\tau^0, t^0) : W_\tau < 0, W_t < 0, MRS_{\tau t}^W < 0 \right\}$$
$$\Omega^{0II} \equiv \left\{ (\tau^0, t^0) : W_\tau > 0, W_t < 0, MRS_{\tau t}^W > 0 \right\},$$
$$\Omega^{0III} \equiv \left\{ (\tau^0, t^0) : W_\tau > 0, W_t > 0, MRS_{\tau t}^W < 0 \right\},$$
$$\Omega^{0IV} \equiv \left\{ (\tau^0, t^0) : W_\tau < 0, W_t > 0, MRS_{\tau t}^W > 0 \right\}.$$

---

[11]We observe that (i) the slope of line $W_\tau = 0$ is steeper than that of line $W_t = 0$ and (ii) the intercept on the t-axis of line $W_\tau = 0$ is larger than that of $W_t = 0$ if and only if $\tau^W > 0$.

As $W(\tau, t)$ is strictly concave in (τ, t), the set $W_+^0 \equiv \{(\tau, t) : W(\tau, t) \geq W(\tau^0, t^0)\}$ is a convex set. Figure 4.1 illustrates the case in which both τ^W and t^W are positive and the initial combination is denoted at point $N \in \Omega^{0I}$ with the iso-welfare contour $W(\tau, t) = W(\tau^0, t^0)$. The set W_+^0 is illustrated as the convex set surrounded by the iso-welfare contour: $W(\tau, t) = W(\tau^0, t^0)$. Therefore, when the import tariff is reduced, any change in the sales tax that satisfies $dt < MRS_{\tau t}^W(\tau^0, t^0)d\tau > 0$ where $d\tau < 0$ and $MRS_{\tau t}^W(\tau^0, t^0) < 0$ and shifts point N in the set W_+^0 can increase social welfare. By applying the similar reasoning to other cases in which (τ^0, t^0) exist in Ω^{0II} to Ω^{0IV}, we can see that there exist welfare-improving sales tax reforms associated with a tariff reduction.[12] Therefore, we have Lemma 4.2.

Lemma 4.2 *If a tariff reduction and the coordinated sales tax reform are infinitesimal in size and if the initial sales tax is not optimal for a given initial tariff that is lower than the optimal level, then there is a welfare-improving tax reform associated with a reduction of import tariff.*

4.3.3 Complete Trade Liberalization and Coordinated Sales Tax Reform

We now turn to study how welfare varies in the continuous tariff reduction process in which the government optimally adjusts the sales tax for each level of the reduced import tariff. We obtain the welfare-maximizing sales tax for a given $\tau \in [0, \tau^P)$ from (4.18):

$$t = \tilde{t}(\tau) \equiv -(A_t)^{-1}(n^e B\tau + \phi_t). \tag{4.20}$$

We see that the government will monotonically raise the sale tax as it reduces the import tariff. Letting t^* be the optimal sales tax when the market is perfectly liberalized, then

$$t^* = -(A_t)^{-1}\phi_t. \tag{4.21}$$

There are three possible cases for the combination of the sign of t^W and t^*: (i) $t^W > 0$, $t^* > 0$, (ii) $t^W < 0$, $t^* < 0$, and (iii) $t^W < 0$, $t^* > 0$. We now examine case (i) to case (iii) consecutively.

Case (i): $t^W > 0$ and $t^* > 0$. Figure 4.2 illustrates the iso-welfare curve of $W(0, t^*)$ as a contour $W^* \equiv W(\tau, t) = W(0, t^*)$. Define $W_+^* \equiv \{(\tau, t) : W(\tau, t) \geq W(0, t^*)\}$.

---

[12]However, we have exceptional cases where the sales tax reforms cannot raise welfare. If the initial sales tax is the optimal level for any given initial import tariff which is lower than the optimal tariff, any change in sales tax associated with a tariff reduction will reduce welfare. In Fig. 4.1, these cases occur when the initial combination of sales tax and import tariff (τ^0, t^0) is on the left-hand segment of the optimal point E on $W_t = 0$ line.

This convex set is illustrated as the set enclosed by iso-welfare contour $W^* = W$ $(0, t^*)$. We observe that if $(\tau^0, t^0) \in W_+^*$, then $W(0, t^*) < W(\tau^0, t^0)$ and that the economy is worse off, when trade is completely liberalized and the welfare-maximizing sales tax is imposed. Conversely, if $(\tau^0, t^0) \notin W_+^*$, then $W(0, t^*) > W(\tau^0, t^0)$ and the economy would be better off. In Sect. 4.2, we have shown that if the initial sales tax is not optimal for a given initial import tariff that is lower than the optimal level, then there are always a welfare-improving one-time infinitesimal coordinated tariff reduction and sales tax reform. However, if the government pursues perfect trade liberalization and sales tax reform, the abovementioned result does not always hold.

To observe how the sales tax should be adjusted optimally and how social welfare changes in the process of trade liberalization, we further divide the set W_+^* into four subsets: $W_+^{*k} \equiv W_+^* \cap \Omega^{0k}$, $(k = I, II, III, IV)$. We consecutively examine the cases in which (τ^0, t^0) is in Ω^{0I} to Ω^{0IV}.

1. Suppose first that $(\tau^0, t^0) \in W_+^{*I} \subset \Omega^{0I}$ and $\tau^0 > \tau^W$. Figure 4.2 illustrates this case. If $t^0 > \tilde{t}(\tau^0)$ (respectively, $t^0 < \tilde{t}(\tau^0)$), the government should first reduce (respectively, raise) the initial sales tax to the optimal level, $t = \tilde{t}(\tau^0)$, and then monotonically increase it along $t = \tilde{t}(\tau) \, \forall \tau \in [0, \tau^0]$ as the import tariff is reduced from τ^0. As τ is reduced, social welfare increases, peaks at (τ^W, t^W), and then starts to decrease monotonically to $W(0, t^*)$ when τ is reduced further to zero. On the other hand, if $\tau^0 < \tau^W$, social welfare monotonically decreases as τ is reduced. If the government can stop reducing τ at a level in the interval: $[\bar{\tau}^0, \tau^0]$, where $\bar{\tau}^0$ is the threshold level at which $W(\bar{\tau}^0, \tilde{t}(\bar{\tau}^0)) = W(\tau^0, t^0) \quad \forall \tau \in [\bar{\tau}^0, \tau^0]$, welfare becomes higher than or equal to the initial level. However, if the import tariff is reduced further, welfare becomes lower than the initial level: $W(\tau, \tilde{t}(\tau)) < W(\tau^0, t^0) \forall \tau \in [0, \bar{\tau}^0]$. On the other hand, if $(\tau^0, t^0) \in (\Omega^{0I} - W_+^{*I})$, then, although the process of trade liberalization and sales tax reform is similar with the abovementioned case, welfare at $(0, t^*)$ is higher than at the initial level. Therefore, the economy would be better off with the perfect market liberalization under the optimal sale tax.

2. In the case that $(\tau^0, t^0) \in \Omega^{0II}$, as $t^0 > \tilde{t}(\tau^0)$, the government should reduce the initial sales tax to $t = \tilde{t}(\tau^0)$ increasing social welfare to $W(\tau^0, \tilde{t}(\tau^0))$. However, as the government reduces τ to zero and increases the sales tax along $t = \tilde{t}(\tau)$ to t^* for $\tau \in [0, \tau^W]$, welfare decreases to $W(0, t^*)$. If $(\tau^0, t^0) \in W_+^{*II}$, then $W(0, t^*) < W(\tau^0, t^0)$ and the economy becomes worse off, whereas if $(\tau^0, t^0) \in (\Omega^{0II} - W_+^{*II})$, the economy would be better off.

3. If $(\tau^0, t^0) \in \Omega^{0III} \cup \Omega^{0IV}$, then $t^0 < \tilde{t}(\tau^0)$. Thus, the government should first raise the initial sales tax to the optimal level, $t = \tilde{t}(\tau^0)$, and further raise it along $t = \tilde{t}$ $(\tau) \, \forall \tau \in [0, \tau^0]$. If $\tau^0 > \tau^W$, welfare initially increases until the import tariff reaches τ^W and then starts to decrease, whereas if $\tau^0 < \tau^W$, welfare monotonically decreases to $W(0, t^*)$ as τ is reduced to zero. Furthermore, if

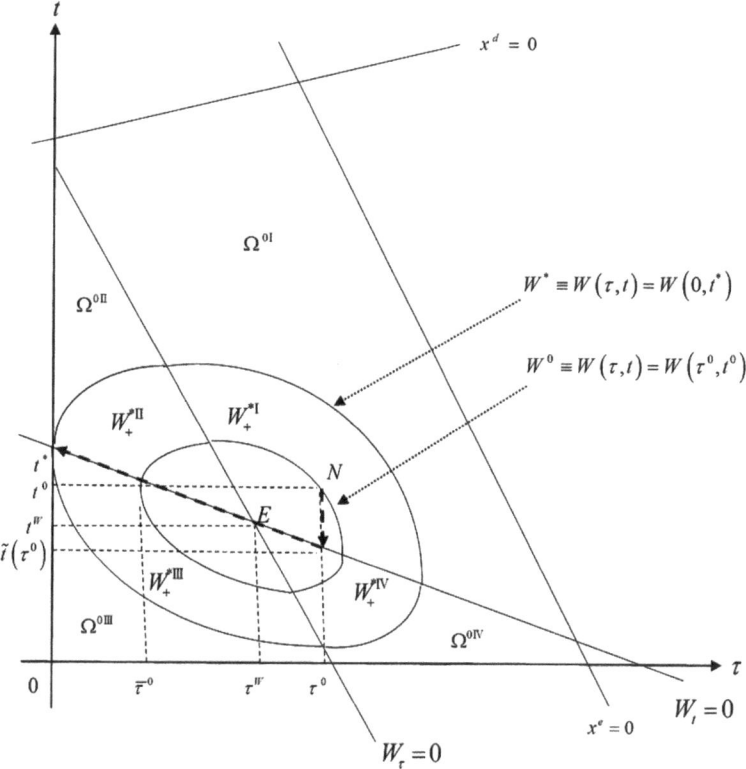

Fig. 4.2 Case (i): $t^W > 0$ and $t^* > 0$

$(\tau^0, t^0) \in W_+^{*III} \cup W_+^{*IV}$, then, when the market is perfectly liberalized, the economy would be worse off than at the initial level, whereas if $(\tau^0, t^0) \in (\Omega^{0II} - W_+^{*II})$, the economy would be better off.

Case (ii): $t^W < 0$ and $t^* < 0$.[13] Figure 4.3 illustrates this case where Ω^{0III} and Ω^{0IV} disappear, so that we have only Ω^{0I} and Ω^{0II}. The initial combination is illustrated as point N in Ω^{0I}.

The government should first turn its initial positive sales tax (t^0) to sales subsidy at the level $t = \tilde{t}(\tau^0) < 0$ and then gradually reduce the size of subsidy to the final level t^* along $t = \tilde{t}(\tau)$ as it reduces the import tariff to zero. If $(\tau^0, t^0) \notin W_+^{*I} \cup W_+^{*II}$ (respectively, $(\tau^0, t^0) \in W_+^{*I} \cup W_+^{*II}$), then welfare when market liberalization is completed and the optimal sales subsidy is imposed becomes higher (respectively,

---

[13]The two special cases in which this sign combination occurs are, for example, (i) $n^f = 0$, $n^d > n^e$, and $c^d \geq c^e$ and (ii) $c^j = c$, ($j = d, e, f$) and $n^f + n^e \leq n^d$.

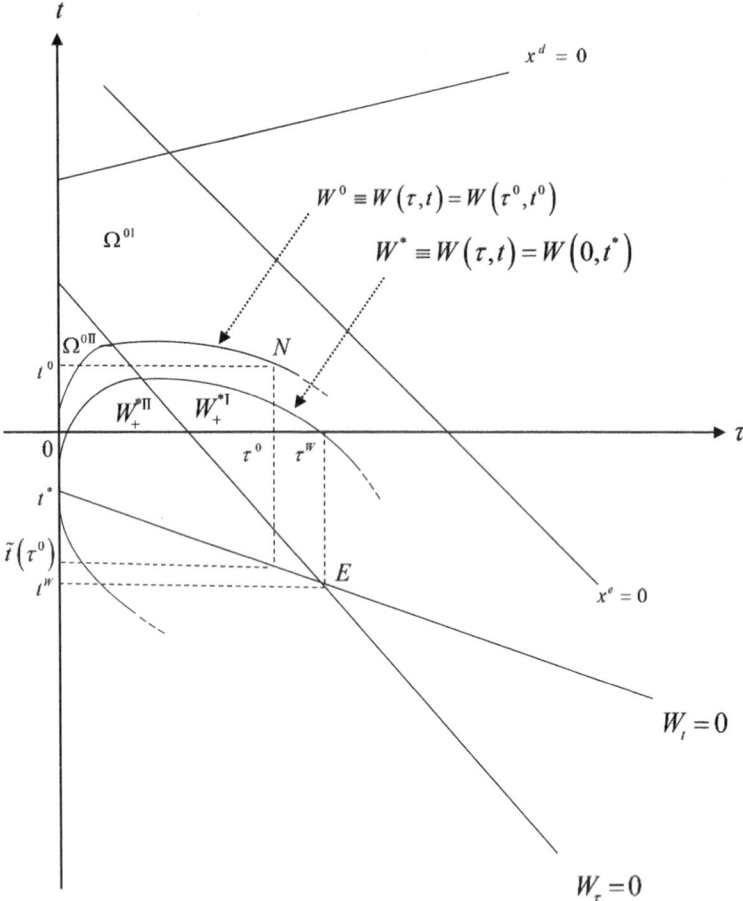

Fig. 4.3 Case (ii): $t^W < 0$ and $t^* < 0$

lower) than the initial level, that is, $W(0, t^*) > W(\tau^0, t^0)$ (respectively, $W(0, t^*) < W(\tau^0, t^0)$).

Case (iii): $t^W < 0$ and $t^* > 0$.[14] Figure 4.4 illustrates this case. The initial combination is point N. As the government reduces the import tariff gradually, it reduces the size of the sales subsidy along $t = \tilde{t}(\tau)$ to zero when the import tariff is reduced to the threshold level $\tilde{\tau}$. Then, as the government reduces the import tariff further, the government changes its sales tax policy from providing the sales subsidy to imposing sales tax and raises the sales tax to t^* when τ reaches zero. If $(\tau^0, t^0) \notin$

---

[14]The special cases in which the combination, $t^W < 0$ and $t^* > 0$, occurs are, for example, (i) $n^f = 0$, $n^e > n^d$, and $c^e \leq c^d$ and (ii) $c^j = c(j = d, e, f)$ and $n^f < n^d < n^f + n^e$.

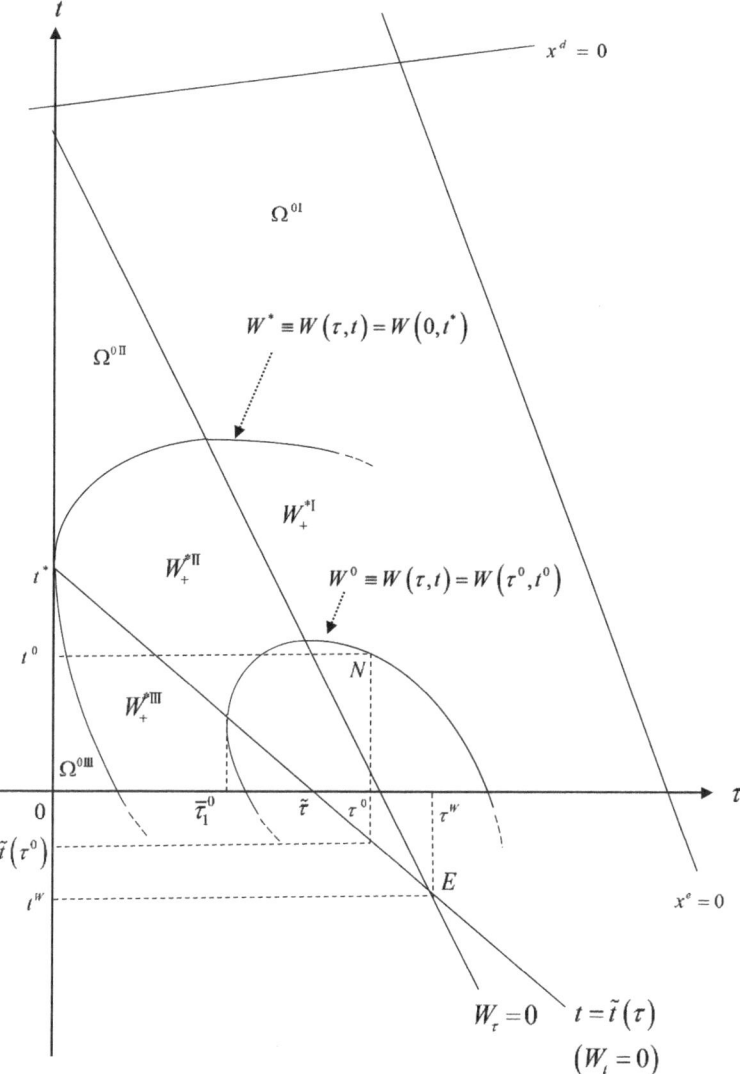

Fig. 4.4 Case (iii): $t^W < 0$ and $t^* > 0$

W_+^* (respectively, $(\tau^0, t^0) \in W_+^*$), then $W(0, t^*) > W(\tau^0, t^0)$ (respectively, $W(0, t^*)$ $< W(\tau^0, t^0)$). If the government can opt for partial trade liberalization to reduce the import tariff to a level in $[\bar{\tau}^0, \tau^0]$, then welfare after partial liberalization is higher or equal to the initial level. We summarize our results in Proposition 4.1.

Proposition 4.1 *Suppose that $(\tau^0, t^0) \in \Omega^0$ and the government pursues complete trade liberalization and sales tax reform. Let t^* be the welfare-maximizing sales tax (subsidy) when trade is completely liberalized ($\tau = 0$), and let $W_+^* \equiv \{(\tau, t) : W(\tau, t) > W(0, t^*)\}$ and $\bar{\tau}^0$ be such that $W(\bar{\tau}^0, \tilde{t}(\bar{\tau}^0)) = W(\tau^0, t^0)$. (i) If $(\tau^0, t^0) \in W_+^*$, then welfare when trade liberalization and sales tax reform are completed is lower than the initial welfare. However, if the government could opt for partial trade liberalization and sales tax reform by reducing the import tariff to a level in $[\bar{\tau}^0, \tilde{t}(\bar{\tau}^0))$, then welfare would be higher or equal to the initial level. (ii) If $(\tau^0, t^0) \notin W_+^*$, then welfare when coordinated trade liberalization and sales tax reform are completed is higher than the initial welfare.*

4.4 Revenue-Neutral Trade Liberalization and Sales Tax Reform

In this section, we study revenue-neutral trade liberalization and sales tax reform in which the sales tax is adjusted so that the initial government revenue is kept unchanged. We examine how the revenue-neutral tariff–sales tax reform affects welfare when the tariff is continuously reduced to zero.

4.4.1 Revenue-Maximizing Import Tariff and Sales Tax

We first derive the formulas of the revenue-maximizing import tariff and sales tax that are necessary in the following analysis. From (4.10), the FOCs for revenue maximization are[15]

$$G_\tau = n^e [a - 2t - 2(1 + n^d + n^f)\tau - (1 + N)c^e + C][b(N + 1)]^{-1}, \text{ and} \quad (4.22)$$
$$G_t = [N(a - 2t) - 2n^e\tau - C][b(N + 1)]^{-1} = 0. \quad (4.23)$$

Thus, we obtain revenue-maximizing tariff and sales tax:

$$\tau^G = [n^d(c^d - c^e) - n^f(c^e - c^f)][2(n^d + n^f)]^{-1} \gtrless 0, \text{ and} \quad (4.24)$$
$$t^G = [n^d(a - c^d) + n^f(a - c^f)][2(n^d + n^f)]^{-1} > 0. \quad (4.25)$$

The revenue function $G(\tau, t)$ is strictly concave in τ and t (see Appendix 4.2), and thus, the pair (τ^G, t^G) is unique and the SOC is satisfied. We should note that the sign

---

[15] $G_i \equiv \partial G/\partial i, (i = \tau, t)$

of τ^G could be both positive and negative.[16] From (4.24), we observe that τ^G is independent of the number of exporting firms e (n^e) and that $\tau^G \gtreqless 0 \Leftrightarrow \alpha^d c^d + \alpha^f c^f \gtreqless c^e$, where $\alpha^j \equiv n^j/(n^d + n^f)$, $(j = d,f)$. Thus, if the marginal cost of exporting firm e is lower (respectively, larger) than the weighted average of the marginal costs of firms d and f, the revenue-maximizing import tariff is positive (respectively, negative). In our setting, tariff revenue is just one of the sources of the government revenue, and the import tariff is levied on the products of exporting firms only, while the sales tax is imposed on the products of all firms in the market and covers a broader range of tax base. Thus, the government manipulates the role of two policies to raise its total revenue by providing an import subsidy to increase market efficiency and by imposing a positive sales tax to shift the profits of foreign subsidiaries and exporters to the government.[17]

On the other hand, the revenue-maximizing sales tax is definitely positive. This result sharply contrasts with the welfare-maximizing sales tax, which can be negative when the government can raise social welfare through increasing market efficiency by providing a sales subsidy to all firms.

4.4.2 Revenue-Neutral Trade Liberalization and Sales Tax Reform: Symmetric Oligopoly Case

We now examine the welfare effects of revenue-neutral trade liberalization and sales tax reform that keeps a government's pre-reform revenue unchanged. To keep tractability of our analysis, we focus on a *symmetric* oligopoly case in which $c^j = c$ and $n^j = n$, $(j = d, e, f)$. In this symmetric oligopoly case, the constraint set Ω in Sect. 4.3 is reduced to the convex set: $\Lambda \equiv \{(\tau, t) : a - t + n\tau \geq c, a - t - (2n + 1)\tau \geq c\}$. We define the set of initial policy combinations $\Lambda^0 \subset \Lambda$ which is the positive quadrant of Λ. We divide it into five subsets, from Λ_0^0 to Λ_4^0.[18] Deleting the redundant subset Λ_0^0, from our analysis, the subsets Λ_1^0 to Λ_4^0 are characterized as follows:

---

[16]The possibility that the revenue-maximizing tariff could be negative cannot appear when the government's revenue consists of tariff revenue only, regardless of whether the market structure is perfectly or imperfectly competitive. From (4.22), we obtain $\tau_{t=0}^G = [2(1 + n^d + n^f)]^{-1}[a - (1 + N)c^e + C] > 0$.

[17]Collie (1991), Larue and Gervais (2002), and Clarke and Collie (2006), among others, compared the maximum welfare tariff with the maximum revenue tariff.

[18]Suppose $(\tau^0, t^0) \in \Lambda_0^0$. Since $G(,)$ is strictly concave and the revenue-maximizing pair is at R in Figure 4.5, the same government revenue as $G(\tau^0, t^0)$ with higher social welfare can be attained by a pair (τ, t) in Λ_1^0 to Λ_4^0. Thus, we assume that the government prefers an initial pair (τ^0, t^0) in Λ_1^0 to Λ_4^0.

$$\Lambda_1^0 \equiv \{(\tau^0, t^0) : W_t < 0, MRS_{\tau t}^W < 0, MRS_{\tau t}^G > 0\},$$
$$\Lambda_2^0 \equiv \{(\tau^0, t^0) : W_t < 0, MRS_{\tau t}^W < 0, MRS_{\tau t}^G < 0\},$$
$$\Lambda_3^0 \equiv \{(\tau^0, t^0) : W_t < 0, MRS_{\tau t}^W > 0, MRS_{\tau t}^G < 0\},$$
$$\Lambda_4^0 \equiv \{(\tau^0, t^0) : W_t > 0, MRS_{\tau t}^W < 0, MRS_{\tau t}^G < 0\}.$$

where

$MRS_{\tau t}^G(\tau^0, t^0) \equiv -G_\tau(\tau^0, t^0)/G_t(\tau^0, t^0)$ is the marginal rate of substitution between τ and t to keep the initial government revenue unchanged.

In Fig. 4.5,[19] the combination of the welfare-maximizing import tariff and sales tax is point E, where $(\tau^W, t^W) = ((a - c)/(3n + 1)^2(5n + 2), 0)$, while the revenue-maximizing pair is point R where $(\tau^G, t^G) = (0, (a - c)/2)$. Recalling that both $W(,)$ and $G(,)$ are strictly concave in (τ, t), we observe that the revenue-neutral welfare-maximizing pair $[\tau^{GW}(\tau^0, t^0), t^{GW}(\tau^0, t^0)]$ for a given $G^0 = G(\tau^0, t^0)$ is the unique solution of the constraint maximization problem to maximize $W(\tau, t)$ subject to $G(\tau, t) = G(\tau^0, t^0)$. We can show the solution pair exists in Λ_2^0 (see Appendix 4.3).

Since the government keeps the initial revenue unchanged, the sales tax is adjusted along the iso-revenue contour of $G(\tau^0, t^0)$, as the import tariff is continuously reduced. We first find that if $(\tau^0, t^0) \in \Lambda_1^0$ or $(\tau^0, t^0) \in \Lambda_2^0$ and $\tau^0 > \tau^{GW}(\tau^0, t^0)$, then social welfare increases as τ is reduced and reaches the maximum welfare at $[\tau^{GW}(.), t^{GW}(.)]$. Thus, we observe that if (τ^0, t^0) is in one of the above sets, the government could raise both revenue and welfare from the initial levels. If τ is reduced further from τ^{GW}, social welfare turns to decrease monotonically. Let t^f be the sales tax that keeps the initial revenue unchanged when the market is completely liberalized: $t^f = \left[3n(a - c) - D^{\frac{1}{2}}\right]/18n^2(a - c)$ where $D \equiv 9[n(a - c)]^2 - 12b^{-1}n$ $(3n + 1)G(\tau^0, t^0)$, which we assume to be positive. We find that $t^f > 0$. If $(0, t^f) \in W_+^0$ [respectively, $(0, t^f) \notin W_+^0$], then the economy will be better off (respectively, worse off) than pre-reform situation at the complete trade liberalization.

We next observe that if $(\tau^0, t^0) \in \Lambda_3^0$ or $(\tau^0, t^0) \in \Lambda_2^0$ and $\tau^0 < \tau^{GW}(\tau^0, t^0)$, then the social welfare monotonically decreases as τ is reduced and, again, if $(0, t^f) \in W_+^0$ [respectively, $(0, t^f) \notin W_+^0$], then the economy would be better off (respectively, worse off) than the pre-reform situation at complete trade liberalization. On the other hand, in the case where $(\tau^0, t^0) \in \Lambda_4^0$, the welfare effect of reduction of import tariff is not unambiguous. We find that if $MRS_{\tau t}^W < MRS_{\tau t}^G$ (respectively, $MRS_{\tau t}^W > MRS_{\tau t}^G$) then, as τ is reduced, the welfare decreases (respectively, increases). Those results are summarized in Proposition 4.2.

Proposition 4.2 *Suppose that the number of oligopoly firms in each group and the marginal costs of all firms are identical and that the government undertakes revenue-neutral partial or complete trade liberalization and sales tax reform. (i) If $(\tau^0, t^0) \in \Lambda_1^0$ or $(\tau^0, t^0) \in \Lambda_2^0$ and $\tau^0 > \tau^{GW}(\tau^0, t^0)$, then social welfare increases as τ is reduced and reaches its maximum level at $[\tau^{GW}(.), t^{GW}(.)]$. If τ is reduced further, social welfare starts to decrease. If $(0, t^f) \in W_+^0$ [respectively, $(0, t^f) \notin W_+^0$], then the economy would be better off (respectively, worse off) than the pre-reform situation at*

---

[19]In Figure 4.5, for the simplicity, lines $x^d = x^f = 0$ and $x^e = 0$ are deleted.

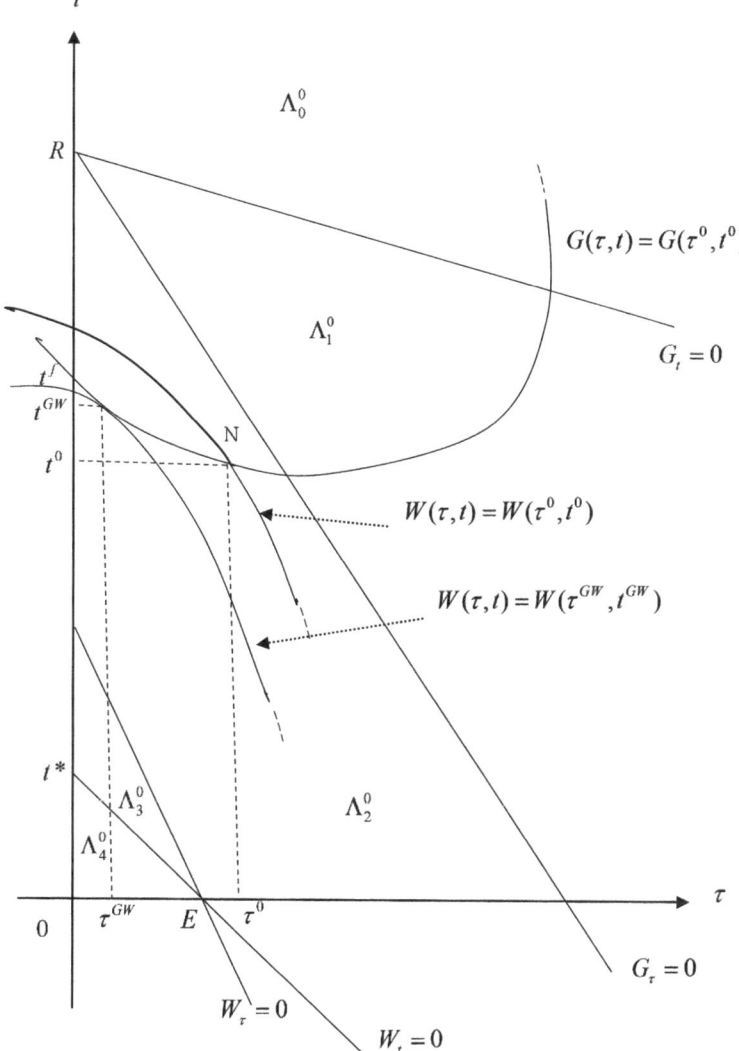

Fig. 4.5 Revenue-neutral reform: symmetric oligopoly case

complete trade liberalization. (ii) If $\left(\tau^0,t^0\right)\in\Lambda_3^0$ or $\left(\tau^0,t^0\right)\in\Lambda_2^0$ and $\tau^0<\tau^{GW}(\tau^0,\text{t}^0)$, then social welfare monotonically decreases as τ is reduced. If $\left(0,t^f\right)\in W_+^0$ [respectively, $\left(0,t^f\right)\notin W_+^0$], then the economy would be better off (respectively, worse off) than the pre-reform situation at complete trade liberalization. (iii) If $\left(\tau^0,t^0\right)\in\Lambda_4^0$ and $MRS_{\tau t}^W<MRS_{\tau t}^G$ (respectively, $MRS_{\tau t}^W>MRS_{\tau t}^G$), then social welfare decreases (respectively, increases) as τ is reduced.

We find that, in the phase in which $\tau<\tau^{GW}$, the government must raise the sales tax increasingly higher than the welfare-maximizing level in order to keep its revenue unchanged. Thus the divergence between a revenue-neutral sales tax and a welfare-maximizing sales tax becomes larger as the reduced tariff approaches zero. This implies that it would be more desirable for the government to switch its revenue-neutral trade liberalization to a mixed policy with a combination of welfare-maximizing reform and lump-sum income transfer that could attain higher welfare by keeping the pre-reform government revenue unchanged.

4.5 Concluding Remarks

This chapter has first examined the welfare effects of one-time infinitesimal tariff reduction with coordinated domestic tax reform to make our results comparable with those obtained by earlier papers. However, trade liberalization process with domestic tax reforms in countries is not of such one-time type and consists of gradual successive process toward partial or complete liberalization. By setting up a simple international oligopoly model, we have seen how welfare varies as the government continues to liberalize trade and reform domestic tax system and shown that, depending on the level of the initial tariff and tax, such reform may decrease the welfare when the import tariff is eliminated.

In the process, domestic firms and the foreign-owned subsidiary firms are hurt by those reforms. Thus, domestic and foreign subsidiary firms might oppose the reform. We observe from simple comparative statics with respect to the marginal cost of domestic firms (c^d) in Eqs. (4.4), (4.9), and (4.10) that $\partial \pi^d / \partial c^d < 0$, $\partial CS / \partial c^d < 0$, and $\partial G / \partial c^d \lessgtr 0 \Leftrightarrow n^e \tau \lessgtr t$. Therefore, a sufficient condition for $\partial W / \partial c^d < 0$ is $n^e \tau < t$. In addition, we can observe from (4.21) that $\partial t^* / \partial c^d = n^d (A_t)^{-1}(1 + 2n^e + 2n^f) > 0$ and that the optimal sales tax at the complete market liberalization becomes lower as the marginal cost of domestic firms becomes lower. Thus, if domestic firms could succeed in increasing their productivity and reducing marginal costs in the process of market liberalization, the firms as well as the economy could be better off than the pre-reform situation when trade liberalization and sales tax reform are completed. The government could provide a production subsidy in a lump-sum fashion to support the R&D activity of domestic firms to raise their productivity and competitiveness.[20]

Acknowledgment We would like to express our gratitude to Professors Binh Tran-Nam, Murray C. Kemp, Xiaochun Li, Hiroshi Ohta, Makoto Tawada, and Martin Richardson and an anonymous reviewer for their helpful comments. This research is financially supported by Grants-in-Aid for Scientific Research (no. 15 K03485). All remaining errors are ours.

---

[20]If the foreign-owned subsidiary firms cannot bear the loss of profits caused by the host countries' tariff–tax reform, the firms will exit the market, although we assume implicitly that the loss would not cause such case and the foreign subsidiary firms would stay in the market.

Appendices

Appendix 4.1: Concavity of **W(τ, t)**

The second-order partial derivatives of $W(\tau, t)$ are

$$\partial^2 W/(\partial \tau)^2 = -(n^e A_\tau/b)(N+1)^{-2} < 0,$$
$$\partial^2 W/(\partial t)^2 = -(A_t/b)(N+1)^{-2} < 0, \quad \text{and}$$
$$\partial^2 W/\partial t \partial \tau = -(n^e B/b)(N+1)^{-2} < 0.$$

The determinant of the Hessian matrix is $D^W = n^e[b^2(N+1)]^{-4}\Phi > 0$, where $\Phi \equiv A_\tau A_t - n^e B^2 = 2(1+N)^2[(n^d + n^f) + n^f(n^e + 2)] > 0$. Thus, $W(\tau, t)$ is strictly concave in τ and t. The set $W_0^+ \equiv \{(\tau, t) | W(\tau, t) \geq W(\tau^0, t^0)\}$ is strictly convex.

Appendix 4.2: Concavity of **G(τ, t)**

The second-order partial derivatives of $G(\tau, t)$ are

$$\partial G/(\partial \tau)^2 = -\left[2n^e\left(n^d + n^f + 1\right)\right]/b(N+1)^{-1} < 0,$$
$$\partial G/(\partial t)^2 = -(2N/b)(N+1)^{-1} < 0, \quad \text{and}$$
$$\partial G/\partial t \partial \tau = -(2n^e/b)(N+1)^{-1} < 0.$$

The determinant of the Hessian matrix is $D^G = 4n^e(n^d + n^f)[b^2(N+1)]^{-1} > 0$. Thus, the revenue function $G(\tau, t)$ is strictly concave, and the optimal combination of (τ^G, t^G) is global maximum.

Appendix 4.3: Uniqueness of Tangency Point (τ^{GW}, t^{GW})

We consider how $MRS_{\tau t}^G(\tau^0, t^0)$ and $MRS_{\tau t}^W(\tau^0, t^0)$ vary in Λ_2^0. In Λ_2^0, as τ decreases, the $MRS_{\tau t}^G(,)$ of an iso-revenue curve monotonically decreases from 0 to some negative value at an intersection point with the $G_\tau = 0$ line, while the $MRS_{\tau t}^W(.)$ of any iso-welfare curve monotonically increases from some negative value to zero at the intersection point on the $W_t = 0$ line. Therefore, there is a unique point (τ^{GW}, t^{GW}) at which $MRS_{\tau t}^G(\tau^{GW}, t^{GW}) = MRS_{\tau t}^W(\tau^{GW}, t^{GW})$ in Λ_2^0 for a given initial iso-revenue curve.

References

Bond, E. W., & Park, J.-H. (2002). Gradualism in trade agreements with symmetric countries. *Review of Economic Studies, 69*, 379–406.

Chisik, R. (2003). Gradualism in free trade agreements: A theoretical justification. *Journal of International Economics, 59*, 367–397.

Clarke, R., & Collie, D. R. (2006). Optimum-welfare and maximum-revenue tariffs under Bertrand duopoly. *Scottish Journal of Political Economy, 53*, 398–408.

Collie, D. R. (1991). Optimum welfare and maximum revenue tariffs under oligopoly. *Scottish Journal of Political Economy, 38*, 398–401.

Fujiwara, K. (2015). Tax principles and tariff-tax reforms under international oligopoly. *Journal of Public Economic Theory, 18*, 84–98.

Hatzipanayatou, P., Michael, M. S., & Miller, S. M. (1994). Win-win indirect tax reform. *Economic Letters, 44*, 147–151.

Haufler, A., Schjelderup, G., & Stähler, F. (2005). Barriers to trade and imperfect competition: The choice of commodity tax base. *International Trade and Public Finance, 12*, 281–300.

Karakosta, O., & Tsakiris, N. (2014). Can tariff and tax reforms deliver welfare improvements under imperfect competition? *Journal of International Trade and Economic Development, 23*, 315–328.

Keen, M., & Ligthart, J. E. (2002). Coordinated tariff reduction and domestic tax reform. *Journal of International Economics, 56*, 489–507.

Keen, M., & Ligthart, J. E. (2005). Coordinated tariff reduction and domestic tax reform under imperfect competition. *Review of International Economics, 13*, 385–390.

Kemp, M. C. (2007). Normative comparison of customs unions and other types of free trade association. *European Journal of Political Economy, 23*, 416–422.

Kemp, M. C., & Wan, H., Jr. (1976). An elementary proposition concerning the formation of customs unions. *Journal of International Economics, 6*, 95–97.

Kemp, M. C., & Wan, H., Jr. (1972). Gains from Free Trade. *International Economic Review, 13*, 509–522.

Kemp, M. C., & Wan, H., Jr. (1993). *The welfare economics of international trade*. Chur, Switzerland: Harwood Academic.

Larue, B., & Gervais, J.-P. (2002). Welfare-maximizing and revenue-maximizing tariffs with a few domestic firms. *Canadian Journal of Economics, 35*, 786–804.

McCorriston, S., & Sheldon, I. (2011). Tariff (de-) escalation with successive oligopoly. *Review of Development Economics, 15*, 587–600.

Michael, S. M., Hatzipanayotou, P., & Miller, S. M. (1993). Integrated reforms of tariff and consumption taxes. *Journal of Public Economics, 52*, 417–428.

Naito, T., & Abe, K. (2008). Welfare- and revenue-enhancing tariff and tax reform under imperfect competition. *Journal of Public Economic Theory, 10*, 1085–1094.

Ohyama, M. (2002). The significance of the GATT/WTO rules. In A. D. Woodland (Ed.), *Economic theory and international trade* (pp. 71–85). Cheltenham: Edward Elgar.

Okawa, M., & Iguchi, T. (2016). Welfare-improving coordinated tariff and sales tax reforms under imperfect competition. *Review of Development Economics, 20*, 475–487.

Panagariya, A., & Krishna, P. (2002). On necessity welfare-enhancing free trade areas. *Journal of International Economics, 57*, 353–367.

Part II
Normative and Welfare Economics Under Gossenian Assumptions

Chapter 5
Normative Trade Theory Under Gossenian Assumptions

Murray C. Kemp

Abstract It is now more than 250 years since Montesquieu wrote a letter to William Domville in which he discussed what would now be called the welfare implications of international trade. In what sense can a country be said to benefit from trade with other countries? Early in the twenty-first century, that question still lacks a complete answer. It was shown by Grandmont JM and McFadden D, J Int Econ 2:109–125, 1972 and by Kemp MC and Wan HY, Int Econ Rev 13:509–522, 1972 that, for a single country, free trade coupled with suitable compensatory lump sum payments confined to that country would leave each resident of that country better off than in autarky. However the normative trade theory of 1972 neglected the fact that all consumption, production and endowment of commodities take time and are subject to a second budget of 24 h a day. The importance of the time constraint was first recognized by Gossen HH, *Entwickelung der gesetz des menschlichen verkehrs*, F. Vieweg und Sohn, Braunschweig, 1854. His book was written in German but was neglected even by German scholars. Eventually the greatest of all economic theorists, Léon Walras (J des Economistes 30:68–90 and 260–261. Walras' article was later published (in slightly abridged form) in English in Spiegel HW, *The development of economic thought. Great economists in perspective*, Chapman and Hall, London, 1952, pp 471–488, 1885, translated Gossen's book into French and ensured that it would not be forgotten. Jevons WS, *The theory of political economy*, 2nd edn. Penguin Books, Harmondsworth, 1879, and Edgeworth FY, Gossen, Hermann Heinrich (1810–1858). In: Palgrave RHI (ed) *Dictionary of political economy*, vol II. Macmillan, London, 1896, were the first to write about Gossen in English, but it was not until 1983 that an English translation of Gossen's book became available. Since then Gossen has become unforgettable for economists. Books about Gossen have become easier to sell than the book by Gossen in 1854. This chapter demonstrates that key propositions in normative trade theory remain valid in the presence of Gossen's time constraint. Each individual must now pool

M. C. Kemp (✉)
School of Economics, UNSW Sydney, Sydney, NSW 2052, Australia

© Springer Nature Singapore Pte Ltd. 2018
B. Tran-Nam et al. (eds.), *Recent Developments in Normative Trade Theory and Welfare Economics*, New Frontiers in Regional Science: Asian Perspectives 26,
https://doi.org/10.1007/978-981-10-8615-1_5

his/her family's time with members of other households. Pooling may extend across the world.

Keywords Time constraint · Time pooling · Gossenian assumptions · Normative trade theory

5.1   Introduction: Normative Trade Theory Without Gossenian Assumptions

It is more than 250 years since Montesquieu (1749) wrote his 'Lettre à William Domville'. In that essay Montesquieu discussed what would now be called the welfare implications of international trade. The chief novelty of the essay lays in its focus on the well-being, not of the Prince but of the People, that is, of the population at large. The central questions suggested by it concern the sense in which a country may be said to benefit from the opportunity to trade with other countries and the variety of circumstances under which trade is indeed beneficial. The first of these questions was answered, although not to everyone's satisfaction, by Pareto (1894), at the end of the nineteenth century.

Early in the twenty-first century, the second question still awaits a complete answer. However, much progress has been made, especially during the last 40 years or so. In particular, it has been shown by Grandmont and McFadden (1972) and by Kemp and Wan (1972) that, for a single country, free trade coupled with a suitable scheme of compensatory lump sum transfers confined to that country would leave each resident of the country better off than in autarky. Both demonstrations were conducted under assumptions of a type made familiar by Arrow and Debreu (1954) and McKenzie (1954), building on Walras (1874). Moreover, since 1972, the proposition has benefited from a considerable weakening of those assumptions. It is now known to accommodate incomplete markets, symmetrical cash-in-advance monetary economies, chaotic trading equilibria and trade-dependent preferences and technologies; it is also known that, subject to the existence of equilibrium, the proposition accommodates non-convex production sets and the associated oligopolistic competition.[1]

Closely related to the 1972 propositions is the so-called Kemp–Wan proposition concerning the possibility of forming Pareto-improving customs unions; see Kemp (1964, p. 176), Vanek (1965), Kemp and Wan Jr. (1976, 1986) and Ohyama (1972). Like the 1972 propositions, the Kemp–Wan proposition was established under assumptions of Walras–Arrow–Debreu or McKenzie type. However, as in the case of the 1972 propositions, it has been possible to relax those assumptions and

---

[1]Since 1972 the proposition has been further extended to accommodate overlapping finite generations and infinite time horizons; see Kemp and Wolik (1995) and Kemp and Wong (1995). However, as shown by Kemp and Fishburn (2013), the extension is conditional upon a non-trivial additional assumption: that the government of each trading country requires all parents and parents-in-law to maintain under free trade their autarkic vectors of bequests.

accommodate incomplete markets, symmetrical cash-in-advance monetary economies and increasing returns to scale and oligopolistic competition; see Kemp (1995,
Chapters 5 and 7) and Kemp (2001, Chapter 20).[2]

Given the current popularity of preferential trading arrangements, the Kemp–
Wan proposition is of special interest to policymakers. Indeed, to meet the
immediate needs of policymakers, the proposition has recently been extended
to accommodate (i) free trade associations that are not also customs unions and
(ii) non-member countries that adjust their tariffs in response to the formation of
free trade associations; see Kemp (2007) and Kemp and Shimomura (2001a),
respectively.

5.2 Normative Trade Theory with Gossenian Time Constraints

The normative trade theory summarized in Sect. 5.1 rests on the conventional
neoclassical model of household behaviour. In that model, consumption is
constrained by household preferences and by a single *financial* budget. Thus the
model neglects the fact that all consumption takes time and that each household is
subject to a second *time* budget of exactly 24 h a day. The importance of the time
constraint was first recognized by Gossen (1854).

Gossen's contribution was virtually ignored during his lifetime but, a generation
later, was acclaimed by Edgeworth (1896) and Pantaleoni (1889). Even earlier,
Jevons (1879) and Walras (1885) had warmly praised Gossen's work, but without
fully appreciating the central importance of Gossen's focus on the constraint of time.
More recently, Gossen's time constraint has been discussed, in an appreciative and
illuminating way but primarily in a context of closed economies, by Georgescu–
Roegen (1983, 1985) and Steedman (2001).[3]

In the present section, it is shown that each of the normative propositions listed in
Sect. 5.1 remains valid under the Gossenian time constraint.

5.2.1 Price-Taking Households

Let us begin by considering a single one-period, pure-exchange economy k with N_k
households and the set of households $\mathbf{N}_k \equiv \{1, 2, \ldots, N_k\}$. The period is partitioned
into a finite number of equal subperiods. Markets open only once, during the first

---

[2]The Kemp–Wan proposition, like the 1972 propositions, has been further extended to accommodate overlapping finite generations and infinite time horizons; see Kemp and Wolik (1995) and
Kemp and Wong (1995).

[3]Indeed it can now be reasonably argued that Gossen's contribution to microeconomics is as
fundamental as that of his illustrious predecessor von Thünen to the theory of economic growth.

finite subperiod, but agreements may be made during that subperiod for delivery during any future subperiods. The commodities are distinguished both by their date of delivery and by their physical and other characteristics. During any subperiod, a household consumes each commodity at a constant (possibly zero) rate; but across subperiods the rate of consumption may vary sharply. For the present, there is no time constraint and no allowance is made for the **joint consumption, production and endowment** of commodities by two or more households. As in the conventional theory of consumer demand, each household i takes commodity prices as given, beyond its control. Finally, it will be assumed that the consumption set of i is closed, convex and bounded below; that the preferences of i are convex and representable by a continuous, ordinal utility function; and that i can survive with less of each component of its endowment bundle. The task of i is to solve the problem

$$\max_{c_k^i} u_k^i\left(c_k^i\right)$$
$$i \in N_k \qquad\qquad (P)$$
$$\text{s.t. } pc_k^i \le pe_k^i$$

where c_k^i is the consumption vector of household i, $u_k^i(c_k^i)$ is the utility function of household i, e_k^i is the endowment vector of household i and p is a given commodity price vector. Notice that (P) requires only that i balance its budget over the whole time period; it allows i to borrow or lend across subperiods. The solution to (P) is $c_k^i(p, e_k^i)$. The autarkic market-clearing prices for country k, assumed to be unique up to a positive multiple, are then obtained as solutions to

$$\sum_{i \in N_k} d_k^i\left(p, e_k^i\right) \equiv \sum_{i \in N_k} c_k^i\left(p, e_k^i\right) - \sum_{i \in N_k} e_k^i = 0 \qquad\qquad (5.1)$$

and if in each country households are price takers, the world free trade market-clearing prices, also assumed to be unique up to a positive multiple, are obtained as solutions to

$$\sum_{k \in K} \sum_{i \in N_k} d_k^i\left(p, e_k^i\right) = 0 \qquad\qquad (5.2)$$

where $\mathbf{K} \equiv \{1, 2, \ldots, K\}$ and K is the number of trading countries. From the 1972 propositions, free trade potentially (after lump sum compensation) benefits each trading country.

Against the above background, let us take a tentative Gossenian step forward, allowing for the constraint of time but not for the pooling of time in **joint consumption, production and endowment**. The task of household i in country k is now to solve the revised problem

$$\max_{c_k^i} v_k^i \left(c_k^i, t_k^i \right)$$

$$i \in \mathrm{N}_k \qquad\qquad (P')$$

$$\text{s.t. } pc_k^i \leq pe_k^i$$

$$\tilde{t}_k^i c_k^i \leq t_k^i$$

where t_k^i is the time available to household i in country k and, in a one-period economy, might be set equal to 1 and where $\tilde{t}_k^i$ is the vector of time needed by household i in country k to consume a bundle of one unit of each commodity. On this approach, household i may consume two or more commodities simultaneously, and those commodities may be related in any way in the household's preferences. However the household may not engage with other households to pool their time in jointly consuming a commodity (eating a meal together, walking in the woods together, playing tennis together, attending a play or concert together, examining a painting together or engaging in a telephone conversation). Evidently, this is an extremely severe restriction; it will be relaxed shortly. It is assumed also that, in each subperiod, household i must use all of the time available to it but can freely dispose of unwanted commodities. Finally, it is assumed that household i's time-adjusted consumption set is non-null, closed, convex and bounded below.[4] Under these assumptions, for each country $k \in \mathrm{K}$ and for each household $i \in \mathrm{N}_k$, v_k^i, viewed as a function of c_k^i only, has properties similar to those of $u_k^i(c_k^i)$. Hence the admission of Gossenian time constraints has almost no bearing on the existence of free trade equilibrium or on the gainfulness of free trade[5]; however, it does help determine the extent of the trade gains.

On a more comprehensive approach, we must allow for the possibility that members of each household pool their time in joint consumption within their household and with members of other households. As Gossen (1983: 110) himself observed, many potential pleasures '... become actual pleasures only if other persons, too, participate in the enjoyment.' To accommodate this observation in our theory, it must be recognized that the utility of household i in country k depends on an enlarged set of variables. In particular, that household's consumption vector must be extended to accommodate the joint consumption of each possible subset of commodities by any price-taking subset of the remaining households in country k.

---

[4]Kemp (2008) provides an example designed to help readers assess the plausibility of this assumption.

[5]In an extreme case, all households in a country might have endowments that are too plentiful to be completely consumed in the available time. In such a case, the country will have no incentive to trade with other countries, whatever the terms of trade. If it has only one potential trading partner, there will be no market-determined international trade and no gains from trade for either country.

Time pooling is by prior agreement among a subset of households. It is possible that members of a tennis or dining club[6] will deliberately exclude other households from membership. However, by itself, this rejection does not imply that harmful externalities have been created by the joint consumption of club members. For if the externalities are limited to the club membership, then, even on our present comprehensive approach, the admission of Gossenian time constraints has no bearing on the existence of a free trade equilibrium or on the potential gainfulness of free trade: The club members jointly produce a public consumption good but the publicness of the consumption does not extend beyond the club membership.

The approach here described can be further broadened to accommodate the pooling of time by households from countries k and j ($j \neq k$). Since international pooling does not take place under autarky, it can present no new problems to governments trying to implement *GMG* (Grandmont and McFadden (1972) and Grinols (1981)) compensation.

Neither does our focus on pure-exchange economies prejudice our conclusions. Thus, one might broaden the definition of 'consumption' to include (painful or enjoyable) activity in alternative occupations, add to the price vector the wage rate for each skill, develop aggregate supply functions for each skill and extend the model to embrace production in trading countries. Production might be of intermediate goods (employed in the production of other goods) or of final consumption goods, it may be of purely domestic or non-traded goods and may be joint or non-joint. Each of the production structures described by Sanyal and Jones (1982), by Kemp et al. (1980) or Kemp et al. (1985) is admitted.

It has been assumed to this point that all market equilibria are unique. However, that assumption was introduced for convenience only. Our reasoning has been essentially that of Grandmont and McFadden (1972) and Kemp and Wan Jr. (1972); and in neither of those papers was uniqueness required.

Having travelled this far, it will be apparent that other well-known normative trade propositions also survive the introduction of Gossenian time constraints, provided of course that v_k^i, viewed as a function of c_k^i only, has properties similar to those of $u_k^i\left(c_k^i\right)$. In particular, this is true of the Kemp–Wan proposition and of the two considerable generalizations of that proposition mentioned in Sect. 5.1.

It should be apparent also that many normative propositions concerning closed economies remain valid under Gossenian constraints. Thus consider a competitive economy in equilibrium on the boundary of its convex production set at, let us say, P_0. If the production set expands uniformly as the result of technical improvements or the discovery of additional resources, then there exists a scheme of lump sum compensation that improves the lot of each household; indeed, as Kemp and Wan (1999) have noted, this is true provided only that P_0 lies in the interior of the new production set.

It seems then that, under Gossenian assumptions, most normative general equilibrium propositions remain valid. In contrast, many descriptive propositions require

---

[6]Gossenian clubs, based on a time-constrained joint consumption, should not be confused with Tiebout (1956)–Buchanan (1965) clubs.

substantial modification under Gossenian assumptions. To appreciate that this is so, we need only recall the familiar $2 \times 2 \times 2$ textbook model of international trade. Almost invariably, the model is presented with representative agents and homothetic preferences, the latter assumption ensuring that neither commodity is inferior in consumption. However, when to the assumptions of representative agents and homothetic preferences are added the Gossenian time constraint (without the pooling of time in joint consumption) and the further requirement that the financial constraint is binding before and after any change in income, at least one commodity must be inferior in consumption; see Kemp (2008). This finding rules out the well-known Mill–Edgeworth result on impoverishing growth; see Mill (1848) and Edgeworth (1894, 1899). The finding also casts doubt on propositions that rest on milder assumptions like 'Hatta normality'; see Hatta (1977).[7] Other examples of the destructive power of the Gossenian constraint have been provided by Georgescu–Roegen (1983, 1985) and Steedman (2001).

To complete these miscellaneous remarks, I note that problem (P') can be partitioned into daytime and nighttime. It is plausible that the now-familiar propositions of normative trade theory survive an extension of this kind.

5.2.2 Price-Making Households

Throughout Sect. 5.2.1, the focus has been on traditional Walras–Arrow–Debreu or McKenzie general equilibrium models with price-taking households. We now briefly note that the recently constructed Kemp–Shimomura (2001b, c) model, which accommodates variable returns to scale, oligopolistic behaviour and even occasional price-taking behaviour (based on misinformation and/or irrationality), can also be extended in Gossenian fashion without sacrificing either of the findings based on it: that, given the existence of equilibrium, free trade is potentially Pareto-improving and that any subset (of possibly tariff-ridden countries) can form a Pareto-improving customs union or, more generally, a Pareto-improving free trade association.

5.3 A Related Problem

Of course, working (the pursuit of income) and consumption (the enjoyment of income) are not the only activities that require time. The absorption of information about the availability of consumption goods also requires time and is rarely

---

[7]For a small country, Hatta normality is a necessary condition of Walrasian (*tâtonnement*) stability, and this fact has served as justification of the assumption. However, it is now known that Walrasian dynamics are internally inconsistent; see Kemp et al. (2002). Thus any defence of Hatta normality based on the assumption of Walrasian stability is without value. In the present paper, we have found that there are other good reasons for mistrusting Hatta normality.

completed so that purchases of consumption goods are generally based on incomplete information. This fact has been emphasized by Simon (1971) and Gabaix et al. (2006) and is of special significance in the case of dynamic economies for which the consumption menu is constantly changing. Nevertheless, even in dynamic economies with consumption decisions based on incomplete information, the gains-from-trade and related propositions discussed in Sect. 5.2 remain valid.

5.4   Two Cautionary Remarks

(i)

Throughout the present paper, whether the immediate focus has been on the 1972 propositions, on the Kemp–Wan proposition or on the two generalizations of the Kemp–Wan proposition, the analysis has rested on one or another of several finite general equilibrium models which share assumptions that together imply market power on the part of all households and firms and which also share the assumption of price taking by all households and firms.

The possible inconsistency of these assumptions has long been overlooked – since the pioneering work of Walras (1874) and continuing through the modern period dominated by Arrow and Debreu (1954) and McKenzie (1954). Only very recently has it attracted attention; see Kemp (2005) and Kemp and Shimomura (2005). Here I note only that internal consistency in the models relied on can be maintained by adding the additional assumption that each household is incompletely informed (about the economy of which it is a member) or incompletely rational (unable to appreciate the implications of membership for its market power) or both. With that additional assumption and, paradoxically, the familiar existence theorem and the fundamental welfare propositions of Arrow, Debreu and McKenzie remain intact and so do the gains-from-trade propositions of 1972 as well as the later results concerning customs unions and other free trade associations. Thus a little carefully delineated ignorance and/or irrationality can be viewed as a good thing. But if the assumption of imperfect knowledge and/or irrationality is unacceptable, for whatever reason, then one must abandon price-taking firms and households and, ipso facto, abandon small-country models of international trade. In these circumstances, one may fall back on the model proposed by Kemp and Shimomura (2001b, c), excluding non-convex production sets while continuing to admit market power on the part of households and firms. Appeal might then be made to the single-economy existence result of Nishimura and Friedman (1981, Theorem 1). However, it must be borne in mind that the Nishimura–Friedman result rests on assumptions unlike those of Walras, Arrow, Debreu and McKenzie in that they are imposed on households' best responses to the strategies of other households, which are normally viewed as endogenous variables, not directly on the customary-defining elements of an economy (preferences, technologies and endowments (including information)). For an unsympathetic discussion of the widespread employment of restrictions on endogenous variables, see Kemp and Wan Jr. (2005).

(ii)

The cautionary remarks (i) were *static*: the theoretical analysis of 1972, 1976 and later was for their stable content only. Now, in our cautionary remarks (ii), we adopt a *dynamic* approach: new ideas are first absorbed; then, in due course, the new ideas are further developed. Once the process of innovation has started, it can continue for many years, both in factory production and in human psychology.

In the present chapter, I have considered general equilibrium models of increasing complexity, beginning with Montesquieu and then passing on to Walras, Arrow–Debreu, McKenzie and Gossen. I cite the papers and books in their periods of greatest influence, not in their times of initial publication. The date of Gossen's initial publication was 1854, but the period of his greatest influence began in 1983 when his book was finally translated into English. As time goes on, economic theory evolves not uniformly and some aspects change slowly while others move quickly.

Acknowledgement   I am grateful to Geoffrey Fishburn, Binh Tran-Nam, Henry Y. Wan, Jr., and an anonymous internal reviewer for their helpful comments. The present chapter is written to honour Ian Steedman (see Kemp 2010). Unlike its predecessor of 2010, which dealt only with consumption, this chapter considers joint consumption, production and endowment.

References

Arrow, K. J., & Debreu, G. (1954). Existence of an equilibrium for a competitive economy. *Econometrica, 32*, 265–290.

Buchanan, J. (1965). An economic theory of clubs. *Economica, 33*, 1–14.

Edgeworth, F. Y. (1894). The theory of international values I. *Economic Journal, 4*, 35–50.

Edgeworth, F. Y. (1896). Gossen, Hermann Heinrich (1810–1858). In R. H. I. Palgrave (Ed.), *Dictionary of political economy* (Vol. II). London: Macmillan.

Edgeworth, F. Y. (1899). On a point in the pure theory of international trade. *Economic Journal, 9*, 125–128.

Gabaix, X., Laibson, D., Moloche, G., & Weinberg, S. (2006). Costly information-acquisition: Experimental analysis of a bounded rational model. *American Economic Review, 96*, 1043–1068.

Georgescu–Roegen, N. (1983). Herman Heinrich Gossen: His life and work in historical perspective. In H. H. Gosen (Ed.), *The laws of human relations and the rules of human action derived therefrom* (pp. xi–cxlv). Cambridge, MA: MIT Press.

Georgescu–Roegen, N. (1985). Time and value in economics and in Gossen's system. *Rivista Internazionale di Scienze Economiche e Commerciali, 32*, 1121–1140.

Gossen, H. H. (1854). *Entwickelung der gesetz des menschlichen verkehrs*. Braunschweig: F. Vieweg und Sohn.

Gossen, H. H. (1983). *The laws of human relations and the rules of human action derived therefrom*. Cambridge, MA: MIT Press. English translation of H. H. Gossen (1854) by R. C. Blitz.

Grandmont, J. M., & McFadden, D. (1972). A technical note on classical gains from trade. *Journal of International Economics, 2*, 109–125.

Grinols, E. L. (1981). An extension of the Kemp–Wan theorem on the formation of customs unions. *Journal of International Economics, 11*, 259–266.

Hatta, T. (1977). A theory of piecemeal policy recommendations. *Review of Economic Studies, 44,* 1–21.

Jevons, W. S. (1879). *The theory of political economy* (2nd ed.). Harmondsworth: Penguin Books.

Kemp, M. C. (1964). *The pure theory of international trade.* Englewood Cliffs: Prentice–Hall.

Kemp, M. C. (1995). *The gains from trade and the gains from aid.* London: Routledge.

Kemp, M. C. (2001). *International trade and national welfare.* London: Routledge.

Kemp, M. C. (2005). Trade gains: The end of the road? *Singapore Economic Review, 50,* 361–368.

Kemp, M. C. (2007). Normative comparisons of customs unions and other types of free trade association. *European Journal of Political Economy, 23,* 416–422.

Kemp, M. C. (2008). How normal is normality in consumption? *Economics Letters, 101,* 44–47.

Kemp, M. C. (2010). Normative trade theory under Gossenian assumptions. In J. Vint, J. S. Metcalfe, H. D. Kuz, N. Salvadori, & P. A. Samuelson (Eds.), *Economic theory and economic thought – Essays in honour of Ian Steedman* (pp. 98–115). London: Routledge.

Kemp, M. C., & Fishburn, G. (2013). Normative trade in the context of overlapping generations and inter-generational bequests. *Global Journal of Economics, 2.* https://doi.org/10.1142/S2251361213500043.

Kemp, M. C., & Shimomura, K. (2001a). A second elementary proposition concerning the formation of customs unions. *Japanese Economic Review, 52,* 64–69.

Kemp, M. C., & Shimomura, K. (2001b). Gains from trade in a Cournot–Nash general equilibrium. *Japanese Economic Review, 52,* 284–302.

Kemp, M. C., & Shimomura, K. (2001c). The Kemp–Wan proposition under increasing returns to scale and oligopolistic competition. In M. C. Kemp (Ed.), *International trade and national welfare* (pp. 158–170). London: Routledge.

Kemp, M. C., & Shimomura, K. (2005). Price taking in general equilibrium. *American Journal of Applied Sciences, 2,* 78–80.

Kemp, M. C., & Wan, H. Y., Jr. (1972). The gains from free trade. *International Economic Review, 13,* 509–522.

Kemp, M. C., & Wan, H. Y., Jr. (1976). An elementary proposition concerning the formation of customs unions. *Journal of International Economics, 6,* 95–97.

Kemp, M. C., & Wan, H. Y., Jr. (1986). The comparison of second-best equilibria: The case of customs unions. In D. Bös & C. Seidl (Eds.), *The welfare economics of the second best, Supplementum 5 to the Zeitschift für Nationalökonomie* (pp. 161–167). Wein: Springer.

Kemp, M. C., & Wan, H. Y., Jr. (1999). On lumpsum compensation. In J. R. Melvin, J. C. Moore, & R. Riezman (Eds.), *Trade, theory and econometrics. Essays in honor of John S. Chipman* (pp. 185–205). New York: Routledge.

Kemp, M. C., & Wan, H. Y., Jr. (2005). *On the existence of equivalent tariff vectors – When the status quo matters.* Singapore Economic Review 50 (pp. 345–359). Reprinted in M. C. Kemp. (2009). *International trade theory: A critical review* (pp. 181–194). London: Routledge.

Kemp, M. C., & Wolik, N. (1995). The gains from trade in a context of overlapping generations. In M. C. Kemp (Ed.), *The gains from trade and the gains from aid* (pp. 129–146). London: Routledge.

Kemp, M. C., & Wong, K.-Y. (1995). Gains from trade with overlapping generations. *Economic Theory, 6,* 283–303.

Kemp, M. C., Manning, R., Nishimura, K., & Tawada, M. (1980). On the shape of the single-country and world commodity-substitution and factor substitution surfaces under conditions of joint production. *Journal of International Economics, 10,* 395–404.

Kemp, M. C., Long, N. V., & Tawada, M. (1985). Sharp points in production surfaces. *Oxford Economic Papers, 37,* 375–381.

Kemp, M. C., Kimura, Y., & Shimomura, K. (2002). A second correspondence principle. In A. D. Woodland (Ed.), *Economic theory and international trade* (pp. 37–56). Aldershot, Hants: Edward Elgar.

McKenzie, L. W. (1954). On equilibrium in Graham's model of world trade and other competitive systems. *Econometrica, 22,* 147–161.

Mill, J. S. (1848). *Principles of political economy with some applications to social philosophy* (1st ed.). London: John W. Parker.

Montesquieu (C.–L. de Secondat, baron de la Brède et de Montesquieu). (1749). Une lettre à William Domville. In A. Masson (Ed.), (1950–1955), *Oeuvres complètes de Montesquieu* (Vol. II, pp. 593–595). Paris: Nagel.

Nishimura, K., & Friedman, J. W. (1981). Existence of Nash equilibrium in *n* person games without quasi-concavity. *International Economic Review, 22*, 637–648.

Ohyama, M. (1972). Trade and welfare in general equilibrium. *Keio Economic Studies, 9*, 37–73.

Pantaleoni, M. (1889). *Manuale die economia pura.* Firenze: Barbera [In 1898, Pantaleoni's book was republished in English under the title Pure Economics. London: Macmeillan].

Pareto, V. (1894). Il massimo di utilita dato dalla biera concorrenza. *Giornale degli Economisti, 10*, 48–66.

Sanyal, K. K., & Jones, R. W. (1982). The theory of trade in middle products. *American Economic Review, 72*, 16–31.

Simon, H. (1971). Designing organizations for an information-rich world. In M. Greenberger (Ed.), *Computers, communications, and the public interest* (pp. 37–72). Baltimore: Johns Hopkins Press.

Steedman, I. (2001). *Consumption takes time: Implications for economic theory.* London: Routledge.

Tiebout, C. (1956). A pure theory of local expenditures. *Journal of Political Economy, 64*, 416–424.

Vanek, J. (1965). *General equilibrium of international discrimination: The case of customs unions.* Cambridge, MA: Harvard University Press.

Walras, L. (1874). *Eléments d'economie politique pure.* Lausanne: L. Corbaz.

Walras, L. (1885). Un économist inconnu. *Journal des Economistes, 30*, 68–90 and 260–261. Walras' article was later published (in slightly abridged form) in English in H. W. Spiegel (1952), The development of economic thought. Great economists in perspective (pp. 471–488). London: Chapman and Hall.

Chapter 6
Time Allocation Under Autarky and Free Trade in the Presence of Time-Consuming Consumption

Binh Tran-Nam

Abstract This chapter examines the impact of incorporating a Gossenian–Beckerian consumption time constraint in a simple general equilibrium model with representative agents. In the closed economy case, the conventional theory is shown to remain more or less intact with the conventional transformation curve being replaced by the generalized transformation curve. In the open economy case, while trade remains welfare improving, the sources of trade gainfulness differ from those in conventional trade models. In particular, the conventionally defined exchange (consumption) and specialization (production) gains vanish. There are, however, positive gains from time reallocation (away from production toward consumption) and specialization associated with this time reallocation. The model produces results which are similar to those obtained from trade theory with an endogenous labour supply.

Keywords Gossen · Becker · Consumption time constraint · Generalized transformation curve · Time reallocation gain

6.1 Introduction and Context

The present chapter is motivated by both theoretical and empirical considerations.[1] First, in current textbook models of the behaviour of economic agents, consumption is typically constrained by a single financial budget. Even in the labour–leisure choice model, no allowance is made for time spent on consuming goods and services. Similarly,

---

[1] In addition, time-consuming consumption represents a current research interest of Professor Murray C. Kemp to whom this chapter is devoted.

B. Tran-Nam (✉)
School of Taxation and Business Law, The University of New South Wales Sydney, Kensington, NSW 2052, Australia

School of Business and Management, RMIT University Vietnam, Ho Chi Minh City, Vietnam
e-mail: b.tran-nam@unsw.edu.au; binh.trannam@rmit.edu.vn

© Springer Nature Singapore Pte Ltd. 2018
B. Tran-Nam et al. (eds.), *Recent Developments in Normative Trade Theory and Welfare Economics*, New Frontiers in Regional Science: Asian Perspectives 26,
https://doi.org/10.1007/978-981-10-8615-1_6

the literature on theory of trade with variable labour supply does not recognize time-consuming consumption.

The absence of a consumption time constraint implies that either consumption is instantaneous or a typical economic agent has a sufficiently large amount of time to consume any finite bundle of commodities. Neither of these assumptions is plausible. Consumption does take time, and every agent has a finite amount of time to allocate between various activities, including work and consumption.

An exception to the above is Becker's (1965) model of household production and a small number of subsequent studies. However, this branch of literature tends to focus on the closed economy and ignore the production side of the economy (see, e.g. Becker 1965; Steedman 2001; Gahvari 2007). There is an apparent lack of interest in time-consuming consumption among general equilibrium (GE) or pure trade theorists.

Secondly, there has been growing anecdotal evidence that workers, especially those in developed nations, feel increasingly stressed because they are time poor (see, e.g. Schulte 2014). They have been spending more time at work so that they do not have sufficient time for leisure and consumption. This suggests that it is no longer sensible to dismiss the importance of time allocation between working and consumption.

The primary purpose of this chapter is to investigate the impact of incorporating a consumption time constraint into a simple general equilibrium (GE) model involving two countries, two goods and two factors. In so doing, it examines the validity or otherwise of some well-known results of the conventional Heckscher–Ohlin–Samuelson (HOS) model. It also seeks to determine how these conventional results need to be modified to take time-consuming consumption into account. In this sense, it can be viewed as an extension of Tran-Nam's (2012) Ricardian model with time-consuming consumption.

The remainder of this chapter is organized as follows. Section 6.2 presents a brief literature review to prepare the ground for the discussions that follow. Section 6.3 focuses on the formulation and interpretation of a consumption time constraint. Section 6.4 then formulates and analyses an autarkic two-good, two-factor model in which consumption requires labour time. In this closed economy case, the conventional theory is shown to remain intact with the conventional transformation curve being replaced by a generalized transformation curve, which captures not only information about resource endowments and productive technology but also consumption technology. A world economy of two trading countries is then examined in Sect. 6.5. In this open economy case, the pattern of trade is dictated by the theory of comparative advantage. However, the sources of trade gains are different from those derived from standard models. Conventionally defined exchange and production gains vanish, but there are positive gains from time reallocation (away from production toward consumption) and specialization associated with this time reallocation. The model produces results which are similar to those obtained from trade theory with an endogenous labour supply. Section 6.6 concludes and offers some remarks about how the model can be extended.

6.2   A Brief Literature Review

The importance of the time constraint on consumption was first emphasized by Gossen (1854), a Prussian civil servant, whose pioneering work was largely ignored by mainstream economists.[2] While neoclassical theorists such as Jevons (1879) and Walras (1885) praised Gossen's contribution to the theory of marginal utility, they did not pay attention to his primary emphasis on the constraint of time. This neglect was later maintained by Marshall (1890).[3]

In more recent times, Gossen's work has been discussed in depth by Georgescu–Roegen (1983), Niehans (1990) and Steedman (2001), primarily in a context of closed economies. Kemp (2009) demonstrated that the normative theory of trade, including the well-known Grandmont–McFadden (1972) and Kemp–Wan (1972) propositions, survives the incorporation of a Gossenian time constraint. Most recently, Tran-Nam (2012) investigated the pattern of and gains from trade in a Ricardian model incorporating a consumption time constraint.

In a related strand of literature, a general theory of time allocation was developed by Becker (1965). His approach emphasizes the role of utility maximizing households as productive agents who combine time and market goods via household production functions to generate vectors of basic commodities that enter directly into household utility functions. Becker's integration of household production and consumption differs fundamentally from the textbook distinction between households as consumption units and firms as production units. It is shown, in the next section, that Becker's formulation may be interpreted as a generalization of Gossen's consumption time constraint.

However, Becker did not refer to Gossen's contribution to the theory of time allocation.[4] This neglect has surprisingly persisted until today, despite the availability of Blitz' English translation of Gossen's book in 1983. This is perhaps most apparent in the optimal commodity taxation literature where many models are formulated in the Gossenian spirit without acknowledging Gossen (see, e.g. Boadway and Gahvari 2006; Gahvari 2007).

There is of course a small number of trade models incorporating variable labour supply (see, e.g. Kemp and Jones 1972; Martin and Neary 1980; Woodland 1982; Mayer 1991). These models differ from one another in one important respect. Unearned income from capital ownership is assumed to be constant in Kemp and

---

[2]Steedman (2001) provided an historical account of this neglect. It is interesting to note that, according to Steedman (2001, p. 21), Gossen began by ignoring the financial budget constraint.

[3]In the first edition of *Principles* (1890) on the last page of Book III, Chapter 1, there was a vague footnote stating that Jevons had been 'anticipated in many of his best thoughts' by Cournot and Gossen. This footnote did not appear in the second and third editions of the *Principles*. However, in the fourth edition (1898), Marshall referred to the 'profoundly original and vigorous, if somewhat abstract reasoning of Gossen' in a footnote (176n).

[4]In an email correspondence with the author, Professor Becker indicated that he was not aware of Gossen's work when developing his 1965 paper. This is not surprising because Gossen's work was obscure to English-speaking economists until the early 1980s.

Jones (1962) and Martin and Neary (1980) but endogenous in Woodland (1982) and Mayer (1991). As will be shown later in the chapter, the present model is consistent with the endogenous capital income approach. However, while all of these trade models take the labour–leisure tradeoff into account, they all fail to recognize that consumption takes time.

6.3   The Consumption Time Constraint

We are now all familiar with Lord Lionel Robbins' (1935, p. 16) famous definition: 'Economics is the science which studies human behaviour as a relationship between ends and scarce means which have alternative uses'. Gossen (1854) saw that what is ultimately scarce is time alone. In his vision, even in the land of Cockaigne where commodities are freely available in unlimited quantities, there will still be an economizing problem.

Even when the importance of a consumption time constraint is recognized, there is still a debate about the treatment of time. Various authors (see, e.g. Winston 1982, p. 164 and Steedman 2001, p. 5) have argued that the approaches of Gossen and Becker are fundamentally different in that time is a context in Gossen case, while it is an input in Becker case. Regardless of how one may interpret the role of time in consumption, it can be shown below that both approaches are similar, at least from a mathematical formulation point of view.

Since Gossen did not express his idea in mathematical form, it is somewhat unclear how his consumption time constraint should be formulated. A simple interpretation, adopted by Niehans (1990) and Steedman (2001), states the consumption time constraint as $a_1X_1 + a_2X_2 + \ldots + a_nX_n \leq L^c$ where X_i refers to the amount of the i-th good purchased, a_i to number of time units required to consume one unit of the i-th good ($i = 1, 2, \ldots, n$), and L^c the total number of time units available for consumption. Expressed in this way, the Gossenian approach can be seen as a special case of Becker's production function approach, $C_i = h_i(X_i, L_i^c)$ and $L_1^c + L_2^c + \ldots + L_n^c \leq L^c$, where C_i refers to the amount of the i-th 'basic commodity' and L_i^c to the number of time units required to consume X_i ($i = 1, 2, \ldots, n$). More specifically, if all h_i take the simple Leontief form, i.e. $C_i = \min\{X_i, L_i^c/a_i\}$ ($i = 1, 2, \ldots, n$), then the Beckerian model simplifies into the Gossenian model.

However, it is interesting to note that Gossen's theory of utility is based on consumptive activities (e.g. the act of eating), not quantities of goods and services consumed. While Gossen's consumptive activities are close to, they are not the same as Becker's (1965: 495) basic commodities described above. In this sense, Becker's household production approach helps to clarify and enhance the Gossenian proposal.

The approach adopted in this chapter is both Gossenian and Beckerian. It is Gossenian in the sense that all consumption technologies take the simple Leontief form. But it is also Beckerian in the sense that time is treated as a labour input to be expended in the consumption process.

6.4 The Closed Economy

6.4.1 Model Assumptions

The economy is stationary and populated by agents who are identical in all respects including preferences, endowments, access to information, etc. Agents are equally endowed with labour and capital where labour (measured in time units) can be alternatively allocated between production and consumption,[5] while capital is employed in production only. Aggregate endowments of capital and labour are denoted by $\bar{K}$ and $\bar{L}$, respectively. For each agent, consumption and production cannot be undertaken simultaneously, and the total amount of time available for consumption and production is equal to 24 h a day minus sleeping time.

In the output market, profit-maximizing and price-taking competitive firms produce two private, intermediate consumption goods with the aid of two homogenous, inelastically supplied factors of production, namely, labour and capital. The aggregate production functions are written as $Q_i = F_i(L_i, K_i)$ where L_i and K_i are the amounts of labour and capital employed in sector i ($i = 1, 2$), respectively. It is assumed that $F_i(0, 0) = 0$ and $F_i(., .)$ is a twice differentiable function that exhibits constant returns to scale, positive and diminishing marginal products with respect to both inputs, and strictly decreasing marginal rate of technical substitution along any isoquant. Thus, F_i is concave. The problem facing the producer of good i is constrained profit maximization, i.e. to maximize $P_i Q_i - W L_i - R K_i$ by the choice of (L_i, K_i) subject to the production constraint and the non-negativity of inputs where P_i is the price of good i ($i = 1, 2$) and W and R are the wage and rental rates, respectively.

Let X_i denote the quantity of the consumption good i that the consumer purchases, and let C_i denote the quantity of the 'final' consumption good i that the consumer wishes to enjoy. To transform X_i into C_i, the consumer needs to use another input, called 'consumption time', L_i^c ($i = 1, 2$). The Leontief consumption technology is assumed, i.e. $C_i = \min\{X_i, L_i^c/a_i\}$ where a_i (> 0) is the technological coefficient associated with good i ($i = 1, 2$). For example, suppose $a_i = 2$, then if the consumer wants $C_i = 1$, he/she needs to choose $X_i = 1$ and $L_i^c = 2$. Note that information search, time spent on purchasing, etc. can be incorporated into the technological coefficients of this Leontief conversion technology.

In order to ensure smooth flows of production and consumption, it is assumed that, at any instant of time, some agents are working, while the others are consuming. However, agents remain identical over the entire period of the model in the sense that they all allocate the same fraction of their labour endowments to production (or consumption). A credit market may be introduced to allow each agent to produce and consume sequentially, while aggregate consumption and production remain steady.

---

[5]The act of consumption can be broadly interpreted to include search, purchase, preparation and consumption.

Since agents are identical in all respects, it is possible to speak of a social utility function. The utility function is summarized as $U(C_1, C_2)$ where $U(., .)$ is supposed to be homothetic and twice differentiable with positive marginal utility and strictly diminishing marginal rate of substitution along any indifference curve. Thus, $U(., .)$ is strictly quasi-concave. We also assume that $MRS_{21} \equiv -dC_2/dC_1 \to \infty$ (0) as $C_1/C_2 \to 0$ (∞).

The consumer's problem is to maximize $U(C_1, C_2)$ by the choice of (C_1, C_2) subject to the financial and time constraints where the financial constraint varies depending on whether the economy is closed or open. Three remarks deserve mention here. Firstly, while pooled consumption (eating or watching TV together) is allowed for, consuming jointly does not give an agent more satisfaction than consuming alone. Secondly, a vast majority of leisure-related activities, such as reading a book, or skiing, involve combining intermediate goods with scarce consumption time. Such active leisure can be accommodated in the present model in a straightforward manner. Thirdly, passive leisure can also be incorporated as a commodity that requires only time to be consumed (neither capital nor any good is needed).

6.4.2 Existence and Uniqueness of an Autarkic Equilibrium

In this representative-agent economy, it is well known that the decentralized market equilibrium can be obtained from the social-optimizing problem. Under autarky, focusing on the real side of the economy, the social problem is to maximize $U(C_1, C_2)$ subject to the following inequality constraints:

$$F_i(L_i, K_i) - Q_i \geq 0, i = 1, 2 \tag{6.1}$$
$$Q_i - X_i \geq 0, i = 1, 2 \tag{6.2}$$
$$\min\{X_i, L_i^c/a_i\} - C_i \geq 0, i = 1, 2 \tag{6.3}$$
$$\bar{L} - L_1 - L_2 - L_1^c - L_2^c \geq 0 \tag{6.4}$$
$$\bar{K} - K_1 - K_2 \geq 0 \tag{6.5}$$
$$K_i \geq 0, L_i \geq 0, L_i^c \geq 0, Q_i \geq 0, x_i \geq 0, C_i \geq 0, i = 1, 2 \tag{6.6}$$

Any vector $y \equiv \{C_1, C_2, x_1, x_2, Q_1, Q_2, K_1, K_2, L_1, L_2, L_1^c, L_2^c\}$ that satisfies (6.1), (6.2), (6.3), (6.4), (6.5) and (6.6) is said to be feasible. An autarkic equilibrium is then a feasible allocation that maximizes $U(C_1, C_2)$. We define the set S of feasible allocations as

$$S \equiv \{y \in \mathbb{R}_+^{12} \text{ such that } (5.1) \text{ to } (5.6) \text{ holds}\} \tag{6.7}$$

By a theorem in Takayama (1974) on concave programming, if all inequality constraints are expressed in the form $g_j(....) \geq 0$, $j = 1, 2, \ldots, m$, and if each of these g_j is a concave function (possibly linear),[6] then the feasible set is a convex and non-empty set.

Next, we define the projection of the feasible set S into the feasible final goods space (C_1, C_2). Call this set S_C.

$$S_C \equiv \left\{ (C1, C2) \in \mathbb{R}_+^2 \text{ such that } y \in S \right\} \tag{6.8}$$

It is well known that the projection of a convex set in $\mathbb{R}_+^m$ into $\mathbb{R}_+^2$ is itself a convex set. S_C is therefore also a non-empty and convex set. The upper boundary of S_C can be written as $C_2 = \phi(C_1)$ where ϕ is concave and strictly decreasing. The graph of ϕ may be termed the generalized transformation curve, which traces out the locus of maximal consumption points under autarky. In this sense it can also be thought of as the autarkic, final good consumption possibility frontier. In capturing information about resource endowments, and production and consumption technologies, the generalized transformation curve plays the same role as the conventional transformation curve in the present model.

In summary, we can now state

Proposition 6.1 *The generalized transformation curve of the economy described in this section exists uniquely and is concave and strictly decreasing.*

It is apparent that, as both a_1 and a_2 approach zero, the generalized transformation curve approaches the conventional transformation curve. Now, the maximization of a strictly quasi-concave function $U(C_1, C_2)$ over a convex set S_C yields a unique solution (C_1^*, C_2^*) (Takayama 1974). Further, this unique autarkic equilibrium is also non-corner in view of the assumption concerning MRS_{21}. We have thus established

Corollary 6.1 *The autarkic equilibrium of the economy described in this section exists uniquely and is a non-corner solution.*

Two quick remarks deserve mention. First, since there are no externalities and no public goods in this economy, the autarkic equilibrium is Pareto optimal. Secondly, the determination of (unique) equilibrium output, commodity prices and factor prices has not yet been demonstrated. Such a determination is provided in Appendix 6.1.

6.4.3   Derivation of the Generalized Transformation Curve

In view of the important role played by the generalized transformation curve, it seems useful to illustrate how such a curve can be derived.

---

[6]It is well known that the function $\min\{.,.\}$ is a concave function.

For given any value $L_M \in (0, \bar{L})$, we define the production possibility set $S_Q \equiv \{(Q_1, Q_2) \in \mathbb{R}_+^2 : Q_i \le F_i(L_i, K_i), L_1 + L_2 \le L_M \text{ and } K_1 + K_2 \le \bar{K}\}$. The upper boundary of the set is the transformation curve and can be represented by the function $Q_2 = \psi(Q_1; L_M, \bar{K})$. The graph of this function is a concave, downward sloping curve. Thus, for each feasible L_M, we can draw two curves: the transformation curve, $Q_2 = \psi(Q_1; L_M, \bar{K})$, and the consumption-time budget line, $Q_2 = [\bar{L} - L_M - a_1 Q_1]/a_2$. These two curves may intersect each other at zero, one or two points in the positive quadrant; see Figs. 6.1a, 6.1b, 6.2a, 6.2b and 6.3, respectively.

Figures 6.1a and 6.1b correspond to what may be termed 'income-poor' and 'time-poor' cases, respectively. Income-poor case refers to a situation in which a typical agent devotes too little time to working so that after consuming all income, he/she still has some surplus time. Time-poor case refers to a situation in which a typical agent devotes too much time to working so that he/she does not have sufficient time to consume all income.

We are ready to state

Fig. 6.1a No intersection (income-poor case)

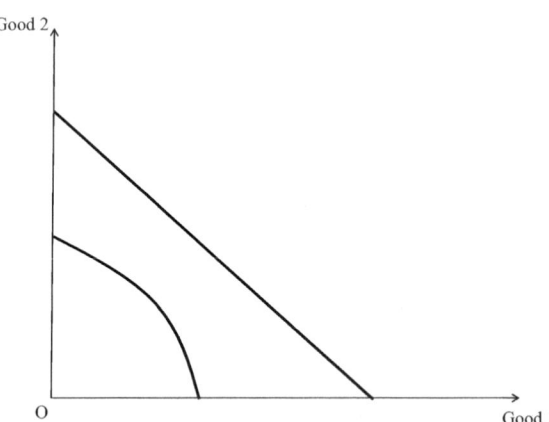

Fig. 6.1b No intersection (time-poor case)

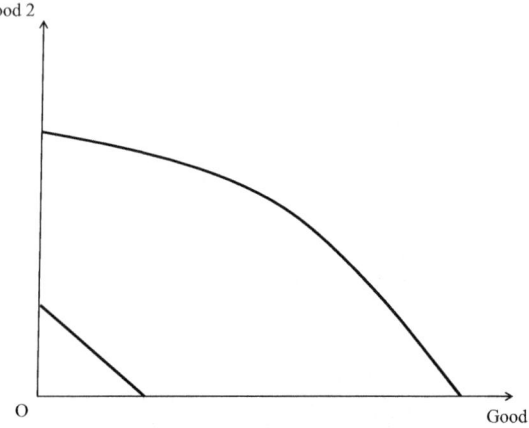

Fig. 6.2a One intersection case

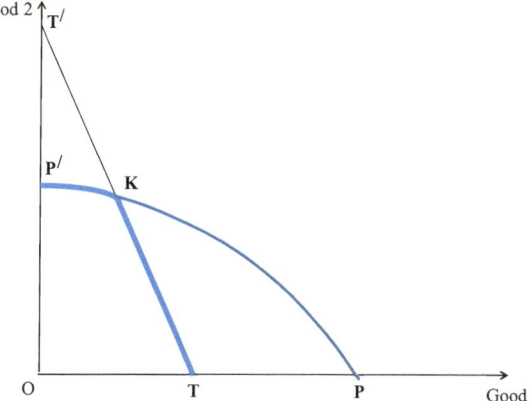

Fig. 6.2b Tangential case

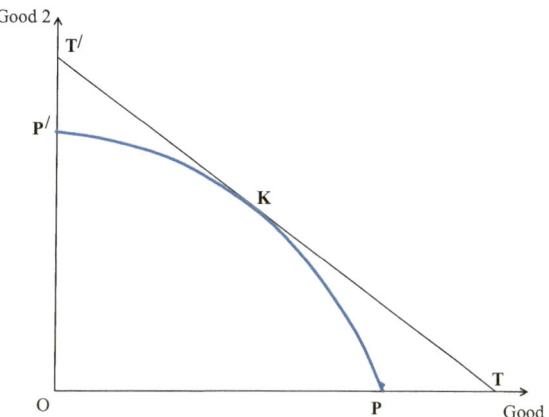

Fig. 6.3 Two intersection case

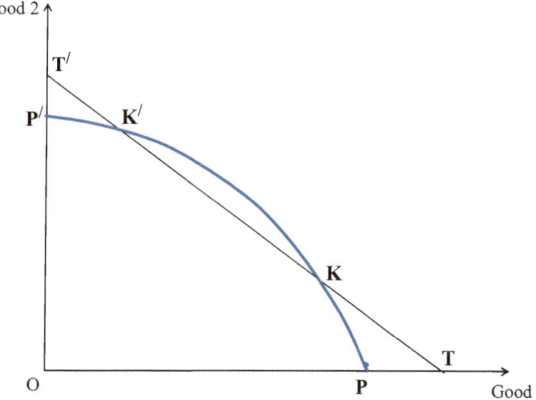

Proposition 6.2 *The generalized transformation curve is the locus of all intersecting or tangential points of a certain family of transformation curves and the corresponding family of consumption-time budget lines.*

Proof
In the income-poor (time-poor) case, none of the points on the transformation curve (consumption-time budget line) can be a maximal point of consumption because economic agents can always consume more of one or both goods by devoting more (less) time to production. Following a similar reasoning, only the point K in Figs. 6.2a and 6.2b or the points K' and K in Fig. 6.3 can be maximal consumption points under autarky.

 QED

The intersection or tangency of the transformation curve and consumption-time budget line narrows down the range of possible values of autarkic equilibrium total amount of labour devoted to production L_M^*.

Corollary 6.2 *The autarkic equilibrium total amount of labour devoted to production L_M^* lies within $(\underline{L_M}, \bar{L}_M)$ where $\underline{L}_M$ and $\bar{L}_M$ are, respectively, the greatest lower and least upper bounds of the solution set to $\psi(Q_1; L_M, \bar{K}) - [\bar{L} - L_M - a_1 Q_1]/a_2 = 0$.*

Proof
When the two curves intersect or are tangential, we have the equation

$$\psi(Q_1; L_M, ; \bar{K}) - [\bar{L} - L_M - a_1 Q_1]/a_2 = 0 \qquad (6.9)$$

Let Ω be the set of $L_M \in (0, \bar{L})$ for which the above equation has a positive solution for Q_1. In view of Proposition 6.1, Ω is not empty. We denote by $\underline{L}_M$ $(\bar{L}_M)$ the greatest lower (least upper) bound of this set. The equilibrium L_M^* must then lie within these two bounds inclusively.

 QED

6.4.4 Properties the Generalized Transformation Curve

Like the transformation curve, the generalized transformation curve is also concave and strictly decreasing. However, the magnitude of the inverse of slope of the transformation curve reflects the relative output price ratio (P_2/P_1) whereas that of the generalized transformation curve represents the relative 'full' or 'virtual' price ratio (π_2/π_1). The full price, π_i, of the final consumption good C_i is the output price, P_i, plus the opportunity cost of L_i^c ($i = 1, 2$). Treating good 1 as numéraire and, without loss of generality, taking P_1 as 1, we have $\pi_1 = 1 + a_1 w$ and $\pi_2 = p + a_2 w$ where $p \equiv P_2/P_1 = P_2$ and w is the wage rate in terms of good one. For the determination of equilibrium commodity and factor prices, refer to Appendix 6.1.

The optimal consumption bundle can then be determined by the tangency between a social indifference curve and the generalized transformation curve, giving the familiar condition that the marginal rate of substitution be equal to the relative full price in equilibrium. As a well-known result from Becker (1965), it can also be shown that the relative full price ratio lies strictly between the relative output price ratio and consumption rate ratio except in the special case in which $p^* = a_2/a_1$ as illustrated in Fig. 6.2b.

Corollary 6.3 *The equilibrium full price ratio in terms of good one is given by* $(p^* + w^*a_2)/(1 + w^*a_1)$, *and it lies strictly between* p^* *(equilibrium output price ratio in terms of good one) and* a_2/a_1, *unless by mere chance* $p^* = a_2/a_1$.

Proof
It is easy to see that if $p^* < (= \text{ or } >)\ a_2/a_1$, then $p^* < (= \text{ or } >)\ (p^* + W^*a_2)/(1 + W^*a_1) < a_2/a_1$.
 QED

6.5   The Open Economy

6.5.1   Assumptions and Derivation of Post-trade Equilibrium

Now we turn our attention to international trade. For simplicity, the world is supposed to consist of two countries, called home (H) and foreign (F). Each country produces two identical private goods with the aid of two essential inputs, labour and capital, as described in Sect. 6.4. It is assumed that labour, capital and final consumption goods cannot be traded, but trade in produced goods is free, costless and balanced.

Suppose that the autarkic equilibrium relative price of intermediate goods in H, p_H^*, differs from that in F, p_F^*. Then there is an incentive for the two countries to trade. In what follows, it is convenient to assume that the good one is always more labour intensive than the good two.

Let the world terms of trade (relative price of good two in terms of good one) be denoted by p^w. The financial constraint (6.2) in the closed economy case of H now becomes the balance of trade constraint

$$(Q_{1H} - X_{1H}) + p^w(Q_{2H} - X_{2H}) \geq 0 \tag{6.2'}$$

Given p^w, it is possible to determine the excess demand of each output. This can be easily done if H's post-trade production is not completely specialized. When both goods are produced, the price-equals-cost conditions uniquely determine the factor prices W_H and R_H: $W_H = W_H(p^w)$ and $R_H = R_H(p^w)$. Then the virtual national income of H, which includes the imputed value of labour used in consumption activities, is

$$Y_H\left(p^w; \bar{L}_H, \bar{K}_H\right) = W_H(p^w)\bar{L}_H + R_H(p^w)\bar{K}_H, \tag{6.10}$$

and the prices of the two final consumption goods are $\pi_{1H} = 1 + a_{1H}W_H(p^w) = \pi_{1H}(p^w)$ and $\pi_{2H} = p^w + a_{2H}W_H(p^w) = \pi_{2H}(p^w)$.

The indirect utility of the representative H consumer is given by

$$V_H = V_H(Y_H, \pi_{1H}, \pi_{2H}). \tag{6.11}$$

By Roy's identity, the consumer demand for final good i is

$$x_{iH} = -(\partial V_H/\partial \pi_{iH})/(\partial V_H/\partial Y_H) = x_{iH}(Y_H, \pi_{1H}, \pi_{2H})$$
$$= x_{iH}\left(p^w; \bar{L}_H, \bar{K}_H\right), i = 1, 2. \tag{6.12}$$

This implies that $L_{iH}^c = a_{iH}x_{iH}(p^w; \bar{L}_H, \bar{K}_H)$, $i = 1, 2$. Then the amount of labour used in manufacturing in country H is

$$L_{MH} = \bar{L}_H - \sum a_{iH}x_{iH}\left(p^w; \bar{L}_H, \bar{K}_H\right). \tag{6.13}$$

This allows us to define G_H, the revenue function, of the manufacturing sector that produces the goods in country H:

$G_H = \max_{L_{iH}, K_{iH}} F_{1H}(L_{1H}, K_{1H}) + p^w F_{2H}(L_{2H}, K_{2H})$ subject to $L_{1H-} + L_{2H} \leq L_{MH}(p^w)$ and

$$K_{1H-} + K_{2H} \leq \bar{K}_H. \tag{6.14}$$

Thus $G_H = G_H(p^w, L_{MH}(p^w), \bar{K}_H)$.

Recalling the standard HOS trade model, we might expect an increase in p^w to increase the supply of good two because the revenue function is convex in prices, given $\bar{K}_H$ and L_{MH}. However, it is conceivable that this well-known result does not hold here because L_{MH} is not constant. In fact we can state

Proposition 6.3 *Unlike the conventional HOS trade model, an increase in p^w may not necessarily lead to an increase the supply of good two.*

Proof
Since $L_{MH} = L_{MH}(p^w)$, the revenue function does not exhibit the conventional property that $dG_H/dp^w = Q_{2H}$. Rather, we have

$$dG_H/dp^w = \partial G_H/\partial p^w + (\partial G_H/\partial L_{MH})(\partial L_{MH}/\partial p^w). \tag{6.15}$$

This is similar to the theory of trade with endogenous labour supply (see, e.g. Mayer 1991). This is not at all surprising because labour devoted to production is endogenous in the present model. Here $\partial G_H/\partial p^w$ (keeping L_{MH} constant) is equal to Q_{2H}, while $\partial G_H/\partial L_{MH} = W_H$, and $\partial L_{MH}/\partial p^w$, depends on how a change in p^w affects Y_H and the demands for L_{1H}^c and L_{2H}^c.

QED

6.5.2 Pattern of Trade

It is well known that the pattern of trade depends on many factors, including endowments, production technologies, consumer preferences and, in this case, consumption technologies. Focusing on endowments as a determinant of trade, the pattern of trade, as anticipated by the HOS model, remains valid in the present open economy model. It is possible to establish

Proposition 6.4 *The HOS theorem concerning the pattern of trade remains valid in a model in which consumption takes time.*

Proof
For simplicity, suppose that H and F are identical in all respects, except that F has more capital endowment. From the standard HOS theory, F is expected to export the relatively capital-intensive good (assumed without loss to be good two). F, having more capital, is richer than H, so F consumers have more to consume, which implies that F requires more L_1^c and L_2^c than H. This makes F's capital–labour ratio $\bar{K}_F/\bar{L}_{MF}$ even greater relative to that of H, $\bar{K}_H/\bar{L}_{MH}$. So, F's relative supply Q_2/Q_1 is greater than that of H.

QED

6.5.3 Gains from Trade

It is well known in the trade literature that the compensating-variational measure of gains from trade can be decomposed into consumption (exchange) gain and production (specialization) gain (see, e.g. Bhagwati and Srinivasan 1983, pp.167–168). Exchange gain refers to the gain that a trading country can enjoy when, in free trade, it was constrained to produce at the autarkic production bundle, whereas consumption was allowed to be at international prices. Specialization gain then refers to the additional gain a trading country can enjoy from being allowed to shift production under free trade from the autarkic equilibrium to the post-trade equilibrium according to the principle of comparative advantage.

In the present model, exchange gain can be interpreted as the gain that would accrue if the home country continued to allocate L_{MH}^* to production and produce the autarkic equilibrium bundle (X_{1H}^*, X_{2H}^*). Under free trade, the home country can now afford a bundle which lies beyond its autarkic equilibrium transformation curve and belongs to an indifference curve that is higher than the autarkic equilibrium one. However, holding the amount of time allocated to consumption constant at L_{CH}^*, agents in the home country are unable to have sufficient time to fully consume that new bundle. This is depicted in Fig. 6.4 where any bundle along the dotted ray A_hB

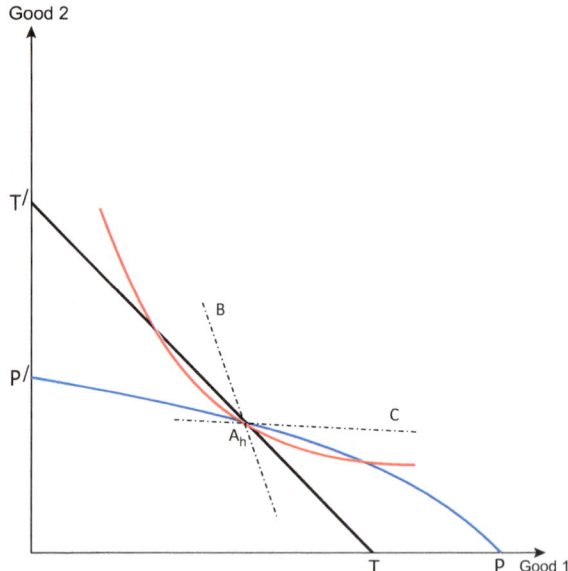

Fig. 6.4 Neither exchange gain nor (conventional) specialization gain from trade

or A_hC (representing world terms of trade) is financially affordable but not time feasible to the home country. Thus, there is no exchange gain in the present model. In fact, more generally, there is no exchange gain for any given allocation of time to consumption.

In general, the home country would become time poor under trade if the autarkic level of time allocation between consumption and production was maintained so that neither exchange gain nor specialization gain would be possible. Thus, for trade to be gainful, there must be first a reallocation of labour time away from production toward consumption. This would eliminate, or at least lessen, time poverty and then allow a reallocation of inputs between the two productive sectors according to the principle of comparative advantage. In this sense, there is a specialization gain associated with time reallocation between consumption and production.

If a trading country devotes less time to production, its transformation curve shifts downward relative to the autarkic transformation curve. By producing at a point where the marginal rate of transformation is equal to the world terms of trade and trading at international prices, the home country can financially afford a bundle that lies beyond its autarkic equilibrium transformation curve. At the same time, having more time available for consumption, economic agents in the home country now also have sufficient time to fully consume this bundle. Note that the post-trade production point is consistent with the theory of comparative advantage in the sense that if $p_H^* > (<) p^w$, the home country will export good two (one).

The above argument is illustrated in Fig. 6.5. In this figure, H is assumed to be relatively more labour abundant than F. H's endowments of capital and labour time are $\bar{K}_H = 100$ and $\bar{L}_H = 200$, respectively, whereas for F, $\bar{K}_F = 160$ and $\bar{L}_H = 150$. For simplicity, assume that $a_1 = a_2 = 1$ for both H and F.

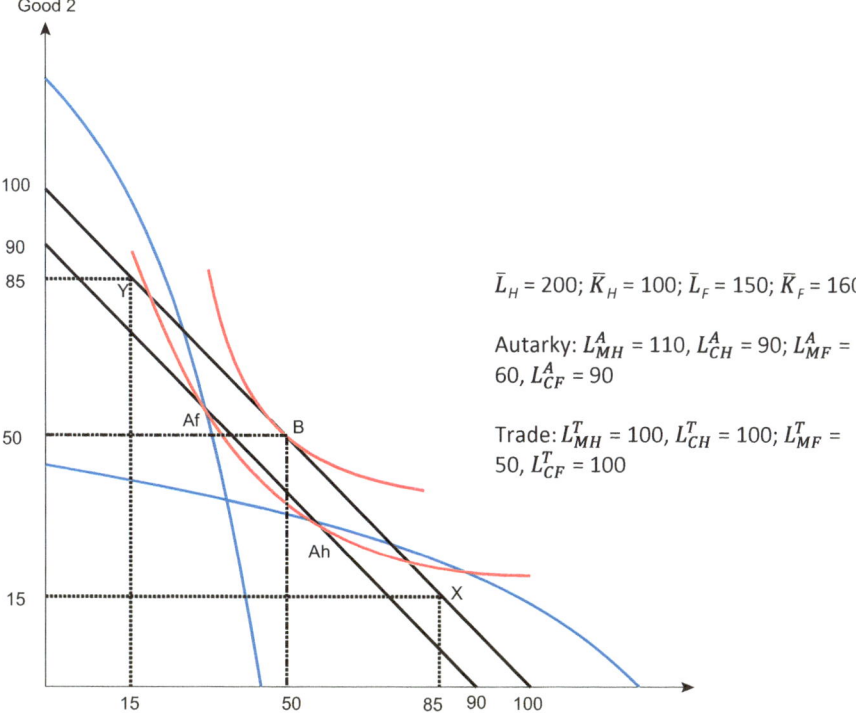

Fig. 6.5 Time reallocation gains from trade ($a_1 = a_2 = 1$)
$\bar{L}_H = 200;\ \bar{K}_H = 100;\ \bar{L}_F = 150;\ \bar{K}_F = 160$
Autarky: $L_{MH}^A = 110;\ L_{CH}^A = 90;\ L_{MF}^A = 60;\ L_{CF}^A = 90$
Trade: $L_{MH}^T = 100;\ L_{CH}^T = 100;\ L_{MF}^T = 50;\ L_{CF}^T = 100$

H's autarkic equilibrium is at point A_H where 60 units of good 1 and 30 units of good 2 are produced. Thus 90 units of labour will be needed in consuming these outputs. H's labour employment in manufacturing under autarky is $L_{MH}^A = 200-90 = 110$. Its transformation curve is $Q_{2H} = \psi(Q_{1H};\ 110,\ 100) \equiv \psi(Q_{1H};\ L_{MH}^A,\ \bar{K}_H)$. F's autarkic equilibrium is at point A_F where 30 units of good 1 and 60 units of good 2 are produced. Thus 90 units of labour will also be needed in consuming these outputs. F's labour employment in manufacturing under autarky is $L_{MF}^A = 150-90 = 60$. Its transformation curve is $Q_{2F} = \psi(Q_{1F};\ 60,\ 160) \equiv \psi(Q_{1F};\ L_{MF}^A,\ \bar{K}_F)$. As drawn, H's autarkic welfare is the same as that of F (note that both countries have the same autarkic consumption-time budget line).

Now allow both countries to trade. H will export good one and import good two, and F will export good two and import good one, according to the pattern of trade discussed above. Both countries become wealthier and can attain the higher level of welfare depicted by point B in Fig. 6.5. At B, each country consumes 50 units of

Fig. 6.6 Specialization
gains from trade

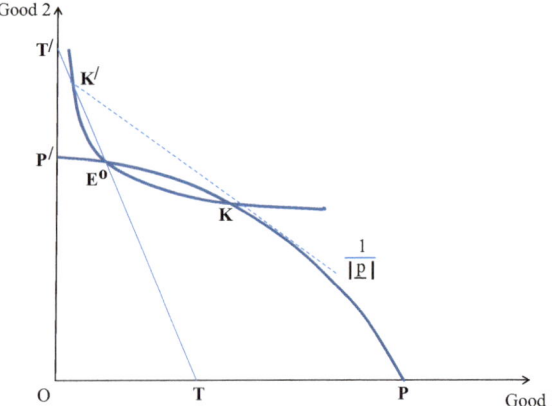

good 1 and 50 units of good 2. This means each of them needs 100 units of labour time
for post-trade consumption. This implies that, as a result of trade, less labour is allocated
to manufacturing in both countries: $L^T_{MH} = 200-100 = 100$ and $L^T_{MF} = 150-100 = 50$.
Their transformation curves are shifted downward (not drawn) to $Q_{2H} = \psi \ (Q_{1H};$
$100, 100) = \psi(Q_{1H}; L^T_{MH}, \bar{K}_H)$ and $Q_{2F} = \psi(Q_{1F}; 50, 160) = \psi(Q_{1F}; L^T_{MF}, \bar{K}_F)$. H
and F post-trade production points are X (85, 15) and Y (15, 85), respectively.

In summary, we may now state

Proposition 6.5 *There is neither exchange gain nor* (*conventional*) *specialization
gain in this simple trading world in which consumption takes time. However, there is
a time allocation gain* (*under which a trading nation will devote more time to
consumption relative to autarky*) *and a specialization gain associated with this
time reallocation.*

Further, the specialization gain is only available for a certain range of world terms
of trade. This is illustrated in Fig. 6.6. In this figure, the autarkic equilibrium
indifference curve intersects the equilibrium transformation curve at K and K'.
Specialization gain is positive only for world terms of trade lying in the range $(\underline{p}^w, \bar{p}^w)$
where $\underline{p}^w$ and $\bar{p}^w$ are the world terms of trade that allow country H to consume after
trade at K and K', respectively.

6.6   Summary and Conclusions

The chapter has examined a simple GE model in which consumption is itself time-
consuming. In the closed economy case, the model generates more general results
than those obtained from the standard model. Assuming a Leontief consumption
technology, a key idea of the model is the replacement of the transformation curve by
the generalized transformation curve which can be defined as the locus of all

maximal consumption points under autarky. As the time required for consumption approaches zero, the present model approaches the traditional GE model.

The model generates interesting results in the open economy scenario. While the pattern of trade as dictated by the law of comparative advantage remains valid in the present model, there are also results which deviate from those derived from the traditional HOS framework. In particular, the model produces some results which are similar to those obtained from trade theory with endogenous labour supply so that some well-known standard trade results do not necessarily hold in the present model.

In addition, the introduction of time-taking consumption implies substantial modification to the conventional decomposition of the gains from trade. This is because trade in produced goods can take place but not trade in time. While trade in goods expands agents' financial affordability, their consumption time constraints remain. As a result, both the exchange and specialization gains, as conventionally defined in the literature, vanish in the presence of a time-taking consumption. There are, however, positive gains from time allocation (shifting labour away from production toward consumption) and specialization associated with that time reallocation.

Like simple GE models in which consumption does not take time, the present model can be extended in several different ways. Some of the extensions such as number of goods and heterogeneity of economic agents can be accommodated within a static framework, while others (e.g. overlapping generations) require a dynamic setup. The following discussion is confined to extensions within the static framework.

For simplicity of analysis and ease of graphical illustration, many simplification assumptions have been made including the number of goods and countries, constant time rate of consumption time and representative agents. It should be apparent that the assumptions concerning the dimensionality of the model are not essential because the reasoning of the model remains valid when there are more than two goods or two countries (see, e.g. Kemp and Wan 1972; Costinot 2009). Similarly, assuming variable rates of consumption, the results of the model also continue to hold if the aggregate consumption-time budget curve is concave.

Heterogeneity of economic agents can be accommodated in a limited way as follows. If all agents have identical homothetic preferences and Leontief consumption technologies, and only differ in labour or capital endowments, the analysis and propositions of the present model remain essentially unchanged. If agents have identical homothetic preferences and different consumption technologies but the ratio $(a_2/a_1)^k$ remains constant for all agents k, then the aggregate consumption-time budget continues to be linear so that the analyses in Sects. 6.4 and 6.5 also remain largely valid.

However, if economic agents have different preferences or different consumption time requirements per unit of any consumption good, then the analysis in Sects. 6.4 and 6.5 requires some modifications. In a GE model of heterogeneous agents with time-consuming consumption, it can be shown, with an additional severe assumption, that an autarkic equilibrium exists, but its uniqueness is no longer assured (see Tran-Nam et al. 2016).

Acknowledgement The author is grateful to invaluable ideas and comments from Professors Ngo Van Long (McGill University) and Murray C. Kemp (UNSW Sydney). The usual caveat applies.

Appendix 6.1: Determination of Equilibrium Output and Commodity and Factor Prices

The optimal consumption bundle (C_1^*, C_2^*) exists uniquely in view of Corollary 6.1. Once (C_1^*, C_2^*) has been determined, we can work out the equilibrium amount of time devoted to consumption of each good $L_i^{C*} = a_i C_i^*$ and the equilibrium total time expended on consumption $L^{C*} \equiv L_1^{C*} + L_2^{C*}$. More generally, given that a country allocates $L^C \equiv L_1^C + L_2^C$ units of labour time to consumption, let $L_M \equiv \bar{L} - L^C$ be the amount of labour time devoted to manufacturing. We define the production possibility set

$$S_Q \equiv \left\{ (Q1, Q2) \in \mathbb{R}_+^2 : Qi \leq Fi(Li, Ki), \;\; L1 + L2 \leq L_M \text{ and } K1 + K2 \leq \bar{K} \right\}.$$

The upper boundary of the set is called the transformation curve and can be represented by the function $Q_2 = \psi(Q_1; L_M, \bar{K})$. The graph of this function is a concave, downward sloping curve.

We are particularly interested in the specific curve $Q_2 = \psi(Q_1; L_M^*, \bar{K})$ where $L_M^* \equiv \bar{L} - L^{C*}$. Given L^{C*}, this curve generates the relevant relative supply curve Q_2/Q_1, as an increasing function of their relative price $p \equiv P_2/P_1$. Since we know $C_2^*/C_1^* = X_2^*/X_1^*$, we can pin down the equilibrium relative supply, $Q_2^*/Q_1^* = X_2^*/X_1^*$, under autarky. This point on the relative supply curve determines the equilibrium relative price $p^* \equiv P_2^*/P_1^*$. Without loss of generality, let $P_1^* = 1$ so that $p^* = P_2^*$.

Given the relative price p^*, we can now work backward to find the equilibrium factor prices, the wage rate w^* and the rental rate r^*(both in terms of good one), by using the conditions that the price of each good is equal to its unit cost (see, e.g. Woodland 1982).

$$c_1(w, r) = 1$$
$$c_2(w, r) = p^*.$$

Assuming that factor intensities differ between the two goods, the above two equations uniquely determine the equilibrium factor prices w^* and r^*.

References

Becker, G. (1965). A theory of the allocation of time. *Economic Journal, 75*, 483–517.
Bhagwati, J. N., & Srinivasan, T. N. (1983). *Lectures on international trade.* Cambridge, MA: MIT Press.

Boadway, R., & Gahvari, F. (2006). Optimal taxation with consumption time as a leisure or labor substitute. *Journal of Public Economics, 90*, 1851–1878.

Costinot, A. (2009). An elementary theory of comparative advantage. *Econometrica, 77*, 1165–1192.

Gahvari, F. (2007). On optimal commodity taxes when consumption is time consuming. *Journal of Public Economic Theory, 9*, 1–27.

Georgescu–Roegen, N. (1983). Herman Heinrich Gossen: His life and work in historical perspective. In H. H. Gossen (1983). *The laws of human relations and the rules of human action derived therefrom*, Cambridge, MA: MIT Press, pp. xi–cxlv.

Gossen, H. H. (1854). *Entwickelung der gesetze des menschlichen verkehrs und der daraus flie ßenden regeln für menschliches handeln*. Braunschweig: Vieweg und Sohn.

Gossen, H. H. (1983). *The laws of human relations and the rules of human action derived therefrom*. Cambridge, MA: MIT Press. English translation by R. C. Blitz of H. H. Gossen (1854).

Grandmont, J. M., & McFadden, D. (1972). A technical note on classical gains from trade. *Journal of International Economics, 2*, 109–125.

Jevons, W. S. (1879). *The theory of political economy* (2nd ed.). Harmondsworth: Penguin Books.

Kemp, M. C. (2009). Normative trade theory under Gossenian assumptions. In J. Vint, S. Metcalfe, H. D. Kurz, N. Salvadori, & P. A. Samuelson (Eds.), *Economic theory and economic thought. Essays in honour of Ian Steedman* (pp. 98–105). London: Routledge.

Kemp, M. C., & Jones, R. W. (1962). Variable labor supply and the theory of international trade. *Journal of Political Economy, 70*, 30–36.

Kemp, M. C., & Wan, H., Jr. (1972). The gains from free trade. *International Economic Review, 13*, 509–522.

Marshall, A. (1890/1961). *Principles of economics*, 9th (variorum) ed., with annotations by C. W. Guillebaud. London: Macmillan.

Martin, J. P., & Neary, J. P. (1980). Variable labor supply and the pure theory of international trade theory: An empirical note. *Journal of International Economics, 10*, 549–559.

Mayer, W. (1991). Endogenous labor supply in international trade theory: Two alternative models. *Journal of International Economics, 30*, 105–120.

Niehans, J. (1990). *A history of economic theory. Classic contributions*. Baltimore: Johns Hopkins University Press.

Robbins, L. (1935). *An essay on the nature and significance of economic science* (2nd ed.). London: Macmillan.

Schulte, B. (2014, February 21). Five reasons why you shouldn't work too hard. *The Washington Post*. Accessed 19 May 2015. http://www.washingtonpost.com/blogs/she-the-people/wp/2014/02/21/5-things-you-get-from-working-too-hard/

Steedman, I. (2001). *Consumption takes time: implications for economic theory*. London: Routledge.

Takayama, A. (1974). *Mathematical economics*. Hinsdale: Dryden Press.

Tran-Nam, B. (2012). An extended Ricardian model incorporating a consumption time constraint. *Review of International Economics, 20*, 1046–1051.

Tran-Nam, B., Le Van, C., Nguyen, T-D-H., & Pham, N-S. (2016, August 11–12). *A simple general equilibrium model in which consumption takes time*. Ninth Vietnam Economists Annual Meeting (VEAM), Danang: University of Danang.

Walras, L. (1885). Un économist inconnu. *Journal des Economistes, 30*, 68–90 & 260–261.

Woodland, A. D. (1982). *International trade and resource allocation*. Amsterdam: North-Holland.

Winston, G. C. (1982). *The timing of economic activities: Firms, households and markets in time-specific analysis*. Cambridgeshire: Cambridge University Press.

Chapter 7
A General Equilibrium Model in Which Consumption Takes Time

Cuong Le-Van, Thi-Do-Hanh Nguyen, Ngoc-Sang Pham, and Binh Tran-Nam

Abstract This chapter examines a general equilibrium competitive economy with many heterogeneous agents. The key feature of the model is that consumption itself takes time so that a typical household is subject to a financial constraint as well as a time constraint. Using the dividend approach proposed by Le-Van and Nguyen (J Math Econ 43:135–152, 2007), it is shown that the economy possesses at least one autarkic Walrasian equilibrium. Sufficient conditions for the uniqueness of the autarkic equilibrium are then derived. Finally, a specific example is provided to illustrate the working of the model, including the derivation of the equilibrium labour allocation and some comparative static results.

Keywords General equilibrium · Heterogeneous households · Quasi-equilibrium · Dividend approach

C. Le-Van
IPAG Business School, Paris School of Economics and Centre National de la Recherche Scientifique, Paris, France
e-mail: cuong.le-van@univ-paris1.fr

T.-D.-H. Nguyen
Center d'Economie de la Sorbonne, University of Paris I Panthon-Sorbonne, Paris, France

N.-S. Pham
Montpellier Business School, Montpellier Research in Management, Montpellier, France
e-mail: ns.pham@montpellier-bs.com

B. Tran-Nam (✉)
School of Taxation and Business Law, The University of New South Wales Sydney, Kensington, NSW 2052, Australia

School of Business and Management, RMIT University Vietnam, Ho Chi Minh City, Vietnam
e-mail: b.tran-nam@unsw.edu.au; binh.trannam@rmit.edu.vn

© Springer Nature Singapore Pte Ltd. 2018   97
B. Tran-Nam et al. (eds.), *Recent Developments in Normative Trade Theory and Welfare Economics*, New Frontiers in Regional Science: Asian Perspectives 26,
https://doi.org/10.1007/978-981-10-8615-1_7

7.1   Introduction

Modern economists have largely accepted Lord Lionel Robbins' approach in defining economics as the science which studies human behaviour as a relationship between ends and scarce means which have alternative uses (Robbins 1935: 16). This approach, which highlights the conflict between human's seemingly infinite wants and their limited resources, has stood unchallenged for more than 80 years. In characterizing the choice problem arising from scarcity, Robbins (1935, p. 15) further stated:

> But, in general, human activity with its multiplicity of objectives has not this independence of time or specific resources. The time at our disposal is limited. There are only twenty-four hours in the day. We have to choose between the different uses to which they may be put... We have neither eternal life nor unlimited means of gratification.

This is indeed an admirable passage! Yet surprisingly, standard economic theory tends to ignore the rather obvious observation that consumption itself takes time. In conventional general equilibrium models, consumers are typically constrained by a financial budget only. While passive leisure is incorporated into the labour−leisure choice model, no allowance is made for time spent on consuming goods and services.

As pointed out in Chaps. 5 and 6 in this edited volume, the formal recognition of the time constraint on consumption goes back to Gossen (1854/1983). In his view, human beings, as mortals, always face an optimizing problem even when commodities are freely available in unlimited quantities to each person. After almost a century of neglect, Gossen's idea of a consumption time constraint was generalized by Becker (1965) in his famous contribution to general theory of time allocation,[1] although there is still a debate on whether time is a context or an input.[2]

There seems to be a lack of interest among general equilibrium theorists in incorporating a consumption time constraint into the general equilibrium model of the economy. A few exceptions are Tran-Nam and Pham (2014) and Tran-Nam et al. (2016). Building on these works, the primary aim of this chapter is to make a modest contribution to the economic theory literature by examining a general equilibrium model in which consumption is itself time consuming. In this chapter, the act of consumption is broadly interpreted to include search, purchase, preparation and consumption. Further, the scope of the chapter is confined to closed economies although it can be seen that results in a closed economy carry over to an open economy in a straightforward manner.

This chapter differs in Chap. 6 in several important respects. First, Chap. 6 is concerned with a representative-agent economy, whereas the present chapter starts with an economy of heterogeneous agents. Secondly, the assumption of two goods in

---

[1]Interestingly enough, Becker (1965) did not refer to the work of Gossen (1854/1983). This is not surprising as Gossen's work was not generally known to English-speaking economists until the English translation of his book became available in 1983.

[2]For an elaboration, the interested reader is referred to Sect. 6.3 of Chap. 6 in this edited volume.

Chap. 6 is abandoned in the present chapter. Thirdly, while the autarkic equilibrium in Chap. 6 is derived as a solution to a central planner problem, the autarkic equilibrium will be derived as a solution to a decentralized Walrasian problem in this chapter. Finally, Chap. 6 extensively utilizes graphical analyses to bring out the intuition of the results, whereas the present chapter will rely mainly on formal mathematics to derive its main results.

The remainder of this chapter is organized as follows. Section 7.2 develops a many-good, two-factor, perfectly competitive economy in which consumption takes time. Agents are heterogeneous in terms of endowment, preferences and consumption technologies. Section 7.3 demonstrates the existence of a market-based equilibrium in such an economy. We employ the dividend approach proposed by Le-Van and Nguyen (2007). This approach introduces an intermediary economy with an additional good that every agent would like to have when he/she reaches satiation. In the new economy, the non-satiation condition is satisfied, and there thus exists an equilibrium. We then show that this equilibrium with dividends will be reduced to a Walrasian equilibrium. Section 7.4 then focuses on deriving conditions to ensure a unique equilibrium. It is shown that when economic agents are homogeneous and the production functions take a less general form, the equilibrium is unique. Section 7.5 provides an illustrative example with representative agents and specific functional forms in order to derive some comparative static results. Section 7.6 concludes.

7.2   The Model

We consider a static, competitive economy having I heterogeneous households and J firms. Each firm produces a different private good using physical capital and labour as essential inputs. The firms and households are further described below.

7.2.1   Firms

Firm j maximizes its profit with a production function F_j, using capital K_j and labour $\tilde{L}_j$:

$$\text{Max}\, p_j F_j\left(K_j, \tilde{L}_j\right) - rK_j - w\tilde{L}_j \tag{7.1}$$

where p_j is the price of good j ($j \in J$) and w and r are the wage and rental rates, respectively. The production set for firms is thus:

$$Y_1 = \{\tilde{y}_1 = (y_1, 0, \cdots, 0, -K_1, -\tilde{L}_1) \in \mathbb{R}_+ \times \{0\}^{j-1} \times \mathbb{R}_-^2 : y_1 \leq F_1(K_1, \tilde{L}_1)\}$$
$$\cdots$$
$$Y_j = \{\tilde{y}_j = (0, \cdots, \tilde{y}_j, \cdots, 0, -K_j - \tilde{L}_j) \in \{0\}^{j-1} \times \mathbb{R}_+ \times \{0\}^{J-j} \times \mathbb{R}_-^2 : y_j \leq F_j(K_j, \tilde{L}_j)\}$$
$$Y_J = \{\tilde{y}_J = (0, 0, \cdots, \tilde{y}_J, -K_J, -\tilde{L}_J) \in \{0\}^{J-1} \times \mathbb{R}_+ \times \mathbb{R}_-^2 : y_1 \leq F_J(K_J, \tilde{L}_J)\}.$$

$$(7.2)$$

We impose the following standard assumptions on the production functions.

Assumption 7.1
For each $j \in J$, the production function F_j is continuous, increasing and concave and exhibits constant returns to scale. Moreover, for all $j \in J$, $F_j(0, L) = F_j(K, 0) = 0$, $\forall K \geq 0$, $\forall L \geq 0$.

Remark 7.1 Under Assumption 7.1, the production set Y_j is nonempty, closed and convex for all $j \in J$.

7.2.2 Households

Aggregate endowments of capital and labour of household i are denoted by $\bar{K}^i$ and L^i, respectively. Denote by $a_j^i (> 0)$ the technological coefficient associated with the consumption of good j by household i, that is, the quantity of time which households i need to consume one unit of good j. The household i purchases the quantity c_j^i of good j and spends $a_j^i c_j^i$ of time to transform these consumption goods to the 'final' consumption goods that the household wishes to enjoy. Household i also allocates L^i of time to work in firms. Each household i faces the time budget constraint

$$a_1^i c_1^i + a_2^i c_2^i + \cdots + a_J^i c_J^i + L^i \leq \bar{L}^i \qquad (7.3)$$

and the financial budget constraint

$$p_1 c_1^i + p_2 c_2^i + \ldots + p_J c_J^i \leq r\bar{K}^i + wL^i. \qquad (7.4)$$

The consumption set for household i is given by

$$X^i = \left\{ x^i = \left(c_1^i, \ldots, c_J^i, 0, -L^i \right) \in \mathbb{R}_+^J \times \{0\} \times \mathbb{R}_- : a_1^i c_1^i + a_2^i c_2^i + \ldots + a_J^i c_J^i + L^i \leq \bar{L}^i \right). \qquad (7.5)$$

Household i chooses $\left(c_1^i, \ldots, c_J^i, L^i \right)$ to maximize $u^i \left(c_1^i, \ldots, c_J^i, L^i \right)$ subject to financial budget constraint (7.4) and consumption time constraint $\left(c_1^i, \ldots, c_J^i, 0, -L^i \right) \in X^i$. We now impose some conditions on the utility functions and the consumption sets.

Assumption 7.2
For each $i \in I$, the utility function u^i is continuous, strictly increasing and concave.

Assumption 7.3

For each $i \in I, \bar{K}^i > 0, \ \bar{L}^i > 0$ and $a_j^i > 0, \forall j \in J$.

Remark 7.2

(i) Under Assumptions 7.2 and 7.3, for each $i \in I$, the consumption set X^i is nonempty, compact and convex.

(ii) Both passive leisure (use of nonworking time without consuming goods) and active leisure (combination of time and leisure goods) can be easily accommodated in this formulation.

(iii) Some acts of consumption can be done by an individual alone (e.g. dining or reading), while other acts require several individuals (e.g. playing chess or soccer). For the former type of consumption, whether an individual chooses to consume alone or jointly with others, the same level of wellbeing is obtained.

We denote the set of satiation points of u^i by S^i:

$$S^i = \left\{ x^{i'} \in X^i : u^i\left(x^{i'}\right) \geq u^i\left(x^i\right) \text{ for any } x^i \in X^i \right\}. \tag{7.6}$$

It is easy to see that the set S^i is closed and convex for all $i \in I$.

The economy can thus be characterized by

$$\varepsilon = \left\{ \left(X^i, u^i, e^i\right)_{i \in I}, \ (Y_j)_{j \in J} \right\} \tag{7.7}$$

where $e^i = \left(0, \ldots, 0, \bar{K}^i, 0\right) \in \{0\}^J \times \mathbb{R}_+ \times \{0\}$.

7.2.3 Equilibrium

Definition 7.1

A list $\left\{ \left(c_1^i, \ldots, c_J^i, L^i\right)_{i \in I}, \ (K_j, \tilde{L}_j)_{j \in J}, \ (p_1, \ldots, p_J, r, w) \right\}$ is said to be an equilibrium if it satisfies

$$(D1)(p_1, \ldots, p_J, r, w) \geq 0, \left(c_1^i, \ldots, c_J^i, 0, -L^i\right) \quad \in X^i, \forall_i \in I \tag{7.8}$$

$(D2)$ *given* $(p_1, \ldots, p_J, r, w), \left(c_1^i, \ldots, c_J^i, L^i\right)$ *solves the problem of household i,* $\forall i \in I$

$$\tag{7.9}$$

$$\forall i \in I, \text{if } (c_1'^i, \ldots, c_J'^i, 0, -L'^i) \in X^i \text{ and } u^i(c_1'^i, \ldots, c_J'^i, 0, -L'^i)$$
$$> u^i(c_1^i, \ldots, c_J^i, 0, -L^i) \text{ then } p_1 c_1'^i + p_2 c_2'^i + \ldots \tag{7.10}$$
$$+ p_J c_J'^i - wL'^i > r\bar{K}^i$$

$(D3)$ *given* $(p_1, \ldots, p_J, r, w), (K_j, \tilde{L}_j)$ *solves the problem of firm j,* $\forall j \in J$ $\tag{7.11}$

$$(D4) \sum_{i \in I} c_j^i = F_j(K_j, \tilde{L}_j), \ \forall j \in J \tag{7.12}$$

$$\sum_{j \in J} K_j = \sum_{i \in I} \bar{K}^i, \text{ and} \tag{7.13}$$

$$\sum_{j \in J} \tilde{L}_j = \sum_{i \in I} L^i. \tag{7.14}$$

Definition 7.2

A list $\left\{ (c_1^i, \ldots, c_J^i, L^i)_{i \in I}, (K_j, \tilde{L}_j)_{j \in J}, (p_1, \ldots, p_J, r, w) \right\}$ is said to be a quasi-equilibrium if it satisfies (7.8), (7.9), (7.11), (7.12), (7.13), (7.14) and a modified version of (7.10):

$$(D2-quasi) \forall i \in I, if (c'_1^i, \ldots, c'_J^i, 0, -L'^i) \in X^i$$
$$\text{and } u^i(c'_1^i, \ldots, c'_J^i, 0, -L'^i) > u^i(c_1^i, \ldots, c_J^i, 0, -L^i), \tag{7.10'}$$
$$\text{then } p_1 c'_1^i + p_2 c'_2^i + \ldots + p_J c'_J^i - wL^i \geq r\bar{K}^i.$$

We note that the consumption set X^i is compact, so there exist satiation points in the preferences of the households and a Walras equilibrium may not exist. Utilizing the idea proposed by Le-Van and Nguyen (2007), we first consider an equilibrium with dividends in which we introduce an additional good that the satiated households want to have.

Definition 7.3

A list $\left\{ (c_1^i, \ldots, c_J^i, L^i)_{i \in I}, (K_j, \tilde{L}_j)_{j \in J}, (p_1, \ldots, p_J, r, w) \right\}$ is said to be an equilibrium (a quasi-equilibrium) with dividends $(d^i)_{i \in I}$ if it satisfies (7.8), (7.11), (7.12), (7.13), (7.14) and

$$(D2 - dividends) \forall i \in I, p_1 c_1^i + p_2 c_2^i + \cdots + p_J c_J^i$$
$$-wL^i \leq r\bar{K}^i + d^i \text{ and}$$
$$for (c'_1^i, \ldots, c'_J^i, 0, -L'^i) \in X^i \text{ and } u^i(c'_1^i, \ldots, c'_J^i, 0, -L'^i) \tag{7.10''}$$
$$\times > u^i(c_1^i, \ldots, c_J^i, 0, -L^i), \text{ then } p_1 c'_1^i + p_2 c'_2^i + \ldots$$
$$+p_J c'_J^i - wL'^i > (\geq) r\bar{K}^i + d^i.$$

Definition 7.4

A list $(c_1^i, \ldots, c_J^i, 0, -L^i)_{i \in I}$ is said to be a feasible allocation if there exists $(0, \ldots, y_j, \ldots, 0, -K_j, -\tilde{L}_j) \in Y_j$ for all $j \in J$ such that (7.3), (7.13), (7.14) and

$$\sum_{i \in I} c_j^i = y_j, \forall j \in J, \tag{7.12'}$$

all hold.

The set of all feasible allocations is denoted by A. Let A^i be the projection of the feasible set A on the consumption set X^i. We assume that any x^i in A^i is not a local satiation point, that is, there exists x'^i in A^i such that $u^i(x'^i) > u^i(x^i)$.

Remark 7.3

The feasible set A is compact.

7.3 Existence of an Equilibrium

To establish the existence of equilibrium, we need to impose an additional assumption.

Assumption 7.4
For each $i \in I$ and $j \in J$, let Z_j^i stand for the maximum real income of household i in terms of good j for all feasible allocations in the feasible set A where real income $= (w\bar{L}^i + r\bar{K}^i)/p_j$. Then, for each $i \in I$, there exist J numbers $\theta_j \in]0, 1[$, $\theta_1 + \ldots + \theta_J = 1$, such that for any $j \in J$, $\theta_j \bar{L}^i > a_j^i Z_j^i$.

Remark 7.4
The above assumption requires (i) each household's labour endowment is sufficiently large and/or (ii) the quantity of time which households i need to consume one unit of good j is sufficiently small, so that each household can at least consume its maximum real income. Assumption 7.4 also implies that $\theta_j \bar{L}^i > a_j^i Z_j^i > a_j^i c_j$ for all $j \in J$ in the feasible allocation set A.

We are now ready to establish the following lemma, which is crucial for the proof of the existence of an equilibrium. Relying on Assumption 7.4, the lemma ensures that there exists no satiation point in the feasible set.

Lemma 7.1 *Suppose that Assumptions 7.1, 7.2, 7.3 and 7.4 hold. For any $i \in I$, if $\left(c_1^i, \ldots, c_J^i, 0, -L^i\right)$ is a feasible allocation, then there exists $\left(c'_1^i, \ldots, c'_J^i, 0, -L'^i\right)$ $\in X^i$ such that $u^i\left(c'_1^i, \ldots, c'_J^i, 0, -L'^i\right) > u^i\left(c_1^i, \ldots, c_J^i, 0, -L^i\right)$.*

Proof
We first consider the case in which $I > 1$. Fix i. If inequality (7.3) is strict, then it is possible to improve the utility of household i by, for example, increasing c_1^i. We claim that if (7.3) is an equality, then $L^i > 0$. Suppose to the contrary that $a_1^i c_1^i + \ldots + a_J^i c_J^i = \bar{L}^i$. This is equivalent to $a_1^i c_1^i / \bar{L}^i + \ldots + a_J^i c_J^i / \bar{L}^i = 1$. Let $\zeta_j = a_j^i c_j^i / \bar{L}^i$ for $j \in J$. We then have $\zeta_j \in]0, 1[$, $\zeta_1 + \ldots + \zeta_J = 1$. If $\zeta_1 \geq \theta_1$, then $c_1^i \geq \theta_1 \bar{L}^i / a_1^i$, which contradicts Assumption 7.4. If $\zeta_1 < \theta_1$, then there exists $k \in J$ such that $\zeta_k \geq \theta_k$, which also leads to a contradiction to Assumption 7.4.

Suppose (7.3) holds with equality with $L^i > 0$. Choose $\varepsilon > 0$ which is sufficiently small and define $L'^i = L^i - \varepsilon > 0$, $c'_1^i = c_1^i + \varepsilon/a_1^i$ and $c'_j^i = c_j^i, \forall j > 1$. We thus have $\left(c'_1^i, \ldots, c'_J^i, 0, -L'^i\right) \in X^i$ such that $u^i\left(c'_1^i, \ldots, c'_J^i, 0, -L'^i\right) > u^i\left(c_1^i, \ldots, c_J^i, 0, -L^i\right)$.

For the special case where $I = 1$, the proof follows basically the same but simpler line of reasoning (with no superscript i).

QED

We will now prove that there is no satiation point in new economy with an additional good. Hence a quasi-equilibrium (and thus, an equilibrium) with dividends exists under our assumptions. We will finally show that this equilibrium with dividends actually corresponds to a Walrasian equilibrium for the initial economy.

Proposition 7.1 *Suppose that Assumptions 7.1, 7.2, 7.3 and 7.4 hold. Then there exists a quasi-equilibrium with dividends* $(d^i)_{i \in I}$.

Proof
We adapt the proof provided in Le-Van and Nguyen (2007). A detailed proof is given in Appendix 7.1.

QED

Proposition 7.2 *Suppose that Assumptions 7.1, 7.2, 7.3 and 7.4 hold. Suppose further that at equilibrium every household is non-satiated. Then a quasi-equilibrium with dividends will be reduced to a quasi-equilibrium. That is, the dividends are zero for every household.*

Proof
We adapt the proof provided in Le-Van and Nguyen (2007). A detailed proof is given in Appendix 7.2.

QED

Proposition 7.3 *Suppose that Assumptions 7.1, 7.2, 7.3 and 7.4 hold. Then there exists an equilibrium.*

Proof
Let $\left\{ \left(c_1^i, \ldots, c_J^i, L^i \right)_{i \in I}, \left(K_j, \tilde{L}_j \right)_{j \in J}, (p_1, \ldots, p_J, r, w) \right\}$ be a quasi-equilibrium. We first prove there exists $\left(c'^i_1, \ldots, c'^i_J, 0, -L'^i \right) \in X^i$ which satisfies $p_1 c'^i_1 + \ldots + p_J c'^i_J - w L'^i < r \bar{K}^i$. Since

$a_1^i c_1^i + a_2^i c_2^i + \ldots + a_J^i c_J^i + L^i = \bar{L}^i$ and $p_1 c_1^i + \ldots + p_J c_J^i - w L^i = r \bar{K}^i$, we can take $L'^i = L^i$ and choose $c'^i_j (j \in J)$ sufficiently small so that $a_1^i c'^i_1 + \ldots + a_J^i c'^i_J + L'^i < \bar{L}^i$ and $p_1 c'^i_1 + \ldots + p_J c'^i_J - w L'^i < r \bar{K}^i$.

Suppose there exists $\left(\hat{c}_1^i, \ldots, \hat{c}_J^i, 0, -\hat{L}^i \right)_{i \in I}$ that satisfies $a_1^i \hat{c}_1^i + \ldots + a_J^i \hat{c}_J^i + \hat{L}^i \leq L^i$, $p_1 \hat{c}_1^i + \ldots + p_J \hat{c}_J^i - w \hat{L}^i = r \bar{K}^i$ and $u^i (\hat{c}_1^i, \ldots, \hat{c}_J^i, 0, -\hat{L}^i). > u^i (c_1^i, \ldots, c_J^i, 0, -L^i)$. For $\lambda \in]0,1[$, define $c_j^i(\lambda) = \lambda \hat{c}_j^i + (1 - \lambda) c'^i_j, j \in J$ and $L^i(\lambda) = \lambda \hat{L}^i + (1 - \lambda) L'^i$. We have $p_1 c_1^i(\lambda) + \ldots + p_J c_J^i(\lambda) - w L^i(\lambda) < r \bar{K}^i$ and $\lambda u^i (\hat{c}_1^i, \ldots, \hat{c}_J^i, 0, -\hat{L}^i) + (1 - \lambda) u^i \left(c'^i_1, \ldots, c'^i_J, 0, -L'^i \right) < u^i (c_1^i(\lambda), \ldots, c_J^i(\lambda), 0, -L^i(\lambda))$. For λ sufficiently close to 1, we have $p_1 c_1^i(\lambda) + \ldots + p_J c_J^i(\lambda) - w L^i(\lambda) < r \bar{K}^i$, and $u^i (c_1^i(\lambda), \ldots, c_J^i(\lambda), 0, -L^i(\lambda)) > u^i (c_1^i, \ldots, c_J^i, 0, -L^i)$, which contradicts that $\{ \left(c_1^i, \ldots, c_J^i, L^i \right)_{i \in I}, \left(K_j, \tilde{L}_j \right)_{j \in J}, (p_1, \ldots, p_J, r, w) \}$ is a quasi-equilibrium.

Therefore, $\qquad p_1\widehat{c}_1^i + \ldots + p_J\widehat{c}_J^i - w\widehat{L}^i > r\bar{K}^i.$ We conclude that $\left\{ \left(c_1^i, \ldots, c_J^i, L^i\right)_{i \in I}, \left(K_j, \tilde{L}_j\right)_{j \in J}, (p_1, \ldots, p_J, r, w) \right\}$ is actually an equilibrium.

QED

Remark 7.4

(i) At equilibrium, because the utilities and the production functions are increasing, the equilibrium prices, wage and rent are strictly positive.

(ii) If, for all $i \in I$ and all $j \in J$, a_j^i approaches zero steadily, then L^i approaches $\bar{L}^i$ for all $i \in I$. The consumption time constraint is gradually disappearing, and the present model is approaching the standard general equilibrium model.

7.4 Sufficient Conditions for a Unique Equilibrium

We have so far demonstrated the existence of an autarkic equilibrium in our model under Assumptions 7.1, 7.2, 7.3 and 7.4. In particular, Assumption 7.4 provides a sufficient condition in ensuring that there is no satiation in the feasible allocation set. However, it is not possible to show that the equilibrium is unique without further conditions. Thus, comparative static analysis cannot be validly conducted in our present model of heterogeneous households.

In Chap. 6 of this book, it has been shown that in a two-by-two model with representative agents, an autarkic equilibrium exists uniquely (Tran-Nam 2018). Thus, a sufficient condition for the existence of a unique equilibrium appears to be the assumption that households are identically homogeneous. The assumption of representative agents is equivalent to the special case of heterogeneous agents with $I = 1$ so the superscript i is no longer necessary.

To preserve the many commodities feature of our original model, we also find it necessary to adopt an assumption concerning the functional form of the production technologies.

Assumption 7.5
For $j \in J$, the j-th production function is given by $F_j(K_j, L_j) = A_j F(K_j, L_j)$ where F satisfies Assumption 7.1.

We can now state Lemma

Lemma 7.2 *Under Assumptions 7.1, 7.2 and 7.3 with $I = 1$ and Assumption 7.5, the financial budget constraint can be written in real variables as*

$$\frac{c_1}{A_1} + \frac{c_2}{A_2} + \ldots + \frac{c_J}{A_J} = F\left(\bar{K}, L\right) \qquad (7.15)$$

where L is the amount of labour that a representative household supplies for work.

Proof

See Appendix 7.3.

QED

Assumption 7.5 is important in deriving Lemma 7.2, which in turn helps us to establish Proposition

Proposition 7.4 *Under Assumptions7.1, 7.2, 7.3 and 7.4 with I = 1 and Assumption 7.5, there exists one and only one autarkic equilibrium if all households are identical.*

Proof

Under Assumptions 7.1, 7.2, 7.3 and 7.4 with $I = 1$, Proposition 7.3 ascertains that there exists an equilibrium. We now proceed to prove that there exist unique positive equilibrium values for $(c_1, c_2, \ldots, c_J)$.

Assume the contrary, there are two distinct equilibria $(c_1, c_2, \ldots, c_J)$ and $(c'_1, c'_2, \ldots, c'_J)$. The associated values of labour are L and L', respectively. The maximum value of utility is thus $\bar{u} = u(c_1, c_2, \ldots, c_J) = u(c'_1, c'_2, \ldots, c'_J)$. Let $\lambda \in]0,1[$ and define $c_j(\lambda) = \lambda c_j + (1 - \lambda)c'_j, j \in J$, and $L(\lambda) = \lambda L + (1-\lambda) L'$. It is easy to see that $(c_1(\lambda), c_2(\lambda), \ldots, c_J(\lambda), L(\lambda))$ satisfies both the time constraint (7.3) and the financial budget constraint (7.15):

$$\sum_{j \in J} a_j c_j(\lambda) + L(\lambda) = \lambda \left[\sum_{j \in J} a_j c_j + L \right] + (1 - \lambda) \left[\sum_{j \in J} a_j c'_j + L' \right] \leq \lambda \bar{L} + (1 - \lambda)\bar{L}$$

$$= \bar{L} \quad \frac{c_1(\lambda)}{A_1} + \frac{c_2(\lambda)}{A_2} + \ldots + \frac{c_J(\lambda)}{A_J} \leq \lambda F(\bar{K}, L)$$

$$+ (1 - \lambda)F(\bar{K}, L') \leq F(\bar{K}, L(\lambda)).$$

But we then obtain a contradiction:

$$u(c_1(\lambda), c_2(\lambda), \ldots, c_J(\lambda)) > \lambda u(c_1, c_2, \ldots, c_J) + (1 - \lambda)u(c'_1, c'_2, \ldots, c'_j) = \bar{u}.$$

Thus, the equilibrium must be unique. Further, since $(c_1, c_2, \ldots, c_J)$ is uniquely determined, so is L.

QED

Remark 7.5

(i) At equilibrium, both the time and financial budget constraints are binding.

(ii) If we add to Assumption 7.2 the familiar Inada condition that $\partial u/\partial c_j \to +\infty$ as $c_j \to 0^+$ for all $j \in J$, then the equilibrium is non-corner.

(iii) Once the equilibrium consumption bundle for each household is obtained, the output composition, commodity prices and factor prices can be determined along the line discussed in Appendix 6.1 of the previous chapter of this book.

7.5 An Illustrative Example

In this section, we specialize the production functions and consumer preferences to characterize the equilibrium and derive some comparative static results. To this end, we consider a representative-agent, two-by-two and closed economy. There are two firms with Cobb–Douglas production functions:

$$F_j(K_j, L_j) = A_j K_j^\alpha L_j^{1-\alpha}, j \in \{1, 2\} \text{ and } \alpha \in (0, 1). \tag{7.16}$$

The utility function takes the logarithmic, separable form:

$$u(c_1, c_2) = \ln(c_1) + \beta \ln(c_2), \beta \in (0, 1). \tag{7.17}$$

In view of Proposition 7.4, a unique equilibrium exists. Let this equilibrium be denoted by $(c_1^*, c_2^*, L^*, K_1^*, K_2^*, L_1^*, L_2^*, p_1^*, p_2^*, r^*, w^*)$. Focusing on the amount of labour employed in production, we can state Proposition

Proposition 7.5 *In the economy described in this section, the equilibrium labour devoted to production L^* is the unique solution to the equation:*

$$\frac{1}{1+\beta}\left[\frac{1}{L^\alpha + (1-\alpha)a_1 A_1 \bar{K}^\alpha} + \frac{\beta}{L^\alpha + (1-\alpha)a_2 A_2 \bar{K}^\alpha}\right] = \frac{L^{1-\alpha}}{\alpha L + (1-\alpha)\bar{K}} \tag{7.18}$$

Proof
Refer to Appendix 7.4.
  QED
  Since the equilibrium is unique, we can sensibly talk about comparative statics. It is particularly interesting to examine how small changes in the consumption technologies impact on the equilibrium total amount of labour employed in production, factor prices and the allocation of labour between industries. To this end, it is possible to establish Proposition

Proposition 7.6
(i) When a_1 or a_2 changes, L^* and r^* will change in the opposite direction, whereas w^* will move in the same direction.
  (ii) L_j^* is decreasing in both a_j for $j = 1, 2$.

Proof
Refer to Appendix 7.5.

                                                                                  QED
  The intuition of Proposition 7.6 (i) is clear. When it is more (less) time consuming to consume goods, the amount of labour available for production necessarily becomes smaller (larger). At constant supply of capital, this will in turn cause

wage rate to rise (fall) and rental rate to fall (rise). Proposition 7.6 (ii) can be interpreted in a similar way. As the total amount of labour available for production declines (rises) as a result of an increase (a decrease) in either a_1 or a_2, the amount of labour allocated to each industry will both decline (rise) in view of their similar functional forms.

Note also that as a_1 or a_2 or both increase, L^* will become smaller and smaller. However, when a_1 or a_2 or both become sufficiently large, Assumption 7.4 will be violated so that the economy described in this section may not possess an equilibrium.

7.6   Final Remarks

In this chapter, we have examined the impact of incorporating a Gossenian–Beckerian time constraint into general equilibrium models of descending level of generality. We started with a very general model with heterogeneous households, two factors, many goods and general production and utility functions. By imposing a plausible assumption (Assumption 7.4) and employing the dividend approach proposed by Le-Van and Nguyen (2007), we were able to demonstrate that such an economy possesses a Walrasian equilibrium. To obtain a stronger result of unique equilibrium, we found it sufficient to adopt the representative-agent assumption and slightly more specific production functional forms. Finally, we assumed a two-by-two, closed economy with Cobb–Douglas production functions and logarithmic, separable utility in order to characterize the (unique) equilibrium and obtain some comparative static results.

The assumption of identical households, together with Assumption 7.5, is sufficient for the existence of a unique autarkic equilibrium. But representative agent is a very restrictive assumption so it is worthwhile to search for weaker sufficient condition(s) for uniqueness. A worthwhile possibility, as suggested in the summary conclusion of Chap. 6, is to explore the case in which households possess the same preferences and consumption technologies but differ in terms of capital and/or labour endowment.

We have confined our analysis to the closed economy case. However, it is apparent that the results that we have obtained can carry over to the open economy case in a straightforward manner. For example, suppose that the economy under study is a small, price-taking open economy. As prices are given by world demand and supply conditions, the determination of the economy's post-trade equilibrium is simpler than the determination of an autarkic equilibrium. Even for a large, price-making open economy, the derivation of the economy's post-trade equilibrium can proceed along a similar line so long as the world prices have been determined.

Acknowledgement The book chapter is a substantially revised version of a conference paper by the same group of authors presented at the *Ninth Vietnam Economist Annual Meeting* (*VEAM*), University of Danang, Vietnam, August 11–12, 2016. It also incorporates materials derived from a working paper by Tran-Nam and Pham (2014).

Appendices

Appendix 7.1: Proof of Proposition 7.1

Step 1. *Introduce the intermediary economy:*

$$\widehat{\varepsilon} = \left\{ \left(\widehat{X}^i, \widehat{u}^i, \widehat{e}^i \right)_{i\in\mathbf{I}}, \left(\widehat{Y}_j \right)_{j\in\mathbf{J}} \right\}$$

where $\widehat{X}^i = X^i \times \mathbb{R}_+, \widehat{e}^i = \left(e^i, \delta^i \right)$ with $\delta^i > 0$ for all $i \in \mathbf{I}$ and $\widehat{Y}_j = (Y_j, 0)$ for $j \in \mathbf{J}$
and the utilities $\widehat{u}^i$:

$$\widehat{u}^i \left(x^i, d^i \right) = \begin{cases} u^i(x^i) & \text{if } x^i \notin S^i \\ u^i(x^i) + \mu d^i = M^i + \mu d^i & \text{if } x^i \in S^i \end{cases}$$

where $\mu > 0$ and $M^i = \max\{u^i(x): x \in X^i\}$.
By denoting for all $i \in \mathbf{I}$ and $j \in \mathbf{J}$:

$$\begin{aligned}
\widehat{x}^i &= \left(x^i, d^i \right) = \left(c_1^i, \ldots, c_J^i, 0, -L^i, d^i \right) \in \widehat{X}^i \\
\widehat{e}^i &= \left(e^i, \delta^i \right) = \left(0, \ldots, 0, \bar{K}^i, 0, \delta^i \right) \\
\widehat{y}_j &= \left(\tilde{y}_j, 0 \right) = \left(0, \ldots, F_j(K_j, \tilde{L}_j), \ldots, 0, -K_j, -\tilde{L}_j, 0 \right) \\
\widehat{p} &= (p, q) = (p_1, \ldots, p_J, r, w, q),
\end{aligned}$$

we can rewrite the definition of quasi-equilibrium with dividends as follows.

A quasi-equilibrium of $\widehat{\varepsilon}$ is a list $\left(\left(\widehat{x}^{*i} \right)_{i\in\mathbf{I}}, \left(y_j^* \right)_{j\in\mathbf{J}}, \widehat{p}^{*i} \right) \in \left(\mathbb{R}^{J+3} \right)^I \times \left(\mathbb{R}^{J+3} \right)^J$
$\times \mathbb{R}^{J+3}$ which satisfies

$$\sum_{i\in\mathbf{I}} \widehat{x}^{*i} = \sum_{i\in\mathbf{I}} \widehat{e}^{*i} + \sum_{j\in\mathbf{J}} \widehat{y}_j^*$$

(a) For each i, one has

$$\widehat{p}^* \cdot \widehat{x}^i = \widehat{p}^{*i} \cdot \widehat{e}^i + \sum_{j\in\mathbf{J}} \theta_{ij} \left(\widehat{p}^* \cdot \widehat{y}_j^* \right)$$

and for each $\widehat{x}^i \in \widehat{X}^i$, with $\widehat{u}^i \left(\widehat{x}^i \right) > \widehat{u}^i \left(\widehat{x}^{*i} \right)$, it holds

$$\widehat{p}^* \cdot \widehat{x}^i \geq \widehat{p}^{*i} \cdot \widehat{e}^i + \sum_{j\in\mathbf{J}} \theta_{ij} \left(\widehat{p}^* \cdot \widehat{y}_j^* \right)$$

(b) For each $j \in \mathbf{J}$, one has $\widehat{y}_j^* \in \widehat{Y}_j$ and $\widehat{p}^* \cdot \widehat{y}_j^* = \sup \left(\widehat{p}^* \cdot \widehat{Y}_j \right) = \sup_{y_j \in \widehat{Y}_j} \left(\widehat{p} \cdot \widehat{y}_j \right)$.

We consider the feasible set $\widehat{A}$ of $\widehat{\varepsilon}$:

$$\widehat{A} = \left\{ \left((\widehat{x}^i)_{i \in I}, (\widehat{y}_j)_{j \in J} \right) : \forall i \in I, \widehat{x}^i \in \widehat{X}^i; \forall j \in J, \widehat{y}_j \in \widehat{Y}_j \text{ and } \sum_{i \in I} \widehat{x}^i \right.$$

$$\left. = \sum_{i \in I} \widehat{e}^i + \sum_{j \in J} \widehat{y}_j \right\}$$

We can see that $\widehat{A}$ is compact.

Step 2. *For each $i \in$ I, the function $\widehat{u}^i$ is strictly quasi-concave, upper semi-continuous and has no satiation point.*

Denote $\mathcal{L}_\alpha^i = \{x^i \in X^i : u^i(x^i) \ge \alpha\}; \widehat{\mathcal{L}}_\alpha^i = \left\{ (x^i, d^i) \in \widehat{X}^i : \widehat{u}^i(x^i, d^i) \ge \alpha \right\}$. It is obvious that $\mathcal{L}_\alpha^i$ and S^i are closed and convex for every α. We will prove that $\widehat{\mathcal{L}}_\alpha^i$ is also closed and convex. We have two cases.

Case 1 $\alpha < M^i$.

If $x \notin S^i$, then $\widehat{u}^i(x^i, d^i) = u^i(x^i)$. So $(x^i, d^i) \in \mathcal{L}_\alpha^i \times \mathbb{R}_+ \Leftrightarrow (x^i, d^i) \in \widehat{\mathcal{L}}_\alpha^i$.
If $x \in S^i$, then $u^i(x^i) = M^i > \alpha$ and $\widehat{u}^i(x^i, d^i) = M^i + \mu d^i > \alpha$; it implies $(x^i, d^i) \in \mathcal{L}_\alpha^i$
$\times \mathbb{R}_+$ and $(x^i, d^i) \in \widehat{\mathcal{L}}_\alpha^i$.

$$\widehat{\mathcal{L}}_\alpha^i = \mathcal{L}_\alpha^i \times \mathbb{R}_+. \qquad \text{(Hence)}$$

Case 2 $\alpha \ge M^i$. Consider $(x^i, d^i) \in \widehat{\mathcal{L}}_\alpha^i$.

If $x^i \notin S^i$, then $u^i(x^i) = \widehat{u}^i(x^i, d^i) \ge \alpha \ge M^i$ contradict the definition of M^i.

Hence $x^i \in S^i$. We have $\widehat{u}^i(x^i, d^i) = M^i + \mu d^i \ge \alpha \Leftrightarrow d^i \ge \dfrac{\alpha - M^i}{\mu}$. It implies that

$$\widehat{\mathcal{L}}_\alpha^i = S^i \times \left\{ d^i : d^i \ge \frac{\alpha - M^i}{\mu} \right\}.$$

We have proved that $\widehat{u}^i$ is upper semi-continuous and quasi-concave for every $i \in$ I.
We now prove that $\widehat{u}^i$ is strictly quasi-concave. Take $(x^i, d^i), (\tilde{x}^i, \tilde{d}^i) \in X^i \times \mathbb{R}_+$ such that $\widehat{u}^i(\tilde{x}^i, \tilde{d}^i) > \widehat{u}^i(x^i, d^i)$. For any $\lambda \in 0, 1[$, we will verify that

$$\widehat{u}^i\left(\lambda x^i + (1-\lambda)\tilde{x}^i, \lambda d^i + (1-\lambda)\tilde{d}^i\right) > \widehat{u}^i(x^i, d^i)$$

We have two cases.

Case 1 $x^i \in S^i$. We have $\widehat{u}^i(x^i, d^i) = M^i + \mu d^i$.
Since $\widehat{u}^i(\tilde{x}^i, \tilde{d}^i) > \widehat{u}^i(x^i, d^i)$, it implies $\tilde{x}^i \in S^i$ and $\tilde{d}^i > d^i$. This follows $\lambda x^i + (1-\lambda)\tilde{x}^i \in S^i$, and we have

$$\widehat{u}^i\left(\lambda x^i + (1-\lambda)\tilde{x}^i, \lambda d^i + (1-\lambda)\tilde{d}^i\right) = M^i + \mu\left(\lambda d^i + (1-\lambda)\tilde{d}^i\right)$$
$$> M^i + \mu\left(\lambda d^i + (1-\lambda)d^i\right)$$
$$= M^i + d^i = \widehat{u}^i(x^i, d^i)$$

Case 2 $x^i \notin S^i$. We have $\widehat{u}^i(x^i, d^i) = u^i(x^i) < M^i$ and $u^i(\tilde{x}^i) > u^i(x^i)$.

If $\lambda x^i + (1 - \lambda)\tilde{x}^i \in S^i$, then

$$\widehat{u}^i(\lambda x^i + (1 - \lambda)\tilde{x}^i, \lambda d^i + (1 - \lambda)\tilde{d}^i) = M^i + \mu(\lambda d^i + (1 - \lambda)\tilde{d}^i)$$
$$> u^i(x^i) = \widehat{u}^i(x^i, d^i).$$

If $\lambda x^i + (1 - \lambda)\tilde{x}^i \notin S^i$, since u^i is concave, we have:

$$\widehat{u}^i(\lambda x^i + (1 - \lambda)\tilde{x}^i, \lambda d^i + (1 - \lambda)\tilde{d}^i) = u^i(\lambda x^i + (1 - \lambda)\tilde{x}^i)$$
$$\geq \lambda u^i(x^i) + (1 - \lambda)u^i(\tilde{x}^i)$$
$$> u^i(x^i) = \widehat{u}^i(x^i, d^i).$$

We have proved that $\widehat{u}^i$ is strictly quasi-concave. We now prove that $\widehat{u}^i$ has no satiation point. Take $(x^i, d^i) \in \widehat{X}^i$; we will verify that there exists $(\tilde{x}^i, \tilde{d}^i) \in \widehat{X}^i$ such that $\widehat{u}^i(\tilde{x}^i, \tilde{d}^i) > \widehat{u}^i(x^i, d^i)$. We consider two cases:

- $x^i \in S^i$. Take $\tilde{x}^i = x^i$ and $\tilde{d}^i > d^i$. We have

$$\widehat{u}^i(\tilde{x}^i, \tilde{d}^i) = M^i + \mu\tilde{d}^i > M^i + \mu d^i = \widehat{u}^i(x^i, d^i).$$

- $x^i \notin S^i$. Take $\tilde{x}^i \in X^i$ such that $u^i(\tilde{x}^i) > u^i(x^i)$ and $\tilde{d}^i = d^i$. We have

$$\widehat{u}^i(\tilde{x}^i, \tilde{d}^i) \geq u^i(\tilde{x}^i) > u^i(x^i) = \widehat{u}^i(x^i, d^i).$$

We have proved that $\widehat{u}^i$ has no satiation point.

Step 3. *We consider a sequence of truncated economies.*

Let $B(0, n)$ denote the ball centred at 0 with radius n. Let

$$\widehat{X}^i_n = \widehat{X}^i \cap B(0, n), \quad i \in \mathbf{I}.$$

Let S be the unit sphere of $\mathbb{R}^{J+4}$. For every $(\widehat{p}, s) \in S \cap (\mathbb{R}^{J+3} \times \mathbb{R}_+)$, define the multivalued mapping

$$\xi^i_n, Q^i_n : S \cap (\mathbb{R}^{J+3} \times \mathbb{R}_+) \to \widehat{X}^i$$

by setting:

$$\xi^i_n(\widehat{p}, s) = \left\{\widehat{x}^i \in \widehat{X}^i_n : \widehat{p} \cdot \widehat{x}^i \leq \widehat{p} \cdot \widehat{e}^i + \sum_{j \in \mathbf{J}} \theta_{ij}\Pi^n_j(\widehat{p}) + s\right\} Q^i_n(\widehat{p}, s)$$

$$= \left\{\widehat{x}^i \in \xi^i_n(\widehat{p}, s) : \text{if} \widehat{x}^{\prime i} \in \widehat{X}^i_n \text{ with } \widehat{u}_i(\widehat{x}^{\prime i}) > \widehat{u}^i(\widehat{x}^i) \text{ then} \widehat{p} \cdot \widehat{x}^{\prime i} \geq \widehat{p} \cdot \widehat{e}^i + \sum_{j \in \mathbf{J}} \theta_{ij}\Pi^n_j(\widehat{p}) + s\right\},$$

where $\Pi^n_j(p) = \max(p \cdot Y^n_j)$ is profit of firm j in truncated economies.

Define the mapping $z_n : S \cap (\mathbb{R}^{J+3} \times \mathbb{R}_+) \to \mathbb{R}^{J+4}$ by setting

$$z_n(\widehat{p}, s) = \left(\sum_{i \in \mathbf{I}} Q_n^i(\widehat{p}, s) - \sum_{i \in \mathbf{I}} \widehat{e}^i - \sum_{j \in \mathbf{J}} \Phi_j^n(\widehat{p}) \right) \times \{-I\}$$

where $\Phi_j^n(\widehat{p}) = \left\{ \widehat{y}_j \in \widehat{Y}_j^n : \widehat{p} \cdot \widehat{y}_j = \max \widehat{p} \cdot \widehat{Y}_j^n \right\}$.

Step 4. *(Lemma Gale–Nikaido–Debreu) Suppose*

(i) *P be a closed nonempty convex cone in the linear space $\mathbb{R}^l$ and S be the unit sphere in $\mathbb{R}^l$.*
(ii) *The multivalued mapping Z from $S \cap P$ to $\mathbb{R}^l$ is upper semi-continuous having nonempty convex compact values.*
(iii) *For every $p \in S \cap P$, $\exists z \in Z(p)$ such that $p \cdot z \leq 0$.*

Then there exists $\bar{p} \in S \cap P$ satisfying

$$Z(\bar{p}) \cap P^0 \neq \emptyset,$$

where $P^0 = \{q \in \mathbb{R}^l : q \cdot p \leq 0, \forall p \in P\}$

Step 5. *For each $i \in \mathbf{I}$, the mapping $\xi_n^i(\widehat{p}, s)$ is upper semi-continuous having nonempty convex compact values.*

By choosing $\widehat{x}^i = (0, \ldots, 0, -\bar{L}^i, \delta^i) \in \widehat{X}^i$, we can easily see that $\xi_n^i(\widehat{p}, s) \neq \emptyset$. If $\{x_k^i\}_k \subset \xi_n^i(\widehat{p}, s)$ and $\lim_{k \to +\infty} x_k^i = \widehat{x}^i$, then $\widehat{x}^i \in \widehat{X}_n^i$ (since $\widehat{X}_n^i$ compact) and $\widehat{p} \cdot \widehat{x}^i \leq \widehat{p} \cdot \widehat{e}^i + s$. Hence $\xi_n^i(\widehat{p}, s)$ is closed, and since it is a subset of compact set $\widehat{X}_n^i$, so $\xi_n^i(\widehat{p}, s)$ is compact.

For every $\widehat{x}^i, \widehat{z}^i \in \xi_n^i(\widehat{p}, s)$ and $\lambda \in [0, 1]$, we have

$$\widehat{p} \cdot [(1 - \lambda)\widehat{x}^i + \lambda \widehat{z}^i] = (1 - \lambda)\widehat{p} \cdot \widehat{x}^i + \lambda \widehat{p} \cdot \widehat{z}^i$$

$$\leq (1 - \lambda) \left(\widehat{p} \cdot \widehat{e}^i + \sum_{j \in \mathbf{J}} \theta_{ij} \Pi_j^n(\widehat{p}) + s \right) + \lambda \left(\widehat{p} \cdot \widehat{e}^i + \sum_{j \in \mathbf{J}} \theta_{ij} \Pi_j^n(\widehat{p}) + s \right)$$

$$= \widehat{p} \cdot \widehat{e}^i + \sum_{j \in \mathbf{J}} \theta_{ij} \Pi_j^n(\widehat{p}) + s.$$

Hence $(1 - \lambda)\widehat{x}^i + \lambda \widehat{z}^i \in \xi_n^i(\widehat{p}, s)$ which means that $\xi_n^i(\widehat{p}, s)$ is convex.

Let $\{\widehat{p}_k, s_k\} \subset S \cap (\mathbb{R}^{J+3} \times \mathbb{R}_+)$ converge to $(\widehat{p}, s)$ and let $\{\widehat{x}_k^i\}$ be a sequence with $\widehat{x}_k^i \in \xi_n^i(p_k, s_k) \forall k$. Since $\{\widehat{x}_k^i\} \subset \widehat{X}_n^i$ and $\widehat{X}_n^i$ is compact, there exists subsequence $\{\widehat{x}_{km}^i\}$ converging to $\widehat{x}^i \in \widehat{X}_n^i$. We have

$$\widehat{p}_{k_m} \cdot \widehat{x}_{k_m}^i \leq \widehat{p}_{k_m} \cdot \widehat{e}^i + \sum_{j \in \mathbf{J}} \theta_{ij} \Pi_j^n(\widehat{p}_{k_m}) + s_{k_m}.$$

Letting $m \to +\infty$, we obtain

$$\widehat{p} \cdot \widehat{x}^i \leq \widehat{p} \cdot \widehat{e}^i + \sum_{j \in \mathbf{J}} \theta_{ij} \Pi_j^n(\widehat{p}) + s.$$

This implies that $\widehat{x}^i \in \xi_n^i(\widehat{p}, s)$. Hence ξ_n^i is upper semi-continuous.

Step 6. *For each $i \in \mathbf{I}$, the mapping $Q_n^i(\widehat{p}, s)$ is upper semi-continuous having nonempty convex compact values.*

Since $\widehat{u}^i$ is an upper semi-continuous function on $\xi_n^i(\widehat{p}, s)$, nonempty compact subset of $\mathbb{R}^{J+3}$, then $\widehat{u}^i$ has a maximum on $\xi_n^i(\widehat{p}, s)$. Let $x \in \xi_n^i(\widehat{p}, s)$ and $\widehat{u}^i(x) = \max\{\widehat{u}^i(\widehat{x}^i) : \widehat{x}^i \in \xi_n^i(\widehat{p}, s)\}$. We will show that $x \in Q_n^i(\widehat{p}, s)$.

Indeed, let $x'^i \in \widehat{X}_n^i$ and $\widehat{u}^i(x'^i) > \widehat{u}^i(x)$ and then $x'^i \notin \xi_n^i(\widehat{p}, s)$ (by identifying x). Since $x'^i \notin \xi_n^i(\widehat{p}, s)$, we have

$$\widehat{p} \cdot x'^i > \widehat{p} \cdot \widehat{e}^i + \sum_{j \in \mathbf{J}} \theta_{ij} \Pi_j^n(\widehat{p}) + s.$$

Hence $x \in Q_n^i(\widehat{p}, s)$ which implies that $Q_n^i(\widehat{p}, s)$ is not empty.

For every $\widehat{x}^i, \widehat{z}^i \in Q_n^i(\widehat{p}, s)$ and $\lambda \in [0, 1]$, we will prove that $w^i := \lambda \widehat{x}^i + (1 - \lambda)\widehat{z}^i \in Q_n^i(\widehat{p}, s)$. Indeed, since $\xi_n^i(\widehat{p}, s)$ is convex and $\widehat{x}^i, \widehat{z}^i \in \xi_n^i(\widehat{p}, s)$, we have $w^i \in \xi_n^i(\widehat{p}, s)$. Let $x'^i \in \widehat{X}_n^i$ with $\widehat{u}^i(x'^i) > \widehat{u}^i(w^i)$. Since $\widehat{u}^i$ is strictly quasi-concave,

$$\widehat{u}^i(w^i) = \widehat{u}^i(\lambda \widehat{x}^i + (1 - \lambda)\widehat{z}^i) > \min(\widehat{u}^i(\widehat{x}^i), \widehat{u}^i(\widehat{z}^i)).$$

It follows that

$$\widehat{u}^i(x'^i) > \min(\widehat{u}^i(\widehat{x}^i), \widehat{u}^i(\widehat{z}^i))$$

since $\widehat{x}^i, \widehat{z}^i \in Q_n^i(\widehat{p}, s)$; we have

$$\widehat{p} \cdot x'^i > \widehat{p} \cdot \widehat{e}^i + \sum_{j \in \mathbf{J}} \theta_{ij} \Pi_j^n(\widehat{p}) + s.$$

Hence $w^i \in Q_n^i(\widehat{p}, s)$ which implies that $Q_n^i(\widehat{p}, s)$ is convex.

Let $(\widehat{p}_k, s_k, \widehat{x}_k^i) \in \operatorname{graph} Q_n^i$ and assume that $(\widehat{p}_k, s_k) \to (\widehat{p}, s); \widehat{x}_k^i \to \widehat{x}^i$. We will show that $(p, s, \widehat{x}^i) \in \operatorname{graph} Q_n^i$.

Since $\widehat{x}_k^i \in Q_n^i(p_k, s_k) \subset \xi_n^i(p_k, s_k)$ and ξ_n^i is closed, we have $\widehat{x}^i \in \xi_n^i(\widehat{p}, s)$.

Let $x'^i \in \widehat{X}_n^i$ with $\widehat{u}^i(x'^i) > \widehat{u}^i(\widehat{x}^i)$. By the upper semi-continuity of $\widehat{u}^i$, we have the set

$$E := \left\{ x : \widehat{u}^i(x) < \widehat{u}^i(x'^i) \right\}$$

which is open in $\mathbb{R}^{J+3}$. Since $\widehat{x}^i \in E$, there exists $\varepsilon > 0$ such that the ball $B(\widehat{x}^i, \varepsilon) \subset E$. On the other hand, since $\widehat{x}_k^i \to \widehat{x}^i$, with that ε, there exists k_0 such that

$\widehat{x}_k^i \in B(\widehat{x}^i, \varepsilon), \forall k > k_0$. Hence $\widehat{u}^i(\widehat{x}_k^i) < \widehat{u}^i(x'^i)$ for all k large enough.Since $\widehat{x}_k^i \in Q_n^i$ (p_k, s_k), we have

$$p_k \cdot x'^i > p_k \cdot \widehat{e}^i + \sum_{j \in J} \theta_{ij} \Pi_j^n(\widehat{p}_k) + s_k;$$

letting $k \to +\infty$, we obtain

$$\widehat{p} \cdot x'^i > \widehat{p} \cdot \widehat{e}^i + \sum_{j \in J} \theta_{ij} \Pi_j^n(\widehat{p}) + s.$$

This implies that $\widehat{x}^i \in Q_n^i(\widehat{p}, s)$. Hence Q_n^i is closed. Moreover,

$$Q_n^i(\widehat{p}, s) \subset \xi_n^i(\widehat{p}, s) \subset \widehat{X}_n^i, \quad \forall (\widehat{p}, s) \in S \cap (\mathbb{R}^{J+3} \times \mathbb{R}_+), n \geq 1$$

and $\widehat{X}_n^i$ is compact; we see that Q_n^i is a compact mapping.

It is obvious that $S \cap (\mathbb{R}^{J+3} \times \mathbb{R}_+)$ is compact. Following with just proven result, Q_n^i is closed. Hence Q_n^i is upper semi-continuous.

Step 7. *Applying Lemma Gale–Nikaido–Debreu for multivalued mapping z_n.*

It is easy to see that the set $\mathbb{R}^{J+3} \times \mathbb{R}_+$ is a closed nonempty convex cone in $\mathbb{R}^{J+4}$ (which satisfied the condition (i) in Lemma GND).

By the result of step 6, it is easy to see that z_n is upper semi-continuous having nonempty convex compact values (the condition (ii) is satisfied).

For every $(\widehat{p}, s) \in S \cap (\mathbb{R}^{J+3} \times \mathbb{R}_+)$, note that $x \in z_n(\widehat{p}, s)$ can be written as

$$x = \left(\sum_{i \in I} \widehat{x}_n^i - \sum_{i \in I} \widehat{e}^i - \sum_{j \in J} \widehat{y}_j^n\right) \times (-I), \quad \text{where} \widehat{x}_n^i \in Q_n^i(\widehat{p}, s), \widehat{y}_j^n \in \Phi_j^n(p).$$

Since $\widehat{x}_n^i \in Q_n^i(\widehat{p}, s) \subset \xi_n^i(\widehat{p}, s)$, we have

$$\widehat{p} \cdot \widehat{x}_n^i \leq \widehat{p} \cdot \widehat{e}_n^i + p \sum_{j \in J} \theta_{ij} \Pi_j^n(p) + s = \widehat{p} \cdot \widehat{e}^i + \sum_{j \in J} \theta_{ij} p \cdot \widehat{y}_j^n + s$$

$$\Rightarrow \widehat{p} \cdot \sum_{i \in I} \widehat{x}_n^i \leq \widehat{p} \cdot \sum_{i \in I} \widehat{e}^i + \sum_{i \in I} \sum_{j \in J} \theta_{ij} p \cdot \widehat{y}_j^n + Is = \widehat{p} \cdot \sum_{i \in I} \widehat{e}^i + p \cdot \sum_{j \in J} \widehat{y}_j^n + Is$$

$$\Rightarrow \widehat{p} \cdot \left(\sum_{i \in I} \widehat{x}_n^i - \sum_{i \in I} \widehat{e}^i - \sum_{i \in J} \widehat{y}_j^i\right) - Is \leq 0$$

$$\Rightarrow (\widehat{p}, s)x \leq 0.$$

Hence $(\widehat{p}, s)x \leq 0$ for every $(\widehat{p}, s) \in S \cap \mathbb{R}^{J+3} \times \mathbb{R}_+$ and $x \in z_n(\widehat{p}, s)$ (the condition (iii) is satisfied).

Let

$$P := \mathbb{R}^{J+3} \times \mathbb{R}_+ = \{a = (a_1, \ldots, a_6) : a_6 \geq 0\}$$
$$P^0 := \{b = (b_1, \ldots, b_6) \in \mathbb{R}^{J+4} : a \cdot b \leq 0, \forall a \in P\}.$$

Note, for $j = \overline{1, J+4}$, $\mathbf{1}_j$, the vector with 1 in component j and 0 elsewhere. By choosing $a = \pm \mathbf{1}_j, j = 1, \ldots, J+4$ and $a = \mathbf{1}_{J+4}$, since $a \cdot b \leq 0$, we obtain

$$b_1 = \cdots = b_l = 0; b_{J+4} \leq 0.$$

Moreover, $b \in \mathbf{O}_{\mathbb{R}^{J+3}} \times \mathbb{R}_-$ satisfies $a \cdot b \leq 0$, $\forall a \in P$. Hence

$$\left(\mathbb{R}^{J+3} \times \mathbb{R}_+ \right)^0 = \mathbf{O}_{\mathbb{R}^{J+3}} \times \mathbb{R}_-.$$

Applying the Gale–Nikaido–Debreu Lemma (see Geistdoerfer–Florenzano 1982), we can conclude that there exists $\left(\widehat{p}_n, s_n \right) \in S \cap \left(\mathbb{R}^{J+3} \times \mathbb{R}_+ \right)$ such that

$$z_n \left(\widehat{p}_n, s_n \right) \cap \mathbf{O}_{\mathbb{R}^{J+3}} \times \mathbb{R}_- = \emptyset.$$

It follows that there exists $\widehat{x}_n \in \mathbb{R}^{J+4}$ such that

$$\widehat{x}_n = \left(\sum_{i \in \mathbf{I}} \widehat{x}_n^i - \sum_{i \in \mathbf{I}} \widehat{e}^i - \sum_{j \in \mathbf{J}} \widehat{y}_j^n \right) \times (-Is_n) \tag{A.7.1}$$

$$\widehat{x}_n^i \in Q_n^i(p_n, s_n) \tag{A.7.2}$$

$$\sum_{i \in \mathbf{I}} \widehat{x}_n^i - \sum_{i \in \mathbf{I}} \widehat{e}^i - \sum_{j \in \mathbf{J}} \widehat{y}_j^n = 0 \tag{A.7.3}$$

From (3), we have $\left(\widehat{x}_n^i, \widehat{y}_j^n \right) \in \widehat{A}$. Since $\widehat{A}$ is compact, without loss of generality, we may assume that

$$\left(\widehat{x}_n^i, \widehat{y}_j^n \right) \to \left(\widehat{x}^{*i}, \widehat{y}_j^* \right), \quad i \in \mathbf{I}, j \in \mathbf{J}.$$

Since $(p_n, s_n) \in S \cap (\mathbb{R}^{J+3} \times \mathbb{R}_+)$ and $S \cap (\mathbb{R}^{J+3} \times \mathbb{R}_+)$ are compact, we can also assume that

$$\left(\widehat{p}_n, s_n \right) \to \left(\widehat{p}^*, s^* \right).$$

We will prove the existence of equilibrium with $\left(\left(\widehat{x}^{*i} \right)_{i \in \mathbf{I}}, \widehat{p}^* \right)$ *that has been found.*

Step 8. *Existence of quasi-equilibrium.*

From (3), let $n \to +\infty$; we obtain

$$\sum_{i \in \mathbf{I}} \widehat{x}^{*i} = \sum_{i \in \mathbf{I}} \widehat{e}^i + \sum_{j \in \mathbf{J}} \widehat{y}_j^*; \tag{A.7.4}$$

hence the condition (a) is satisfied.
From (A.7.2), we have $\widehat{x}_n^i \in \xi_n^i(\widehat{p}_n, s_n)$; this implies

$$\widehat{p}_n \cdot \widehat{x}_n^i \leq \widehat{p}_n \cdot \widehat{e}^i + \sum_{j \in \mathbf{J}} \theta_{ij} \Pi_j^n(p_n) + s_n, \quad \forall i \in \mathbf{I}.$$

Letting $n \to +\infty$, we obtain

$$\widehat{p}^* \cdot \widehat{x}^{*i} \leq \widehat{p}^* \cdot \widehat{e}^i + \sum_{j \in \mathbf{J}} \theta_{ij} \Pi_j(p^*) + s^*, \quad \forall i \in \mathbf{I} \tag{A.7.5}$$

Let $\widehat{x}^i \in \widehat{x}_n^i$ with $\widehat{u}^i(\widehat{x}^i) > \widehat{u}^i(x_i^*)$. Let $\lambda \in 0, 1]$. Define

$$\widehat{x}_\lambda^i : (\lambda \widehat{x}^i) + (1 - \lambda)\widehat{x}^{*i}.$$

Since $\widehat{u}^i$ is strictly quasi-concave, we have

$$\widehat{u}^i(\widehat{x}_\lambda^i) > \widehat{u}^i(x_i^*).$$

Since $\widehat{u}^i$ is upper semi-continuous and $\widehat{x}_n^i \to \widehat{x}^{*i}$, for all n large enough, we have

$$\widehat{u}^i(\widehat{x}_\lambda^i) > \widehat{u}^i(\widehat{x}_n^i).$$

From (A.7.2), $\widehat{x}_n^i \in Q_n^i(\widehat{p}_n, s_n)$, we obtain

$$\widehat{p}_n \cdot \widehat{x}_\lambda^i \leq \widehat{p}_n \cdot \widehat{e}^i + \sum_{j \in \mathbf{J}} \theta_{ij} \Pi_j^n(p_n) + s_n$$

$$\Leftrightarrow \widehat{p}_n \cdot (\lambda \widehat{x}^i + (1 - \lambda)\widehat{x}^{*i}) \geq \widehat{p}_n \cdot \widehat{e}^i + \sum_{j \in \mathbf{J}} \theta_{ij} \Pi_j^n(p_n) + s_n.$$

Let $n \to +\infty$; we obtain

$$\widehat{p}^* \cdot (\lambda \widehat{x}^i + (1 - \lambda)\widehat{x}^{*i}) \geq \widehat{p}_n \cdot \widehat{e}^i + \sum_{j \in \mathbf{J}} \theta_{ij} \Pi_j(p^*) + s^*. \tag{A.7.6}$$

Let $\lambda \to 0$; we have

$$\widehat{p}^* \cdot \widehat{x}^{*i} \geq \widehat{p}^* \cdot \widehat{e}^i + \sum_{j \in \mathbf{J}} \theta_{ij} \Pi_j(p^*) + s^*. \tag{A.7.7}$$

Then from (A.7.5) and (A.7.7), follows

$$\widehat{p}^* \cdot \widehat{x}^{*i} \geq \widehat{p}^* \cdot \widehat{e}^i + \sum_{j \in \mathbf{J}} \theta_{ij} \Pi_j(p^*) + s^* \quad \forall i \in \mathbf{I}$$

$$\Leftrightarrow \widehat{p}^* \cdot \widehat{x}^{*i} = \widehat{p}^* \cdot \widehat{e}^i + \sum_{j \in \mathbf{J}} \theta_{ij} \widehat{p}^* \cdot \widehat{y}_j^* + s^* \quad \forall i \in \mathbf{I} \tag{A.7.8}$$

Hence

$$\widehat{p}^* \cdot \sum_{i \in \mathbf{I}} \widehat{x}^{*i} = \widehat{p}^* \cdot \sum_{i \in \mathbf{I}} \widehat{e}^i + \sum_{i \in \mathbf{I}} \sum_{j \in \mathbf{J}} \theta_{ij} \widehat{p}^* \cdot \widehat{y}_j^* + Is^* \quad \forall i \in \mathbf{I}$$

$$\Leftrightarrow \widehat{p}^* \cdot \left(\sum_{i \in \mathbf{I}} \widehat{x}^{*i} - \sum_{i \in \mathbf{I}} \widehat{e}^i - \sum_{i \in \mathbf{I}} \widehat{y}_j^* \right) = Is^*.$$

From (A.7.4), follows

$$s^* = 0.$$

Since $(\widehat{p}^*, s^*) \in S$, it follows that $\widehat{p}^* \neq 0$

Moreover, by substituting $\lambda = 1$ and $s^* = 0$ into (A.7.6), we obtain that

$$\widehat{p}^* \cdot \widehat{x}^i \geq \widehat{p}^* \cdot \widehat{e}^i + \sum_{j \in J} \theta_{ij} \sup \left(p^* \cdot Y_j \right)$$

for all $\widehat{x}^i \in \widehat{x}^i$ with $\widehat{u}^i(\widehat{x}^i) > \widehat{u}^i(\widehat{x}^{*i})$. Hence the condition (b) is satisfied.

Thus $\left((\widehat{x}^{*i})_{i \in I}, \widehat{p}^* \right)$ is a quasi-equilibrium.

Appendix 7.2: Proof of Proposition 7.2

From Proposition 7.1, there exists a quasi-equilibrium (with dividends) $\left((x^{*i}, d^{*i})_{i \in I}, (y_j^*, 0)_{j \in J}, (p^*, q^*) \right)$ which satisfies

1. $\sum_{i \in I} x^{*i} = \sum_{i \in I} e^i + \sum_{j \in J} y_j^*; \sum_{i \in I} d^{*i} = \sum_{i \in I} \delta^i$

2. For any $i \in I$

$$p^* \cdot x^{*i} + q^* d^{*i} = p^* \cdot e^i + \sum_{j \in J} \theta_{ij} \sup \left(p^* \cdot Y_j \right) + q^* \delta^i.$$

For each $(x^i, d^i) \in X^i \times \mathbb{R}_+$, with $\widehat{u}^i(x^i, d^i) > \widehat{u}^i(x^{*i}, d^{*i})$, it holds

$$p^* \cdot x^i + q^* d^i \geq p^* \cdot e^i + \sum_{j \in J} \theta_{ij} \sup \left(p^* \cdot Y_j \right) + q^* \delta^i.$$

3. For any $j \in J : p^* \cdot y_j^* = \sup \left(p^* \cdot Y_j \right)$.

We will prove that $q^* = 0$ and $p^* \neq 0$.

If $x^{*i} \notin S^i$, then there exists $x^i \in X^i : u^i(x^i) > u^i(x^{*i})$. Let $(x^i, 0) \in \widehat{X}^i : u^i(x^i) = \widehat{u}$ $(x^i, 0) > \widehat{u}(x^{*i}, d^{*i}) = u(x^{*i})$. We then have

$$p^* \cdot x^i \geq p^* \cdot e^i + \sum_{j \in J} \theta_{ij} \sup \left(p^* \cdot Y_j \right) + q^* \delta^i$$
$$= p^* \cdot x^{*i} + q^* d^{*i}.$$

Let $x_\lambda = \lambda x^i + (1 - \lambda) x^{*i}$ for any $\lambda \in \,]0, 1[$. From the concavity of u, we have

$$u(x_\lambda) = u\left(\lambda x^i + (1 - \lambda) x^{*i} \right) \geq \lambda u(x^i) + (1 - \lambda) u(x^{*i}) > u(x^{*i}).$$

We then have

$$p^* \cdot x_\lambda \geq p^* \cdot x^{*i} + q^* d^{*i}$$
$$\Leftrightarrow p^* \cdot (\lambda x^i + (1-\lambda)x^{*i}) \geq p^* \cdot x^{*i} + q^* d^{*i}.$$

Letting λ converge to 0, we obtain $q^* d^{*i} \leq 0$. Hence $q^* d^{*i} = 0$ for all $i \in \mathbf{I}$. Because $\sum_{i \in \mathbf{I}} d^{*i} = \sum_{i \in \mathbf{I}} \delta^i > 0$, then $q^* = 0$.

If $p^* = 0$, we then have $q^* \delta^i = q^* d^{*i} = 0$, $\forall i \in \mathbf{I}$; it implies $q^* = 0$ contradiction with $(p^*, q^*) \neq (0,0)$.

Hence we obtain $\left(\left(x^{*i}\right)_{i \in \mathbf{I}}, \left(y_j^*\right)_{j \in \mathbf{J}}, p^* \right)$ is a quasi-equilibrium.

Appendix 7.3: Proof of Lemma 7.2

Consider the problem of firm j. The FOCs give (for all $j \in \mathbf{J}$)

$$p_j A_j \frac{\partial F}{\partial K} (K_j, L_j) = r$$
$$p_j A_j \frac{\partial F}{\partial L} (K_j, L_j) = w.$$

This implies

$$p_j A_j \frac{\partial F}{\partial K} \left(\frac{K_j}{L_j}, 1 \right) = r \qquad\qquad (A.7.9)$$

$$p_j A_j \frac{\partial F}{\partial L} \left(1, \frac{K_j}{L_j} \right) = w. \qquad\qquad (A.7.10)$$

Dividing (A.7.9) by (A.7.10), we obtain

$$\frac{r}{w} = \frac{\dfrac{\partial F}{\partial K} \left(\dfrac{K_j}{L_j}, 1 \right)}{\dfrac{\partial F}{\partial L} \left(1, \dfrac{L_j}{K_j} \right)}, \quad \forall j \in \mathbf{J}.$$

Hence

$$\frac{K_1}{L_1} = \frac{K_2}{L_2} = \cdots = \frac{K_J}{L_J} = \Phi\left(\frac{r}{w}\right),$$

and

$$\frac{K_1 + K_2 + \ldots + K_J}{L_1 + L_2 + \ldots + L_J} = \frac{\bar{K}}{L} = \Phi\left(\frac{r}{w}\right).$$

Observe that

$$rK_j + wL_j = p_jA_jF(K_j, L_j), \quad \forall j \in \mathbf{J}$$

or

$$r\frac{K_j}{L_j} + w = p_jA_jF\left(\frac{K_j}{L_j}, 1\right), \quad \forall j \in \mathbf{J}$$

$$\Rightarrow r\frac{\bar{K}}{L} + w = p_jA_jF\left(\frac{\bar{K}}{L}, 1\right), \quad \forall j \in \mathbf{J}$$

Hence $p_1A_1 = p_2A_2 = \ldots = p_JA_J$. Write $\varsigma = p_1A_1 = p_2A_2 = \ldots = p_JA_J$. We also have

$$F(K_1, L_1) + F(K_2, L_2) + \cdots + F(K_J, L_J)$$
$$= L_1F\left(\frac{K_1}{L_1}, 1\right) + L_2F\left(\frac{K_2}{L_2}, 1\right) + \cdots + L_JF\left(\frac{K_J}{L_J}, 1\right)$$
$$= L_1F\left(\frac{\bar{K}}{L}, 1\right) + L_2F\left(\frac{\bar{K}}{L}, 1\right) + \cdots + L_JF\left(\frac{\bar{K}}{L}, 1\right)$$
$$= (L_1 + L_2 + \cdots + L_J)F\left(\frac{\bar{K}}{L}, 1\right) = LF\left(\frac{\bar{K}}{L}, 1\right) = F(\bar{K}, L)$$

and

$$cr\bar{K} + wL = p_1A_1F(K_1, L_1) + p_2A_2F(K_2, L_2) + \cdots + p_JA_JF(K_J, L_J)$$
$$= \varsigma\left(F(K_1, L_1) + F(K_2, L_2) + \cdots + F(K_J, L_J)\right)$$
$$= \varsigma F(\bar{K}, L).$$

The budget constraint

$$p_1c_1 + p_2c_2 + \ldots + p_Jc_J \leq \varsigma F(\bar{K}, L).$$

Dividing by $\varsigma = p_1A_1 = p_2A_2 = \ldots = p_JA_J$, we get

$$\frac{c_1}{A_1} + \frac{c_2}{A_2} + \ldots + \frac{c_J}{A_J} \leq F(\bar{K}, L).$$

Appendix 7.4: Proof of Proposition 7.5

1. Consider the problem of consumer

$$\max_{c_1, c_2, L \geq 0} \ln(c_1) + \beta \ln(c_2)$$

subject to

$$\frac{c_1}{A_1} + \frac{c_2}{A_2} = \bar{K}^\alpha L^{1-\alpha} \tag{A.7.11}$$

$$a_1 c_1 + a_2 c_2 + L = \bar{L}. \tag{A.7.12}$$

We have the FOCs ($\lambda_1 > 0$, $\lambda_2 > 0$, $\lambda_3 > 0$)

$$\frac{1}{c_1} = \lambda_2 \frac{1}{A_1} + \lambda_3 a_1 \tag{A.7.13}$$

$$\frac{\beta}{c_2} = \lambda_2 \frac{1}{A_2} + \lambda_3 a_2 \tag{A.7.14}$$

$$\lambda_1 = \lambda_2 \alpha \bar{K}^{\alpha-1} L^{1-\alpha} \tag{A.7.15}$$

$$\lambda_3 = \lambda_2 (1-\alpha) \bar{K}^\alpha L^{-\alpha}. \tag{A.7.16}$$

From (A.7.13) and (A.7.14), we have

$$1 = \lambda_2 \frac{c_1}{A_1} + \lambda_2 (1-\alpha) \bar{K}^\alpha L^{-\alpha} a_1 c_1$$

$$\beta = \lambda_2 \frac{c_2}{A_2} + \lambda_2 (1-\alpha) \bar{K}^\alpha L^{-\alpha} a_2 c_2$$

which implies that

$$1 + \beta = \lambda_2 \left(\frac{c_1}{A_1} + \frac{c_2}{A_2} \right) + \lambda_2 (1-\alpha) \bar{K}^\alpha L^{-\alpha} (a_1 c_1 + a_2 c_2).$$

Combining with (A.7.11) and (A.7.12), we have

$$1 + \beta = \lambda_2 \bar{K}^\alpha L^{1-\alpha} + \lambda_2 (1-\alpha) \bar{K}^\alpha L^{-\alpha} (\bar{L} - L)$$

$$\Leftrightarrow \frac{1}{\lambda_2} = \frac{1}{1+\beta} \bar{K}^\alpha L^{-\alpha} [\alpha L + (1-\alpha)\bar{L}]. \tag{A.7.17}$$

In the other side, consider (A.7.13) and (A.7.14):

$$c_1 = \frac{A_1}{\lambda_2 + \lambda_3 a_1 A_1} = \frac{A_1}{\lambda_2 + \lambda_2 (1-\alpha) \bar{K}^\alpha L^{-\alpha} a_1 A_1}$$

$$= \frac{1}{\lambda_2} \frac{A_1}{1 + (1-\alpha) \bar{K}^\alpha L^{-\alpha} a_1 A_1} \tag{A.7.18}$$

$$c_2 = \frac{\beta A_2}{\lambda_2 + \lambda_3 a_2 A_2} = \frac{\beta A_2}{\lambda_2 + \lambda_2 (1-\alpha) \bar{K}^\alpha L^{-\alpha} a_2 A_2}$$

$$= \frac{1}{\lambda_2} \frac{\beta A_2}{1 + (1-\alpha) \bar{K}^\alpha L^{-\alpha} a_2 A_2} \tag{A.7.19}$$

substituting c_1 and c_2 into the equation (A.7.11)

$$\frac{1}{\lambda_2}\frac{1}{1+(1-\alpha)\bar{K}^\alpha L^{-\alpha}a_1A_1} + \frac{1}{\lambda_2}\frac{\beta}{1+(1-\alpha)\bar{K}^\alpha L^{-\alpha}a_2A_2}$$
$$= \bar{K}^\alpha L^{1-\alpha} \Leftrightarrow \frac{1}{1+\beta}\bar{K}^\alpha L^{-\alpha}[\alpha L + (1-\alpha)\bar{L}]$$
$$\times \left(\frac{1}{1+(1-\alpha)^\alpha L^{-\alpha}a_1A_1} + \frac{\beta}{1+(1-\alpha)\bar{K}^\alpha L^{-\alpha}a_2A_2}\right)$$
$$= \bar{K}^\alpha L^{1-\alpha} \Leftrightarrow \frac{1}{1+\beta}\left[\frac{1}{1+(1-\alpha)^\alpha L^{-\alpha}a_1A_1} + \frac{\beta}{1+(1-\alpha)\bar{K}^\alpha L^{-\alpha}a_2A_2}\right]$$
$$= \frac{L}{\alpha L + (1-\alpha)\bar{L}}.$$

We obtain

$$\frac{1}{1+\beta}\cdot\frac{\beta}{L^\alpha + (1-\alpha)a_1A_1\bar{K}^\alpha 1} + \frac{\beta}{1+\beta}\cdot\frac{1}{L^\alpha + (1-\alpha)a_2A_2\bar{K}^\alpha} = \frac{L^{1-\alpha}}{\alpha L + (1-\alpha)\bar{L}}.$$
$$(A.7.20)$$

Equation (A.7.20) allows us to identify L^*. Denote

$$B_j = (1-\alpha)a_jA_j\bar{K}^\alpha, j = 1,2$$
$$\beta_1 = \frac{1}{1+\beta}; \quad \beta_2 = \frac{\beta}{1+\beta}.$$

Consider the function

$$f(L,B_1,B_2) = \frac{\beta_1}{L^\alpha + B_1} + \frac{\beta_2}{L^\alpha + B_2} - \frac{L^{1-\alpha}}{\alpha L + (1-\alpha)\bar{L}}.$$

We have

$$f(0,B_1,B_2) = \frac{\beta_1}{B_1} + \frac{\beta_2}{B_2} > 0$$
$$f(\bar{L},B_1,B_2) = \frac{-\beta_1}{\bar{L}^\alpha + B_1} + \frac{\beta_2}{\bar{L}^\alpha + B_2} - \frac{L^{1-\alpha}}{\alpha\bar{L} + (1-\alpha)L}$$
$$< \frac{\beta_1}{\bar{L}^\alpha} + \frac{\beta_2}{\bar{L}^\alpha} - \frac{1}{\alpha} = 0.$$

Equation (A.7.20) has a solution $L^* = L(B_1,B_2) \in (0,\bar{L})$. From Proposition 7.3, $L^* \in (0,\bar{L})$ is the unique solution to (A.7.20).

Appendix 7.5: Proof of Proposition 7.6

(i) We now claim that L^* is decreasing in B_j, for $j = 1, 2$. By using partial derivatives of $f(L(B_1, B_2), B_1, B_2) = 0$ with respect to B_1, we have

$$
\left[-\frac{\alpha\beta_1 L^{\alpha-1}}{(L^\alpha + B_1)^2} - \frac{\alpha\beta_2 L^{\alpha-1}}{(L^\alpha + B_2)^2} - \frac{(1-\alpha)^2 \bar{L} L^{-\alpha} - \alpha^2 L^{1-\alpha}}{(\alpha L + (1-\alpha)\bar{L})^2} \right] \frac{\partial L}{\partial B_1}
$$

$$
-\frac{\beta}{(L^\alpha + B_1)^2} = 0 \Leftrightarrow \left[\frac{\alpha\beta_1}{(L^\alpha + B_1)^2} - \frac{\alpha\beta_2}{(L^\alpha + B_2)^2} - \frac{(1-\alpha)^2 \bar{L} L^{1-2\alpha} - (\alpha L^{1-\alpha})^2}{(\alpha L + (1-\alpha)\bar{L})^2} \right]
$$

$$
\times \frac{\partial L}{\partial B_1} = \frac{\beta L^{1-\alpha}}{(L^\alpha + B_1)^2}.
$$

$$(A.7.21)$$

We will prove that

$$
\frac{\alpha\beta_1}{(L^\alpha + B_1)^2} - \frac{\alpha\beta_2}{(L^\alpha + B_2)^2} \geq \frac{(\alpha L^{1-\alpha})^2}{(\alpha L + (1-\alpha)\bar{L})^2}. \qquad (A.7.22)
$$

Indeed

$$
\left(\frac{\alpha L^{1-\alpha}}{\alpha L + (1-\alpha)\bar{L}} \right)^2 = \left(\frac{\alpha\beta_1}{L^\alpha + B_1} + \frac{\alpha\beta_2}{L^\alpha + B_2} \right)^2
$$

$$
\leq \alpha \left(\frac{\alpha\beta_1}{(L^\alpha + B_1)^2} + \frac{\alpha\beta_2}{(L^\alpha + B_2)^2} \right)
$$

$$
\leq \frac{\alpha\beta_1}{(L^\alpha + B_1)^2} + \frac{\alpha\beta_2}{(L^\alpha + B_2)^2}
$$

that gives us (A.7.22). Hence $\frac{\partial L}{\partial B_1} < 0$. By using the same argument with B_2, we get $\frac{\partial L}{\partial B_j} < 0$ for all $j = 1, 2$. When a_j increases, B_j increases, and L^* decreases. Consider the problem of firm j:

$$
\max_{K_j, L_j \geq 0} p_j A_j K_j^\alpha L_j^{1-\alpha} - r K_j - w L_j.
$$

The FOC is following:

$$
\alpha p_j A_j K_j^{\alpha-1} L_j^{1-\alpha} = r
$$
$$
(1-\alpha) p_j A_i K_j^\alpha L_j^{-\alpha} = w.
$$

We obtain

$$
\frac{r}{w} = \frac{\alpha}{1-\alpha} \frac{L_j}{K_j}
$$
$$
\alpha^\alpha (1-\alpha)^{1-\alpha} p_j A_j = r^\alpha w^{1-\alpha}.
$$

Hence

$$\frac{K_1}{L_1} = \frac{K_2}{L_2} = \frac{K_1 + K_2}{L_1 + L_2} = \frac{\bar{K}}{L} = \frac{\alpha}{1 - \alpha r}\frac{w}{} \qquad p_1 A_1 = p_2 A_2 = \frac{r^\alpha w^{1-\alpha}}{\alpha^\alpha (1 - \alpha)^{1-\alpha}}.$$

We can represent w and r as functions of L and $\bar{K}$ as follows:

$$\begin{aligned} w &= \alpha^\alpha (1 - \alpha)^{1-\alpha} p_j A_j \left(\frac{w}{r}\right)^\alpha = \alpha^\alpha (1 - \alpha)^{1-\alpha} p_j A_j \left(\frac{1-\alpha}{\alpha}\frac{\bar{K}}{L}\right)^\alpha \\ &= (1 - \alpha) p_j A_j \left(\frac{\bar{K}}{L}\right)^\alpha \end{aligned} \tag{A.7.23}$$

$$r = \frac{L}{\bar{K}}\frac{\alpha}{1-\alpha}w = \frac{L}{\bar{K}}\frac{\alpha}{1-\alpha}(1-\alpha)p_j A_j \left(\frac{\bar{K}}{L}\right)^\alpha = \alpha p_j A_j \left(\frac{L}{\bar{K}}\right)^{1-\alpha}. \tag{A.7.24}$$

This implies that w^* increases and r^* decreases when L^* decreases.

(ii) From Eqs. (A.7.18), (A.7.19) and (A.7.20),

$$\begin{aligned} c_1^* &= \frac{1}{1+\beta}\frac{A_1 \bar{K}^\alpha L^{*-\alpha}[\alpha L^* + (1-\alpha)\bar{L}]}{1 + (1-\alpha)\bar{K}^\alpha L^{*-\alpha}a_1 A_1} \\ c_2^* &= \frac{\beta}{1+\beta}\frac{A_2 \bar{K}^\alpha L^{*-\alpha}[\alpha L^* + (1-\alpha)\bar{L}]}{1 + (1-\alpha)\bar{K}^\alpha L^{*-\alpha}a_2 A_2}. \end{aligned}$$

Market clearing conditions give

$$\begin{aligned} L_1^* &= \frac{c_1^*}{A_1 \bar{K}^\alpha L^{*-\alpha}} = \frac{1}{1+\beta}\frac{[\alpha L^* + (1-\alpha)\bar{L}]}{1 + (1-\alpha)\bar{K}^\alpha L^{*-\alpha}a_1 A_1} \\ L_2^* &= \frac{c_1^*}{A_1 \bar{K}^\alpha L^{*-\alpha}} = \frac{\beta}{1+\beta}\frac{[\alpha L^* + (1-\alpha)\bar{L}]}{1 + (1-\alpha)\bar{K}^\alpha L^{*-\alpha}a_2 A_2}. \end{aligned}$$

If a_1 increases, L^* decreases and $L^{*-\alpha}a_1$ increases, this implies that L_1^* decreases.

References

Becker, G. (1965). A theory of the allocation of time. *Economic Journal, 75*, 483–517.

Geistdoerfer–Florenzano, M. (1982). "The Gale–Nikaido–Debreu lemma and the existence of transitive equilibrium with or without the free-disposal assumption". *Journal of Mathematical Economics, 9*, 113–134.

Gossen, H. H. (1854). *Entwickelung der gesetze des menschlichen verkehrs und der daraus fließenden regeln für menschliches handeln*. Braunschweig: Vieweg und Sohn.

Gossen, H. H. (1983). *The laws of human relations and the rules of human action derived therefrom*. Cambridge, MA: MIT Press. English translation by R. C. Blitz of H. H. Gossen (1854).

Le-Van, C., & Nguyen, B. M. (2007). No-arbitrage condition and existence of equilibrium with dividends. *Journal of Mathematical Economics, 43*, 135–152.

Robbins, L. (1935). *An essay on the nature and significance of economic science* (2nd ed.). London: Macmillan.

Tran-Nam, B. (2018). Time allocation under autarky and free trade in the presence of time-consuming consumption. In B. Tran-Nam, M. Tawada, & M. Okawa (Eds.), *Recent developments in normative trade theory and welfare economics* (Chapter 6 to be derived directly from this edited volume). Singapore: Springer.

Tran-Nam, B., & Pham, N-S. (2014). *A simple general equilibrium model incorporating the assumption that consumption takes time*, Mimeo, UNSW Sydney.

Tran-Nam, B., Le-Van, C., Nguyen, T-D-H., & Pham, N-S. (2016, August 11–12). *A simple general equilibrium model in which consumption takes time. Ninth Vietnam Economists Annual Meeting (VEAM)*. Danang: University of Danang.

Part III
Selected Issues in Trade Policy

Chapter 8
The Effects of Tourism Promotion on Unemployment and Welfare in the Presence of Environmental Protection and an Agricultural Subsidy

Shigemi Yabuuchi

Abstract Tourism is an important strategy for economic development especially in many developing countries. Actually, tourism promotion has been successful in some developing countries. Thus, policymakers have a special interest in tourism promotion in the hope that it can improve welfare and decrease unemployment. However, tourism promotion has negative impacts on the economy by exacerbating the environmental situation through deforestation, ocean pollution, air contamination, and so on. Thus, introducing a pollution tax in order to mitigate these negative effects of pollution is natural. It is known in the literature that, under certain conditions, tourism promotion coupled with a pollution tax expands the tourism sector and improves welfare while increasing unemployment. This suggests that an additional policy is required in order to alleviate the problem of unemployment. Thus, in this chapter, we develop a three-good general equilibrium model with both the pollution tax and an agricultural subsidy and examine the effects of tourism promotion on production, welfare, and (un)employment.

Keywords Tourism promotion · Environment protection · Unemployment · Welfare

8.1 Introduction

Tourism is recognized as an important strategy for economic development, especially in many developing countries. The promotion of tourism has been successful in some countries, for example, Peru, Cambodia, and Turkey. However, tourism promotion has negative effects on the economy by exacerbating the environmental situation. On one hand, the construction of hotels and other tourist sites deteriorate the quality of life through deforestation and pollution. We call this

S. Yabuuchi (✉)
Aichi University, Nagoya, Aichi, Japan
e-mail: yabuuchi@aichi-u.ac.jp

© Springer Nature Singapore Pte Ltd. 2018
B. Tran-Nam et al. (eds.), *Recent Developments in Normative Trade Theory and Welfare Economics*, New Frontiers in Regional Science: Asian Perspectives 26, https://doi.org/10.1007/978-981-10-8615-1_8

127

the consumption externality of pollution. On the other hand, the activity has negative effects on other industries, especially agriculture, through contaminated air and/or water. We call this the production externality of pollution. Thus, introducing a pollution tax in order to mitigate these negative effects of pollution is natural. Various aspects of the interrelation between tourism and environment have been discussed by trade and development theorists, such as Copeland (1991), Hazari and Ng (1993), Hazari and Kaur (1995), Hazari et al. (2003), Hazari and Nowak (2003), Nowak et al. (2003), Tetsu (2006), Beladi et al. (2007), and Yabuuchi (2013, 2015).

Policymakers have a special interest in tourism promotion because it may reduce unemployment. Thus, there are many studies on the effects of tourism promotion on (un)employment, including Wang (1990), Beladi and Frasca (1999), Daitoh (2003, 2008), Tawada and Sun (2010), Daito and Omote (2011), and Yabuuchi (2013, 2015). Among others, Yabuuchi (2015) examines the effects of tourism promotion on production, (un)employment, and welfare in a model including a pollution tax, the production and consumption externalities of pollution, and unemployment in the manner of Harris and Todaro (Harris and Todaro, 1970). His main message is that under certain conditions, tourism promotion expands the tourism sector and improves welfare while *increasing* unemployment. Thus, his result on unemployment is pessimistic but an important concern for policymakers in many developing countries. This suggests that an additional policy is required in order to alleviate the problem of unemployment.

Tourism promotion has negative effects on production and employment by reducing agricultural output through contaminated water, air, and soil. Thus, in this study, we examine the effects of tourism promotion on production, welfare, and (un)employment by introducing a subsidy to agricultural sector and a pollution tax. An agricultural subsidy is often used to compensate the sector damaged by pollution. However, the effect of the subsidy and its relation with the pollution tax and environmental externalities have not yet been examined in this context. The main findings of this study are that under certain conditions, tourism promotion expands the tourism sector, *reduces* unemployment, and improves welfare. Thus, we derive the precise conditions for these results and interpret the economic reasoning behind them.

The remainder of the paper is organized as follows. In Sect. 8.2, we set out the basic model and list the assumptions made therein. Section 8.3 examines the implications of tourism promotion for output and (un)employment in the model with an agricultural subsidy, a pollution tax, and environmental externalities. In Sect. 8.4, we investigate the consequences of tourism promotion on welfare in the model. Finally, Sect. 8.5 provides concluding remarks.

8.2   The Model and Assumptions

Following Yabuuchi (2013, 2015), consider a small open economy with three sectors: an agricultural sector A, a manufacturing sector M, and a tourism sector T. It is assumed that there are two areas in the economy, urban and rural, that sector M is located in the urban area, and that sectors T and A are located in the rural area. The tourism sector produces tourism goods, for example, hotels and resort sites. The tourism sector contributes economic growth and employment, but it has harmful effects on the environment of the economy. First, it directly reduces national welfare because of environmental and health damages by pollution. It also has negative effects on agricultural production through contaminated water and/or soil. Thus, it is natural to introduce both a pollution tax on the tourism sector and a subsidy to the agricultural sector in order to mitigate the detrimental effects of the tourism activities. Other aspects of the model are the same as those employed by Yabuuchi (2013, 2015). Thus, following Yabuuchi (2013, 2015), a three-good general equilibrium model with both a pollution tax and an agricultural subsidy is formulated as follows.

The equations for price equal to marginal (and average) cost for the goods are

$$a_{Lm}w_m + a_{Km}r = p_m, \tag{8.1}$$
$$a_{Lt}w + a_{Kt}r^* = p_t - t, \text{ and} \tag{8.2}$$
$$a_{La}w + a_{Ka}r = 1 + s \tag{8.3}$$

where a_{ij} is the amount of input i used in sector j to produce one unit of the output. Note that w_m and w are the urban and rural wage rates, respectively, and r and r^* are the returns to domestic and foreign capital, respectively. Furthermore, p_m and p_t are the prices of manufacturing and tourism goods, respectively, s is the agricultural subsidy, and t is the pollution tax.

Suppose that the agricultural good is exported and is *numeraire*, so that its price equals unity. In addition, assume that the tax revenue is used to finance the agricultural subsidy. Thus, it holds that

$$tX_t = sX_a \tag{8.4}$$

where X_t and X_a are the outputs of tourism and agricultural goods, respectively.

Following Harris and Torado (1970), the labor allocation mechanism between the areas is as follows.

$$w(1 + \lambda) = w_m \tag{8.5}$$

where $\lambda = L_u/L_m$ is the unemployed-to-employed ratio in the urban area. This plays an important role in our analysis.

The employment conditions in the factor markets are

$$a_{La}X_a + a_{Lt}X_t + (1 + \lambda)a_{Lm}X_m = L, \tag{8.6}$$
$$a_{Ka}X_a + a_{Km}X_m = K, \text{and} \tag{8.7}$$
$$a_{Kt}X_t = K^* \tag{8.8}$$

where X_m is the output of the manufacturing good, K^* is the inflow of foreign capital, and L and K are the endowment of labor and capital, respectively.

The tourism sector generates pollution, causing environmental depletion and degradation. The amount of pollution is denoted by Z. Without loss of generality, it is assumed that one unit of production of the tourism good generates one unit of pollution. Thus, it holds that

$$Z = X_t. \tag{8.9}$$

We assume that the tourism goods and services are exclusively consumed by foreign tourists because sector T has foreign-owned luxury hotels and resorts. This is partly because domestic residents cannot afford to consume them, or the number of residents is sufficiently small compared with foreign visitors.[1] Thus, the equilibrium condition of the tourism market is

$$D_t(p_t, Z, T^*) = X_t, \tag{8.10}$$

where D_t is the demand function of tourism and T^* is a shift parameter that shows the level of tourism promotion. The demand for tourism decreases with the amount of pollution discharged by the sector, while it increases if T^* increases because foreigners' spending increases, the tourist sites are designated as United Nations Education, Scientific and Cultural Organization (UNESCO) world heritage sites, or the country's currency depreciates.

Pollution has a harmful effect on agricultural production because of problems such as water contamination and air pollution. This phenomenon can be captured using the following production function:

$$X_a = g_a(X_t)F^a(L_a, K_a), \tag{8.11}$$

where $g_a(X_t)$ describes the role of the output-generated externality and is a negative function of the output of the tourism sector defined on $(0, \infty)$. We assume that F^a (L_a, K_a) is homogeneous of degree one in the inputs.

---

[1]Beladi et al. (2007) and Yabuuchi (2013) assumed a model in which both domestic residents and foreign tourists consume the tourist good without the production externality of pollution. However, Tetsu (2006) and Yabuuchi (2015) assumed that only foreign tourists consume the tourist good.

8.3 Tourism Promotion and Unemployment

Yabuuchi (2015) shows that tourism promotion increases the level (and rate) of unemployment, though it succeeds to expand the output of the tourism sector. The reduction in the rural wage rate induces the rural labor force to migrate to urban areas. Not all migrant workers can be employed in the urban manufacturing sector, and some workers become unemployed. Thus, tourism promotion eventually increases unemployment because of the unexpected resource allocation effect. The effects of the negative externality of pollution on agricultural production boost resource allocation and exacerbate the problem of unemployment.

Policymakers intend to alleviate chronic unemployment through tourism promotion. However, the result here is pessimistic. Thus, in this section, we reexamine the issue by introducing an agricultural subsidy in the model by Yabuuchi (2015). A favorable effect on unemployment is expected through the positive effect on agricultural production.

Differentiating (8.1), (8.2), (8.3), (8.4), (8.5), (8.6), (8.7), (8.8), (8.9), (8.10) and (8.11) and arranging terms, the result can be expressed in the matrix form as

$$
\begin{bmatrix}
\theta_{Lt} & \theta_{Kt} & -\pi & 0 & 0 & 0 \\
\theta_{Lt} & 0 & 0 & -(\xi+\tau) & \tau & 0 \\
0 & 0 & \alpha & -(1+\gamma) & 0 & 0 \\
\theta_{Lt}\sigma_t & -\theta_{Lt}\sigma_t & 0 & 1 & 0 & 0 \\
-C & \lambda_{Lt}\theta_{Kt}\sigma_t & 0 & 0 & B & \lambda_{La} & (1+\lambda)\lambda_{Lm} \\
\lambda_{Ka}\theta_{La}\sigma_a & 0 & 0 & 0 & -\lambda_{Ka}\xi & \lambda_{Ka} & \lambda_{Km}
\end{bmatrix}
\begin{bmatrix}
\widehat{w} \\
\widehat{r}^* \\
\widehat{p}_t \\
\widehat{X}_t \\
\widehat{X}_a \\
\widehat{X}_m
\end{bmatrix}
=
\begin{bmatrix}
-\delta\widehat{t} \\
\tau\widehat{t} \\
-\eta\widehat{T}^* \\
0 \\
0 \\
0
\end{bmatrix}
$$

$$(8.12)$$

where θ_{ij} is the distributive share of factor i in sector j, for example, $\theta_{Lt} = wa_{Lt}/(p_t - t)$, and λ_{ij} is the allocative share of factor i in sector j, such as $\lambda_{Ka} = a_{Ka}X_a/K$ and $\pi = p_t/(p_t - t)$. Note that $\widehat{A} = dA/A$ for any variable A, $\delta = t/(p_t - t)$ is the pollution tax rate, and $\tau = s/(1 + s)$ is the rate of subsidy. Here, $\xi = X_t g_a'/g_a$ is the elasticity of the negative externality of the tourism sector on the agricultural sector, and $\sigma_t = (\widehat{a}_{Kt} - \widehat{a}_{Lt})/(\widehat{w} - \widehat{r}^*)$ and $\sigma_a = (\widehat{a}_{Ka} - \widehat{a}_{La})/(\widehat{w} - \widehat{r})$ are the elasticities of factor substitution in sectors T and A, respectively. Furthermore, $\alpha = (p_t/D_t)(\partial D_t/\partial p_t) < 0$, $\gamma = -(Z/D_t)(\partial D_t/\partial Z) > 0$, $\eta = (T^*/D_t)(\partial D_t/\partial T^*) > 0$, $B = \lambda_{Lt} - \lambda_{La}\xi$, and $C = (1 + \lambda)\lambda_{Lm} + (\lambda_{La}\theta_{Ka}\sigma_a + \lambda_{Lt}\theta_{Kt}\sigma_t)$.

Thus, (8.12) can be solved for the change in the wage rate ($\widehat{w}$) with respect to $\widehat{T}^*$ as

$$\widehat{w}/\widehat{T}^* = \eta\pi\sigma_t[\theta_{Lt}\Lambda\{(\xi+\tau) - \xi\tau\} + \lambda_{Km}\lambda_{Lt}\tau]/\Delta, \tag{8.13}$$

where $\Lambda = \lambda_{Km}\lambda_{La} - (1 + \lambda)\lambda_{Lm}\lambda_{Ka}$ and Δ is the determinant of the coefficient matrix of Eq. (8.12). Here, $\Delta > 0$ if we assume the stability of the equation system (see the Appendix 8.1). Following the convention employed in the Harris–Todaro literature, it is assumed that the manufacturing sector is capital-intensive relative to the agricultural sector in the value sense, that is, $rK_m/w_mL_m > rK_a/wL_a$, where K_j and L_j are capital and labor employed in sector j ($j = A$ and M). This implies that $K_m/(1 + \lambda)L_m > K_a/L_a$, because $w_m = (1 + \lambda)w$, and thus, $\lambda_{Km}/(1 + \lambda)\lambda_{Lm} > \lambda_{Ka}/\lambda_{La}$. Therefore, it holds that $\Lambda = \lambda_{Km}\lambda_{La} - (1 + \lambda)\lambda_{Lm}\lambda_{Ka} > 0.$[2]

From (8.4), it can be shown that

$$\hat{\lambda} = -(1 + \lambda)\hat{w}/\lambda. \tag{8.14}$$

Thus, the unemployed-to-employed ratio in the manufacturing sector (λ) changes opposite to the change in the wage rate (w). This leads to the following proposition.

Proposition 8.1 *Tourism promotion decreases the unemployed-to-employed ratio in the manufacturing sector (λ) if $(-\xi) < s$.*

Before interpreting the result on unemployment, it is useful to examine the effect of tourism promotion on the output of the sectors. Solving (8.12) for the change in outputs with respect to $\hat{T}^*$, we obtain

$$\hat{X}_t/\hat{T}^* = \eta\pi\theta_{Lt}\sigma_t\big[\theta_{La}\Lambda + \tau\{(\lambda_{Ka}\theta_{La}\sigma_a + \lambda_{Km})(1 + \lambda)\lambda_{Lm} + \lambda_{Km}\lambda_{La}\theta_{Ka}\sigma_a\}\big]/\Delta, \tag{8.15}$$

$$\hat{X}_a/\hat{T}^* = \eta\pi\sigma_t\big[-\theta_{La}\lambda_{Lt}\lambda_{Km} + (\xi + \tau)\theta_{Lt}\lambda_{Km}\{(1 + \lambda)\lambda_{Lm} + \theta_{La}\sigma_a\} + \theta_{La}\theta_{Lt}\{\xi - (\xi + \tau)\sigma_a\}\Lambda\big]/\Delta, \tag{8.16}$$

$$\hat{X}_m/\hat{T}^* = -\eta\pi\sigma_t\big[(\tau\sigma_a - 1)\theta_{La}\lambda_{Lt}\lambda_{Ka} + \theta_{Lt}\lambda_{Ka}\{\lambda_{La}\sigma_a + (1 + \lambda)\lambda_{Lm}\}\{(\xi + \tau) - \tau\xi\}\big]/\Delta. \tag{8.17}$$

Thus, it is easy to see from (8.15) that tourism promotion successfully expands the production of the tourism goods. However, the changes in outputs of the agricultural and manufacturing sectors are somewhat complex. The results are summarized in the following proposition.

Proposition 8.2 *If $(-\xi) > \tau$ and $\sigma_a < \xi/(\xi + \tau)$ then $\hat{X}_a/\hat{T}^* < 0$; and, if $(-\xi) < s$ and $\sigma_a > 1/\tau$ then $\hat{X}_m/\hat{T}^* < 0$.*

As stated here, tourism promotion naturally expands sectors T, as the policy intends. As discussed in Yabuuchi (2015), in an economy without the agricultural subsidy, tourism promotion reduces agricultural production if $\sigma_a < 1$. Furthermore, it increases manufacturing production because the expansion of tourism production absorbs labor from the traditional sectors. This is because the reduction in labor from the traditional sectors tends to reduce the production of the labor-intensive

---

[2]The manufacturing sector is capital-intensive relative to the agricultural sector in the physical sense if the manufacturing sector is capital-intensive in the value sense because $(\lambda_{Km}\lambda_{La} - \lambda_{Lm}\lambda_{Ka}) > \{\lambda_{Km}\lambda_{La} - (1 + \lambda)\lambda_{Lm}\lambda_{Ka}\} > 0$.

agricultural sector A and increase the production of the capital-intensive sector M according to the Rybczynski theorem. This can be confirmed by setting $\tau = 0$ in Eqs. (8.16) and (8.17).

Equations (8.16) and (8.17) can be rewritten as

$$\widehat{X}_a/\widehat{T}^* = \eta\pi\sigma_t\big[-\theta_{La}\lambda_{Lt}\lambda_{Km}$$
$$+\xi\{\theta_{Lt}\lambda_{Km}\{(1+\lambda)\lambda_{Lm}+\theta_{La}\sigma_a\}+\theta_{La}\theta_{Lt}(1-\sigma_a)\Lambda\}$$
$$+\tau\theta_{Lt}\{(1+\lambda)\lambda_{Lm}(\lambda_{Km}+\theta_{La}\lambda_{Ka}\sigma_a)+\theta_{Ka}\lambda_{Km}\lambda_{La}\sigma_a\big]/\Delta, \quad (8.18)$$

$$\widehat{X}_m/\widehat{T}^* = \eta\pi\sigma_t\big[\theta_{La}\lambda_{Lt}\lambda_{Ka}-\xi\theta_{Lt}\lambda_{Ka}\{\lambda_{La}\sigma_a+(1+\lambda)\lambda_{Lm}\}$$
$$-\tau\lambda_{Ka}\{\theta_{La}\lambda_{Lt}\sigma_a+\theta_{Lt}(1-\xi)\{\lambda_{La}\sigma_a+(1+\lambda)\lambda_{Lm}\}\}\big]/\Delta. \quad (8.19)$$

Thus, the introduction of or increase in the agricultural subsidy tends to increase agricultural production and decrease manufacturing production, resulting in a possible eventual reduction in manufacturing production; furthermore, agricultural production may increase eventually. The reduction amount in agricultural production is small compared with that in the case without the subsidy even if production eventually contracts.

Next, we investigate the change in the level and rate of unemployment. Because the unit coefficient of labor in sector M (a_{Lm}) is constant, the definition of λ shows that

$$\widehat{\lambda} = \widehat{L}_u - \widehat{L}_m = \widehat{L}_u - (\widehat{a}_{Lm}+\widehat{X}_m) = \widehat{L}_u - \widehat{X}_m. \quad (8.20)$$

Thus, from Propositions 8.1 and 8.2, we establish the following proposition.

Proposition 8.3 *Tourism promotion reduces the level of unemployment (L_u) and the rate of unemployment (L_u/L) if $(-\xi) < s$ and $\sigma_a > 1/\tau$.*

In the case without agricultural subsidy, tourism promotion increases the level and rate of unemployment. This is because tourism promotion increases the output of the manufacturing sectors and reduces that of the agricultural sector, which is accompanied by the migration of labor from the rural area to the urban area. However, not all migrant workers can be employed in the urban manufacturing sector, and some workers become unemployed. This eventual increase in urban unemployment exacerbates the problem of unemployment because of the resource allocation effect and the negative externality of pollution on agricultural production. However, in the present case with an agricultural subsidy, the subsidy tends to increase agricultural production compared with the case without subsidy even if the output eventually decreases. The rural wage rate increases if $(-\xi) < s$ because the unemployed-to-employed ratio in the urban area (λ) changes opposite to the rural wage rate. This also induces the rural workers to stay in the rural area and reduce urban unemployment.

8.4   Tourism Promotion and Welfare

Next, let us investigate the consequences of tourism promotion on welfare by paying special attention to the implication of the agricultural subsidy. Let U be an index of social utility. Thus, a strictly quasi-concave social utility function is expressed as

$$U = U(D_a, D_m, Z), \tag{8.21}$$

where D_a and D_m are the consumption of the agricultural and manufacturing goods, respectively, and Z is the level of pollution. The consumption of each good has a positive effect on welfare, whereas pollution has a negative effect because pollution harms the general public. Foreign capital is assumed to remit the factor income to the home country. Here, the economy's budget constraint requires the value of expenditure to be determined by the value of income:

$$D_a + p_m D_m = X_a + p_t X_t + p_m X_m - r^* K^*. \tag{8.22}$$

Here,

$$
\begin{aligned}
(1+s)dX_a &+ (p_t - t)dX_t + p_m dX_m \\
&= \{wdL_a + rdK_a + (1+s)g_a{}'F^a dX_t\} + (w_m dL_m + rdK_m) + wdL_t \quad (8.23) \\
&= -wL_m d\lambda + (1+s)g_a{}'F^a dX_t.
\end{aligned}
$$

Differentiating (8.21) and (8.22), and because p_m and K^* are constant, we obtain

$$
\begin{aligned}
dU/U_a\widehat{T}^* &= -wL_m\lambda(\widehat{\lambda}/\widehat{T}^*) + \{(1+s)X_a\xi + X_t(t-q)\}(\widehat{X}_t/\widehat{T}^*) \\
&\quad - r^*K^*(\widehat{r}^*/\widehat{T}^*) + p_t X_t(\widehat{p}_t/\widehat{T}^*) - sX_a(\widehat{X}_a/\widehat{T}^*),
\end{aligned} \tag{8.24}
$$

where $U_a = \partial U/\partial D_a > 0$ and $q = -(\partial U/\partial Z)/U_a > 0$ express the marginal utility of an agricultural good and the marginal disutility of pollution, respectively.

Solving (8.12) for $\widehat{p}_t$ and $\widehat{r}^*$ with respect to $\widehat{T}^*$, we have

$$
\begin{aligned}
\widehat{p}_t/\widehat{T}^* = \ &\eta\big[\theta_{Kt}\theta_{La} + \theta_{Lt}\sigma_t\{(1-\tau)\xi + \tau\}\Lambda + \tau\{\lambda_{Km}(\lambda_{Lt}\sigma_t + \theta_{Kt}\theta_{Ka}\lambda_{La}\sigma_a) \\
&+ \theta_{Kt}(1+\lambda)\lambda_{Lm}(\lambda_{Km} + \theta_{La}\lambda_{Ka}\sigma_a)\}\big]/\Delta,
\end{aligned} \tag{8.25}
$$

$$\widehat{r}^*/\widehat{T}^* = \eta\pi\{\theta_{La} + (\xi+\tau)\theta_{Lt}\sigma_t\}\Lambda/\Delta. \tag{8.26}$$

Then, (8.13) and (8.14) together yield

$$\widehat{\lambda}/\widehat{T}^* = -\eta\pi\{\theta_{La} + (\xi+\tau)\theta_{Lt}\sigma_t\}\Lambda(1+\lambda)/\lambda\Delta. \tag{8.27}$$

Substituting (8.15), (8.16), (8.25), (8.26), and (8.27) into (8.24), we have

$$
\begin{aligned}
(dU/\widehat{T}^*)(\Delta/U_a) \;=\; & \eta\pi\theta_{Lt}\sigma_t[\{w\xi L + (t-q)\theta_{La}X_t\} + w_m L_m \tau\{(1-\xi)\Lambda + \lambda_{Km}\} \\
& + \tau\{(1+s)X_a\xi + (t-q)X_t\}\{(\lambda_{Ka}\theta_{La}\sigma_a + \lambda_{Km})(1+\lambda)\lambda_{Lm} + \lambda_{Km}\lambda_{La}\theta_{Ka}\sigma_a\} - \tau r^* K^* \Lambda] \\
& + \tau\eta p_t X_t\{\theta_{Lt}\sigma_t(1-\xi)\Lambda + \lambda_{Km}(\theta_{Lt}\sigma_t + \lambda_{La}\theta_{Kt}\theta_{Ka}\sigma_a) + \theta_{Kt}(1+\lambda)\lambda_{Lm}(\lambda_{Km} + \theta_{La}\lambda_{Ka}\sigma_a)\} \\
& - s\eta\pi X_a[-\theta_{La}\lambda_{Lt}\lambda_{Km}\sigma_t + (\xi+\tau)\theta_{Lt}\sigma_t\lambda_{Km}\{(1+\lambda)\lambda_{Lm} + \lambda_{La}\sigma_a\} + \theta_{La}\theta_{Lt}\sigma_t\{\xi - (\xi+\tau)\sigma_a\}].
\end{aligned}
\tag{8.28}
$$

This looks complex, but it can be easily interpreted. Equation (8.28) is reduced to

$$
\left(dU/\widehat{T}^*\right)(\Delta/U_a) = \eta\pi\theta_{Lt}\sigma_t\{w\xi L + (t-q)\theta_{La}X_t\},
\tag{8.29}
$$

if there is no agricultural subsidy (i.e., $\tau = s = 0$). Thus, in this case, tourism promotion improves welfare if $t > q + (-\xi)wL/\theta_{La}X_t$ (Yabuuchi, 2015). The following lengthy terms shows the effect of the subsidy. It can be shown that $\{(1+t)X_a\xi + (t-q)X_t\} > 0$ if $t > q + (-\xi)wL/\theta_{La}X_t$ (i.e., $\{w\xi L + (t-q)\theta_{La}X_t\} > 0$) because

$$
\begin{aligned}
(t-q)X_t > (-\xi)wL/\theta_{La} &= (-\xi)wL/\{wa_{La}/(1+s)\} \\
&= (-\xi)(1+s)L/a_{La} > (-\xi)(1+s)L_a/a_{La} \\
&= (-\xi)(1+s)X_a.
\end{aligned}
\tag{8.30}
$$

Thus, the residual terms following τ are all positive if $(-\xi) > \tau$ and $\sigma_a < \xi/(\xi + \tau)$ because the last bracketed term in (8.28) is positive, that is,

$$
-s\eta\pi X_a\big[-\theta_{La}\lambda_{Lt}\lambda_{Km}\sigma_t + (\xi+\tau)\theta_{Lt}\sigma_t\lambda_{Km}\{(1+\lambda)\lambda_{Lm} + \lambda_{La}\sigma_a\} \\
+ \theta_{La}\theta_{Lt}\sigma_t\{\xi - (\xi+\tau)\sigma_a\}\big] > 0.
\tag{8.31}
$$

This term captures the distortion cost caused by the subsidy. Thus, the distortion cost decreases because the agricultural production decreases under these conditions.

The following proposition summarizes the result.

Proposition 8.4 *Tourism promotion improves welfare if* $t > q + (-\xi)wL/\theta_{La}X_t$, $(-\xi) > \tau$, *and* $\sigma_a < \xi/(\xi + \tau)$.

8.5   Concluding Remarks

Tourism promotion has complex effects on pollution, (un)employment, output, and welfare of the national economy. Thus far, Yabuuchi (2015) shows that in an economy without a subsidy for agriculture, tourism promotion expands the tourism sector and increases unemployment; furthermore, it improves welfare if the tax rate is sufficiently high such that $t > q + (-\xi)wL/\theta_{La}X_t$. Thus, the results indicate, "tourism promotion succeeds in expanding the tourism sector and may improve welfare at the risk of unemployment and agricultural production" (Yabuuchi, 2015). This has an important implication indicating that a supporting policy for agriculture is necessary to compensate for the negative cost of pollution and alleviate the problem of unemployment.

In this study, we examined the effect of tourism promotion on production, welfare, and (un)employment by introducing a subsidy to the agricultural sector in a model with only a pollution tax. An agricultural subsidy is often used to compensate the sector damaged by pollution. However, the effect of the subsidy itself and the relation with the pollution tax and environmental externalities have not yet been examined in this context prior to our study. The results show that tourism promotion is likely to reduce unemployment by introducing an agricultural subsidy and also expand the sector and improve welfare. This is because the subsidy raises the rural wage rate and keeps otherwise migrant workers in the area if the subsidy is sufficiently high compared with the negative externality (i.e., $s > (-\xi)$). This has an important implication for policymakers in labor-surplus developing economies that depend heavily on tourism.

However, our results depend on the assumptions that the tourism sector is located in rural areas and that only foreign tourists consume the tourism good. These assumptions may be unrealistic in the case of some developing economies. Since the tourism sector is located in rural areas, it pays the competitive rural wage to the workers, or it need not pay higher wage in the area in labor-surplus developing countries even if it uses foreign capital and ruled under modern management. The sector is expected to create employment opportunities in the rural area. The lower wage is a kind of subsidy from the local government. However, it is also possible to suppose that the workers in the tourism sector obtain the higher urban wage if the sector is located in the urban area or it gives more priority to wage income than employment due to, for example, modern management or powerful labor union. Furthermore, the assumption that only foreign tourists consume the tourism good is rather limited, and a general case that both of domestic residents and foreign tourists demand for the tourism good should be considered. Thus, in a future work, I intend to analyze the issue under alternative assumptions.

Acknowledgment I would like to express my gratitude to Professors Murray C. Kemp and an anonymous reviewer for their many useful comments and suggestions.

Appendix 8.1

Herberg and Kemp (1969) have shown that the price-output response may be ambiguous in the presence of externality. Mayer (1974) has shown that the output of a given commodity responds positively to an increase in its relative price in a dynamically stable system. Following Mayer (1974), let us consider the following dynamic adjustment mechanism.

$$\dot{X}_t = a_1\{(p_t - t) - (a_{Lt}w + a_{Kt}r^*)\}, \tag{A8.1}$$
$$\dot{X}_a = a_2\{(1 + s) - (a_{La}w + a_{Ka}r)\}, \tag{A8.2}$$
$$\dot{p}_t = a_3\{D_t(p_t, Z, T^*) - X_t\}, \tag{A8.3}$$
$$\dot{r}^* = a_4(a_{Kt}X_t - K^*), \tag{A8.4}$$
$$\dot{w} = a_5\{a_{La}X_a + a_{Lt}X_t + (1 + \lambda)a_{Lm}X_m - L\}, \tag{A8.5}$$
$$\dot{r} = a_6\{a_{Ka}X_a + a_{Km}X_m - K\}, \tag{A8.6}$$

where "." denotes differentiation with respect to time and a_j is the positive coefficient measuring the speed of adjustment. We assume a Marshallian adjustment process in the tourism and agricultural good production and a Walrasian adjustment mechanism in the tourism good and factor markets.[3]

The Jacobian matrix of the system of simultaneous Eqs. (A8.1) and (A8.6) is

$$J = \begin{bmatrix} -a_{Lt} & -a_{Kt} & 1 & 0 & 0 & 0 \\ -a_{La} & 0 & 0 & -(1+s)(\xi+\tau)/X_t & -s/X_a & 0 \\ 0 & 0 & \alpha X_t/p_t & -(1+\gamma)X_t & 0 & 0 \\ a_{Kt}X_t\theta_{Lt}\sigma_t/w & -a_{Kt}X_t\theta_{Lt}\sigma_t/r^* & 0 & a_{Kt} & 0 & 0 \\ -\tilde{C} & a_{Lt}X_t\theta_{Lt}\sigma_t/r^* & 0 & \tilde{B} & a_{La} & (1+\lambda)a_{Lm} \\ a_{Ka}X_a\theta_{La}\sigma_a/w & 0 & 0 & -a_{Ka}X_aX_t\xi & a_{Ka} & a_{Km} \end{bmatrix},$$

$$\tag{A8.7}$$

where

$$\tilde{B} = a_{Lt} - a_{La}X_a/X_t,$$
$$\tilde{C} = \{a_{Lm}(1 + \lambda)X_m + a_{La}X_a\theta_{Ka}\sigma_a + a_{Lt}X_t\theta_{Kt}\sigma_t\}/w.$$

Thus, $J = \Pi\tilde{\Delta}\Omega$, where

$$\Pi = \begin{bmatrix} p_t - t & 0 & 0 & 0 & 0 & 0 \\ 0 & 1 + s & 0 & 0 & 0 & 0 \\ 0 & 0 & X_t & 0 & 0 & 0 \\ 0 & 0 & 0 & K^* & 0 & 0 \\ 0 & 0 & 0 & 0 & L & 0 \\ 0 & 0 & 0 & 0 & 0 & K \end{bmatrix},$$

---

[3] See Mayer (1974) for the adjustment mechanism in the economy with variable returns to scale.

$$\tilde{\Delta} = \begin{bmatrix} -\theta_{Lt} & -\theta_{Kt} & \pi & 0 & 0 & 0 \\ -\theta_{La} & 0 & 0 & (\xi+\tau) & -\tau & 0 \\ 0 & 0 & \alpha & -(1+\gamma) & 0 & 0 \\ \theta_{Lt}\sigma_t & -\theta_{Lt}\sigma_t & 0 & 1 & 0 & 0 \\ -C & \lambda_{Lt}\theta_{Kt}\sigma_t & 0 & B & \lambda_{La} & (1+\lambda)\lambda_{Lm} \\ \lambda_{Ka}\theta_{La}\sigma_a & 0 & 0 & -\lambda_{Ka}\xi & \lambda_{Ka} & \lambda_{Km} \end{bmatrix},$$

$$\Omega = \begin{bmatrix} 1/w & 0 & 0 & 0 & 0 & 0 \\ 0 & 1/r^* & 0 & 0 & 0 & 0 \\ 0 & 0 & 1/p_t & 0 & 0 & 0 \\ 0 & 0 & 0 & 1/X_t & 0 & 0 \\ 0 & 0 & 0 & 0 & 1/X_a & 0 \\ 0 & 0 & 0 & 0 & 0 & 1/X_m \end{bmatrix}.$$

Here,

$$|J| = \left[(1+s)K^*LK/wr^*X_aX_m(-1)^2\right]\left|\tilde{\Delta}\right|$$

$$= [(1+s)K^*LK/wr^*X_aX_m]|\Delta|, \tag{A8.8}$$

because $(-1)^2\left|\tilde{\Delta}\right| = |\Delta|$.

According to the Routh–Hurwitz theorem, a necessary condition for local stability of the system is that $|J| > 0$. Thus, if we assume that the equilibrium is stable, it can be seen that $\Delta > 0$.

References

Beladi, H., & Frasca, R. (1999). Pollution control under an urban binding minimum wage. *Annals of Regional Science, 33*, 523–533.

Beladi, H., Chao, C., & Hazari, B. R. (2007). *Tourism and the environment* (Working Paper 0001ECO-414-2007). College of Business, University of Texas at San Antonio.

Copeland, B. R. (1991). Tourism, welfare and de-industrialization in a small open economy. *Economica, 58*, 515–529.

Daitoh, I. (2003). Environmental protection and urban unemployment: Environmental policy reform in a polluted dualistic economy. *Review of Development Economics, 7*, 406–509.

Daitoh, I. (2008). Environmental protection and trade liberalization in a small open dual economy. *Review of Development Economics, 12*, 728–736.

Daitoh, I., & Omote, M. (2011). The optimal environmental tax and urban unemployment in an open economy. *Review of Development Economics, 15*, 168–179.

Harris, J. R., & Todaro, M. (1970). Migration, unemployment, and development: A two-sector analysis. *American Economic Review, 60*, 126–142.

Hazari, B. R., & Kaur, C. (1995). Tourism and welfare in the presence of pure monopoly in the non-traded good sector. *International Review of Economics and Finance, 4*, 171–177.

Hazari, B. R., & Ng, A. (1993). An analysis of tourists' consumption of non-traded goods and services on the welfare of the domestic consumer. *International Review of Economics and Finance, 2*, 43–58.

Hazari, B. R., & Nowak, J. (2003). Tourism, taxes and immiserization: A trade theoretic analysis. *Pacific Economic Review, 8*, 279–287.

Hazari, B. R., Nowak, J., Sahli, M., & Zravevski, D. (2003). Tourism and regional Immiserization. *Pacific Economic Review, 8*, 269–278.

Herberg, H., & Kemp, M. C. (1969). Some implications of variable returns to scale. *Canadian Journal of Economics, 3*, 403–415.

Mayer, W. (1974). Variable returns to scale in general equilibrium theory: Comment. *International Economic Review, 15*, 225–235.

Nowak, J., Sahli, M., & Sgro, P. M. (2003). Tourism, trade and domestic welfare. *Pacific Economic Review, 8*, 245–258.

Tawada, M., & Sun, S. (2010). Urban pollution, unemployment and national welfare in a dualistic economy. *Review of Development Economics, 14*, 311–322.

Tetsu, K. (2006). Tourism promotion and regional development in low-income developing countries. *Pakistan Development Review, 45*, 417–424.

Wang, L. F. S. (1990). Unemployment and the backward incidence of pollution control. *Journal of Environmental Economics and Management, 18*, 292–298.

Yabuuchi, S. (2013). Tourism, the environment, and welfare in a dual economy. *Asia-Pacific Journal of Accounting and Economics, 20*, 172–182.

Yabuuchi, S. (2015). Environmental protection and tourism promotion with urban unemployment. *The International Economy, 18*, 31–41.

Chapter 9
International Immigration via Two Different Types of Midstream Countries

Kenji Kondoh

Abstract Employing the basic model of illegal migration by Bond and Chen (J Int Econ 23:315−328, 1987) and Yoshida (Indian Econ Rev 28:111−115, 1993), we study the recent trends of illegal migrants in Europe. Initially, they cross the border of marginal countries (e.g., Greece or Italy), which are part of a large economic bloc (i.e., the European Union), with the intention of moving within the bloc to find good job opportunities in more developed countries (e.g., Germany); this is facilitated by a lack of passport controls among member countries. Particularly, we focus on the optimal policies of a highly developed country, as the final destination of immigrants from two different routes (i.e., via one country with border control or via another country without any restriction). We find one available policy that encourages a border country to enhance the level of restriction is not sustainable. On the other hand, introducing border control between border countries without any restriction will be welfare improving under certain reasonable conditions.

Keywords Border control · Internal enforcement · The Schengen Agreement · Illegal immigration

9.1 Introduction

In the summer of 2015, a large number of refugees from Middle East countries including Syria began to rush toward Europe, and European Union (EU) countries have made efforts to receive them.[1] With the hope of finding better lives, the movement of illegal immigrants from poor Africa and the Middle East to rich

---

[1] According to the Washington Post (by Griff Witt, May 18, 2015), the European border control agency − Frontex − reported that 283,532 illegal border crossings were detected in 2014. Syrians fleeing civil war accounted for the largest group of migrants or almost one in three. People from

K. Kondoh (✉)
School of Economics, Chukyo University, Nagoya, Japan
e-mail: kkondo@mecl.chukyo-u.ac.jp

© Springer Nature Singapore Pte Ltd. 2018
B. Tran-Nam et al. (eds.), *Recent Developments in Normative Trade Theory and Welfare Economics*, New Frontiers in Regional Science: Asian Perspectives 26,
https://doi.org/10.1007/978-981-10-8615-1_9

European developed countries has been in existence for several decades following the onset of globalization. In reality, there are many economic refugees, and it is quite difficult to distinguish genuine refugees from others. Anyway, those immigrants' final destinations are developed countries that are in good economic conditions like Germany, Sweden, and France.[2] These immigrants usually travel by land or sea in order to avoid the air routes because of higher costs and strict border controls. As a result, two ordinary immigration routes have been established. The first is the Mediterranean Sea route, which is from North Africa to Germany via Italy. The second is the Balkan Peninsula route, which is from Middle East and Turkey to Germany via Greece, Serbia, Hungary, and Austria. Since there is no border control between the members of the Schengen Agreement, it is almost impossible for final destination countries like Germany to restrict illegal immigrants if they smuggled themselves into the gateway countries, that is, Italy or Greece. Therefore, for Germany, political adjustments and cooperation between those gateway countries are quite important and indispensable.

Generally, the restriction policies for illegal immigrants are classified into two types, namely, border control and internal enforcement. Border control is the policy enacted at the immigration gate. Unfortunate immigrants who are detected when they intend to pass the border sometimes need to pay penalty charges and have to return to their home countries. Therefore, they have no opportunities for employment in the host countries, and after return, they will be employed on the same conditions with those left behind in their home countries. On the other hand, internal enforcement is the restriction policy adopted within the host countries. The government detects illegal immigrants when they are employed. They live with the fear of detection throughout their stay. If detected, they must return to their home country; however, their employers are penalized. Thus, employers pay discounted wage rates to illegal immigrants, considering this risk. Regarding the economic effects of these different two restriction methods of illegal immigration on factor prices and economic welfare, we have several accumulated studies, and among all, contributions by Ethier (1986), Bond and Chen (1987), Yoshida (1993), and Kondoh (2000) are important.

We can categorize two types of illegal immigration in Europe depending on the economic situations of the countries that manage the border of the Schengen Agreement. The first case is, as we can see at the Balkan Peninsula, the gateway country is at a medium level of development, and the economic condition is fairly bad like Greece. In this case, it is quite difficult for illegal immigrants to find job opportunities, and even if they do, the wage rate is much lower than that of neighboring developed countries, which are in better economic condition. Most

---

sub-Saharan Africa constituted the next largest group. The number of illegal crossings in 2015 was more than double than in the same period a year before.

[2]According to the Washington Post (e.g., Witte 2015), the number of migrants seeking asylum in Europe has more than tripled since 2008. Germany, Sweden, Italy, and France together received more than half of all new asylum applications in 2014.

immigrants do not consider employment in the gateway country and prefer moving to better countries. This gateway country is just a means of transit for global labor flow; therefore, there is no motivation for this gateway country to bear the costs of restricting immigration. This implies that developed countries such as Germany are drowning in a flood of illegal immigration because of the free entry of workers from gate countries and developed countries can only practice the internal enforcement policy. Otherwise, by destroying or suspending the agreement, those countries might possibly introduce border controls between the gateway country. In this case, the developed countries have two political methods simultaneously, border control and internal enforcement.

The second case is, in the Mediterranean Sea, gateway countries are developed, and their economic condition is of a medium level similar to Italy (better than Greece but worse than Germany). Illegal immigrants find employment in such countries, but the wage rate is relatively lower than in developed countries. Immigrants choose their country of residence by optimally comparing the expected wage rate in the gateway country with that of the final destination country, considering the possibility of detection by internal enforcement policies. In equilibrium, these two expected wage rates should be equal. The government of the gateway country is motivated to restrict the inflow of illegal immigrants because in equilibrium, some of them prefer to stay in that country, which may cause negative effects on the country's economic welfare. Therefore, the gateway country, which is just a quasi-transit country, adopts border control, while the final destination country adopts internal enforcement. They can independently decide on the optimal restriction policies.

Several studies on immigration control policies apply to a two-country model; however, few studies consider the interaction between more than three countries. We consider two types of gateway countries which stand midstream in international labor flow and play the role of just a transit or quasi-transit country. Kondoh (2014) is one of the few examples that focused on the optimal economic policies of the midstream countries. However, Kondoh (2014) focused on the optimal policies of countries such as Thailand, which is confronted simultaneously with both illegal unskilled immigrants from much less developed neighboring countries and skilled workers brain drain to much developed countries. His main interest is different from that of the present study. On the other hand, there are other studies about the migrants' choice of destinations such as Giordani and Ruta (2013). They focused on the standard of restriction policies by the cooperation of multiple countries compared with the optimal level. Coniglio and Kondoh (2015) also adopted a three-country model where the immigration restriction concepts held by the two host countries are different; one country is quality-based, while the other is quantity-based. They studied the liberalization of the labor market between two host countries.

In this chapter, we focus on a final destination developed country that is confronted with illegal immigration via two different types of midstream country. In Sect. 9.2, we present the basic model. In Sect. 9.3, we focused on the economy of the final destination country and studied the effects caused by introduction of one of the two available policies. We find one available policy that encourages a border country to enhance the level of restriction not sustainable. On the other hand, introducing border control between border countries without any restriction will be welfare improving under certain reasonable conditions. Section 9.4 is devoted to the concluding remarks.

9.2   The Model

We develop a simple two-country model of international illegal migration, following Bond and Chen (1987) and Yoshida (1993). Both countries are developed, and the existing firms produce a single manufactured good using constant returns to scale technology. The production functions of the two countries, Countries D and I, are $F(L, K)$ and $F^*(L^*, K^*)$, where L and L^* denote labor inputs and K and K^* denote capital inputs. The price of the good is assumed the numeraire. The primary factors of production are labor and capital. Technologies differ between countries. We assume that Country D is the highly developed country and because of accumulated capital endowment, this country is relatively capital abundant. On the other hand, Country I is also developed but relatively labor abundant compared with Country D. We assume free capital mobility between these countries, and as a result, Country D exports while Countries I imports capital, and rental prices of capital in these countries are equalized, that is, $r = r^*$. We also assume that due to the technology difference between countries, there exist initial wage gap between three countries, and the wage rate of Country D is higher than that in Country I, that is, $w > w^*$. In addition, we consider another medium developed country, Country G. Due to the high unemployment rate caused by poor economic policies, we assume the expected wage rate of this country, w^{**}, is lower than that of Country I, w^*.[3]

All of three countries, D, I and G, are members of large economic blocs like the EU where all markets of goods and factors are integrated. Although a perfectly free border is realized between the members of this bloc, like the Schengen Agreement, we assume no migration of domestic workers between these countries. The reason for this prudence is moving costs. We consider domestic workers' moving costs, which consists of basic trip and additional setup costs. In international migration, workers must dispose of their assets and make special efforts to find new houses, job opportunities, and good schools for their children. Considering the ordinary discount rate, as this additional cost dominates the expected lifelong wage gap, we assume that there is no motivation of migration for domestic workers.

---

[3]We reasonably assume that the main industry of medium developed Country G is agriculture and the primary factors of production are land and labor. Internal labor mobility from rural to urban occurs by excess supply of labor, but due to the insufficient job opportunities, quite a lot of workers remain unemployed in the urban area. Without necessary infrastructure, there is no modern manufacturing industry in Country G, and this is the reason why no capital inflow from Country D or I.

Now we consider that this economic bloc is confronted with the inflow of international immigration from developing countries. Generically, we name them Country S. We assume that Countries I and G locate the border of the economic bloc, which is just next to Country S. Thus, workers immigrate to Country I or G at first. As opposed to domestic workers, there is no setup cost for immigrants from developing countries. Those who just entered in Country I or G are eager to move to Country D because of its higher wage rate especially if the basic trip cost is sufficiently small. In other words, Country D is the final destination for foreign immigrants, and Country I and G are just the gateway.

Countries D and I know that introducing immigrants enhances GDP or national income, as shown by Kemp (1993) and Wong (1995).[4] In order to protect the domestic workers' income, those countries have the intention to introduce restriction policies. In country D, immigration from Country S is illegal. Since Country D does not share borders with Country S, and free mobility for illegal immigrants is guaranteed by the no-passport control within integrated developed countries, the only available option is internal enforcement policies to control the number of immigrants. If firms employing such workers are detected, they must pay penalty costs, and immigrants are deported to their home country.[5] Penalty fees should finance the cost of this restriction policy, that is, financial balances should be satisfied through policy sustainability. On the other hand, the immigration control by Country I, which shares borders with Country S, is border enforcement. We assume border restrictions require public expenditure while it is almost impossible to collect penalty fees from detected and repulsed workers who have no money, as they are not employed in Country I yet.

Following Bond and Chen (1987) and Yoshida (1993), illegal immigrants are assumed to be indifferent between working in Country I (after successfully breaking through the border) and working illegally in Country D, provided that they are given the same expected wage. We consider two different ways for illegal immigrants to enter the economic bloc. The first way is, as mentioned before, via Country I. In equilibrium, some of the immigrants who successfully entered the bloc are employed in Country I, and others are employed in Country D with the same expected wage rate. Another way is via the third country, Country G. This country is also one of the bloc's members, but because of low expected wage rate, no immigrants will intend to stay in Country G to find job opportunities. Country G is just a transit country for immigrants, and all immigrants can go straight to Country D without any border control because Country G is also the member of border-free agreement. Let H denote the number of illegal immigrants in Country D via Country G, and let M denote the number of illegal immigrants to Country D via Country I. Note again that even with a low expected wage rate, domestic workers in Country G do not try to migrate because of the existing setup costs.

---

[4]Applying two gains-from-trade theorems, the gainfulness of trade for a single free-trading country and the existence of gainful custom unions, Kemp (1993) deduced general propositions about the gains from international migration.

[5]The illegal immigrants detected must return to Country I; however, the same numbers of immigrants return, and we have the exact same equilibrium in the next period.

The firm in Country D is risk neutral and is indifferent between domestic and illegal workers from two different routes. The cost of employing an illegal immigrant consists of the worker's wage and the expected value of the penalty fine if the authorities detect illegal employment. In equilibrium, the following equation is satisfied:

$$w = w^* + p(E, M + H)z, \tag{9.1}$$

where E is the level of enforcement, z is the fine which firms pay for each illegal worker caught by the government's internal enforcement policy, and $p(E, M + H)$ is the probability that illegal immigrants are detected, with $p(0, H) = 0$, $p \leq 1$, $p_1 \equiv \partial p/\partial E > 0$, $p_{11} \equiv \partial^2 p/\partial E^2 < 0$, $p_2 \equiv \partial p/\partial (M + H) < 0$, and $p_{22} \equiv \partial^2 p/ \partial (M + H)^2 < 0$.

Additionally, following Yoshida (1993), the production function of a firm in Country D can be rewritten as $F(L, K) = Kf(\lambda)$, where $\lambda = L/K$ and $f' > 0, f'' < 0$. Under perfect competition, the first-order conditions for a firm's profit maximizing condition yields

$$f'(\lambda) = w, \tag{9.2}$$
$$f(\lambda) - \lambda f'(\lambda) = r. \tag{9.3}$$

From (9.2), we easily obtain

$$\lambda = \lambda(w), \quad \lambda' = 1/f'' < 0. \tag{9.4}$$

Similarly, the production functions of a firm in Country I can be rewritten by F^* $(L^*, K^*) = K^* f^*(\lambda^*)$ where $\lambda^* = L^*/K^*$ and $f^{*'} > 0, f^{*''} < 0$.

Let us examine the equilibrium condition in the factor markets. In the market of Country D, we have

$$\lambda(w^* + p(E, M + H)z)(\bar{K} - K_M) = \bar{L} + M + H, \tag{9.5}$$

where $\bar{K}$ and $\bar{L}$ are the initial factor endowments of Country D, K_M denotes the capital outflow from Country D to Country I, and M is the number of illegal immigrants from Country I.

In Country I, the following condition holds in equilibrium:

$$\lambda^*(w^*)(\bar{K}^* + K_M) = \bar{L}^* + N - M, \tag{9.6}$$

where $\bar{K}^*$ and $\bar{L}^*$ are the initial domestic factor endowments of Country I before migration to D. We need to remark that in Country I, there exist illegal immigrants who had already come outside from the economic bloc. N denotes those illegal immigrants from Country S. Again, we need to remark that the national income of Country I only includes domestic capital and labor incomes.

We assume that the enforcement policy of Country D is endogenously determined to satisfy the revenue-neutrality condition.[6] Let v denote the cost associated with returning illegal immigrants to Country I and collecting fines from firms caught hiring them. Additionally, let us assume that the level of enforcement E is also the cost of catching illegal immigrants, which implies that the additional expenditure to detect illegal immigrants will linearly enhance the enforcement level. Thus, the financial balance condition that implies that the government's net income from restriction policy is null, can be expressed as

$$\Psi \equiv (z - v)p(E, M + H)[M + H] - E = 0. \tag{9.7}$$

By totally differentiating (9.1), (9.2), and (9.3), we have

$$dr = -\lambda dw = -\lambda(dw^* + zdp). \tag{9.8}$$

The effect of increasing exogenous variables on r is opposite to its effect on w. Similarly, we obtain the equations for Country I as follows:

$$\lambda^* = \lambda^*(w^*), \quad d\lambda^*/dw^* = 1/f^{*''} < 0. \tag{9.9}$$

Additionally, the relationship between the effects on factor prices of Country I is derived as follows:

$$dr^* = -\lambda^* dw^*. \tag{9.10}$$

From (9.10), it is clear that the effect of changing exogenous variables on r^* is opposite to its effect on w^*, as was the case in Country D.

Free capital mobility guaranteed within the economic bloc yields

$$r = r^*. \tag{9.11}$$

Now we introduce welfare functions of Countries D: $W(M + H) = Y(M + H) - \zeta(M + H)$, where Y denotes gross national income or GNP of Country D and ζ denotes the negative externalities caused by immigrants. We have $Y' > 0$ and $Y'' < 0$, while we reasonably assume that the property of the negative externality function as $\zeta' > 0$ and $\zeta'' > 0$. Let us assume that at the initial equilibrium, due to revenue-

---

[6]The level of enforcement is usually determined considering several complex factors. Maximizing national welfare or income of the host country seems the most reasonable. In the usual case, national welfare includes the term of social safety or stability, which is considered a decreasing function of the number of illegal immigrants. This is the reason why host countries restrict immigration, which causes negative effects on national income. Moreover, concerning international harmony or global welfare, this self-complacent policy, which usually obtains profits from detecting illegal immigrants, might not be favored by foreign countries. Here, instead, we introduce financial balance as a more acceptable and sustainable restriction policy target.

neutrality condition, $W' < 0$ are satisfied, which justifies the stricter restriction policies by Country D as intended.[7]

9.3 Analysis

9.3.1 Choice of Optimal Routes

We now focus on the border enforcement policy by Country I and the optimal choice of migration routes by potential migrants in Country S. Let us consider that all potential migrants in Country S are uniformly distributed in the territory, which spans a large area and is located next to both Countries I and G. Each country has only one possible gate. A potential migrant must pay trip cost, which depends on the distance between his residence area and the entrance gate. Let us define the distance between the two gates in terms of units and assume L_S as the number of potential migrants living in every continuous spot between the two gates. Remember that Country I enforces border control. Therefore, some migrants can fail to enter. To simplify our analysis and adopt a realistic assumption, we ignore penalty charges imposed on detected illegal immigrants at the border. Let α denote the probability of success to enter Country I illegally, μ denote the necessary unit one-way trip cost, and $\underline{w}$ denote the wage rate of Country S.

We need to remark that from (9.1), regardless of the traveling routes, the expected wage rate of every illegal immigrants who confront internal enforcement by the government of Country D is w^*, which is equal with the wage rate of Country I in equilibrium. Now the expected income for a potential migrant traveling the distance t from his home to the gate of Country I can be expressed as $\alpha w^* + (1 - \alpha)\underline{w} - t\mu$ if he intends to migrate to Country I. We assume that a potential immigrant who is not successful in crossing the border will find his job opportunities at the border town of Country S. Thus, he does not return to his home town. On the other hand, his residence is located $(1 - t)$ far from Country G's gate. Since there is no border control at this gate, he straightforwardly can move to Country D; thus, the expected income in this case can be expressed as $w^* - (1 - t)\mu$. Let us define $\tilde{t}$ as the point that satisfies

$$\alpha w^* + (1 - \alpha)\underline{w} - \tilde{t}\mu = w^* - (1 - \tilde{t})\mu, \qquad (9.12)$$

where at the residence $\tilde{t}$, potential workers' expected income from illegal migration to Country I is just equal to that of Country D via Country G. From (9.12), we have

---

[7]In our model, z is exogenously given and fixed. By simple calculation, it is easy to obtain $dw/dz > 0$ and $dW/dz > 0$. However, we dare to exclude the availability of this policy because it is based on the exploitation which implies further wage gap between domestic workers and illegal immigrants even though their productivities are the same.

$$\tilde{t} = \frac{1}{2} - \frac{(1-\alpha)(w^* - \underline{w})}{2\mu}, \tag{9.13}$$

and we easily recognize that $\tilde{t}$ is an increasing function of α.[8] Workers whose residence area is less (larger) than $\tilde{t}$ optimally choose to migrate to Country I (G), respectively. Moreover (9.13) can be rewritten as

$$\mu = \frac{-(1-\alpha)(w^* - \underline{w})}{2\tilde{t} - 1}, \tag{9.14}$$

and to make sense of the positive trip cost, $\mu > 0$, we only need to consider the case of $\tilde{t} < 1/2$.

9.3.2 Stricter Border Control Policy by Country I

Let us assume that Country I starts to adopt stricter border control that results in decreasing α as a result of political cooperation between two developed countries and Country D encourages Country I to enhance the level of border control.[9] We need to remark that immigrants from Country S can now be expressed as $H = (1 - \tilde{t})L_S$ and $N = \alpha \tilde{t} L_S$. We also need to remark that stricter border enforcement will cost more, that is, $B(\alpha) < 0$. Totally differentiating (9.5), (9.6), (9.7), (9.12), and (9.11), we have the following equation system which endogenously determines w^*, M, E, $\tilde{t}$, and K_M under the political choice of α.

$$\begin{bmatrix} \lambda' \bar{K} p_2 z - 1 & \lambda' \bar{K} & \lambda' p_1 z \bar{K} & -(\lambda' \bar{K} p_2 z - 1) L_S & -\lambda \\ 1 & \lambda^{*'} \bar{K}^* & 0 & -\alpha L_S & \lambda^* \\ \partial \Psi / \partial M & 0 & \partial \Psi / \partial E & -(\partial \Psi / \partial M) L_S & 0 \\ 0 & 1 - \alpha & 0 & 2\mu & 0 \\ p_2 \lambda z & \lambda - \lambda^* & p_1 \lambda z & -p_2 \lambda z L_S & 0 \end{bmatrix} \begin{bmatrix} dM \\ dw^* \\ dE \\ d\tilde{t} \\ dK_M \end{bmatrix}$$

$$= \begin{bmatrix} 0 \\ \tilde{t} L_S \\ 0 \\ w^* - \underline{w} \\ 0 \end{bmatrix} d\alpha, \tag{9.15}$$

---

[8]We assume that (9.13) is positive in sign. If (9.13) is negative, all potential migrants in Country S move to the gate of Country G.

[9]As we do not consider the penalty charge which should be paid by the illegal immigrants detected at the border, there is no revenue-neutrality constraint of Country I. Country I determines the level of B or α exogenously to fit political target.

where by the assumption of the existence of the financial balance level of enforcement and $p_{11} \equiv \partial^2 p/\partial E^2 < 0$, we can assert $\partial \Psi/dE = (z - v)p_1(M + H) - 1 < 0$. We also can assert that $\partial \Psi/dM = \partial \Psi/dH = (z - v)[p + p_2(M + H)] > 0$ because increasing the number of immigrants usually reduce the probability of detection for each immigrant but it will enhance the number of detected immigrants in total. Under the assumption $\Theta \equiv p_2 + (z - v)pp_1 > 0$ which implies that the probability of detection is not sufficiently elastic by an increase in illegal immigrants, the determinant of the LHS matrix of (9.15) is $\Delta = -2\mu\{(\lambda^2\lambda^{*'} + \lambda^{*2}\lambda')K^*z\Theta + (\lambda - \lambda^*)^2 (\partial\Psi/\partial E)\} > 0$. By simple calculation, we have

$$dw^*/d\alpha = \frac{(w^* - \underline{w})(1 - \alpha)(4\tilde{\imath} - 1)L_S\lambda^2 z\Theta}{\Delta(2\tilde{\imath} - 1)}, \tag{9.16}$$

$$d\tilde{\imath}/d\alpha = (\Delta)^{-1}\{[\tilde{\imath}\lambda^2 z(1 - \alpha)L_S - (w^* - \underline{w})z(\lambda^2\lambda^{*'}\bar{K}^* + \lambda^*2\lambda'\bar{K})]\Theta \\ -(\partial\Psi/\partial E)(\lambda - \lambda^*)^2(w^* - \underline{w})\} > 0. \tag{9.17}$$

$$\frac{dw}{d\alpha} = \frac{dw^*}{d\alpha} + z\frac{dp}{d\alpha} = \left(1 - \frac{\lambda - \lambda^*}{\lambda}\right)\frac{dw^*}{d\alpha} = \lambda^*\frac{dw^*}{d\alpha}, \tag{9.18}$$

The sign of (9.16) depends on the degree of initial border enforcement of Country I. If Country I has not adopted a sufficiently strict enforcement to satisfy $1/4 < \tilde{\imath} < 1/2$, we conclude that $dw^*/d\alpha < 0$. Furthermore, from (9.18), we also can conclude that $dw/d\alpha < 0$. These imply that at the beginning, in case that border control level is not yet sufficiently strict, additionally enforced border control by Country I will enhance the wage rates of both two developed countries. On the other hand, if Country I's border control is already sufficiently strict to satisfy $\tilde{\imath} < 1/4$, we conclude $dw^*/d\alpha > 0$ and $dw/d\alpha > 0$, which implies that additional enforced border control by Country I will reduce the wage rates of both two developed countries. Moreover, from (9.17), stricter border control will reduce the critical value of $\tilde{\imath}$. Therefore, even though stricter border control could contribute to enhance the wage rates of both Countries I and D at the beginning of the introduction of the cooperated immigration policy, sooner or later, this policy reversely starts to cause negative effects on the wage rates.

From (9.10), if $\tilde{\imath} < (>)1/4$, we have $dr^*/d\alpha < (>)0$ and as

$$\begin{aligned} dY^*/d\alpha &= \bar{L}^*(dw^*/d\alpha) + \bar{K}^*(dr^*/d\alpha) - dB/d\alpha \\ &= (\bar{L}^* - \lambda^*\bar{K}^*)(dw^*/d\alpha) - dB/d\alpha \\ &= -(N - M)(dw^*/d\alpha) - dB/d\alpha, \end{aligned} \tag{9.19}$$

we also can obtain that $dY^*/d\alpha > 0$ if $\tilde{\imath} > 1/4$, where Y^* denotes GNP of Country I.[10] It is necessary to remark that even in case that if $\tilde{\imath} < 1/4$, as $dB/d\alpha < 0$ which implies stricter border enforcement implies higher cost, we cannot conclude $dY^*/d\alpha < 0$ straightforwardly. Moreover, under the assumption of $W*' < 0$, we also can conclude that $dW^*/d\alpha < 0$ if $\tilde{\imath} > 1/4$.

---

[10]We need to remark that $M < N$, which implies that not all illegal immigrants from Country S to I migrate to Country D.

Similar to the case of Country I but there is no additional cost for Country D, we also have $dr/d\alpha < (>)0$, $dY/d\alpha < (>)0$, and $dW/d\alpha > (<)0$ if $\tilde{t} < (>)1/4$.

The above results imply that if Country D cooperates with Country I and encourage to enhance the level of border control by Country I, it may be beneficial for Country D (and I) at the beginning (during $\tilde{t} > 1/4$). By the way, as $d\tilde{t}/d\alpha > 0$, stricter border control makes change in marginal potential immigrants' choice from migration to Country I to Country G, and sooner or later, $\tilde{t} < 1/4$ will be realized. Then, on the other hand, additional enhancement of the level of border control by Country I may reduce the welfare level of Country D. In other words, for Country D, encouraging border control by Country I is not a sustainable policy.[11]

Now we establish the following proposition.

Proposition 9.1 *For the cooperation between two countries, D and I, to reduce illegal immigration and enhance economic welfare of country D, the initial positive effects from the introduction of stricter border control by country I are not sustainable.*

9.3.3 Introduction of Border Control Between Countries D and G

Finally, let us consider the case where Country D starts to introduce border control between Country G to reduce the inflow of illegal immigrants from Country S via Country G.[12] Let β denote the probability of success to enter Country D from G illegally. All the failed workers must go back to Country G, and their expected wage rate in Country G is w^{**}.[13] Now let us define $\hat{t}$ as the point that satisfies

$$\alpha w^* + (1 - \alpha)\underline{w} - \hat{t}\mu = \beta w^* + (1 - \beta)w^{**} - (1 - \hat{t})\mu, \qquad (9.20)$$

where at residence $\hat{t}$, the potential workers' expected income from illegal migration to Country I is just equal to that of Country D via Country G. We note that

---

[11]It might be necessary to mention that this political cooperation is costless for Country D. If Country D should spend public fund to support Country I's restriction policy, due to the revenue-neutrality condition, which will reduce the level of possible internal enforcement. As a result, the probability of political gain will shrink.

[12]In 2016, Sweden temporarily introduced border control with Denmark to prevent the free inflow of refugees already inside the Schengen area.

[13]As mentioned in Introduction, it is quite difficult for illegal immigrants to find job opportunities in Country G, and therefore w^{**} is quite low level, and it might be lower than $\underline{w}$. In that case, we may consider the possibility that all returned immigrants prefer to go back to Country S, and in this case, instead of w^{**}, we need to apply the failed workers' wage rate is $\underline{w}$, and there is no motivation for Country G to introduce any reaction toward Country D regardless of introduction of border control. If we consider another case that Country D pays necessary money and makes Country G to introduce border control. Also in this case, the failed workers expected wage is $\underline{w}$.

immigrants from Country S can be expressed as $H = \beta(1 - \hat{\imath})L_S$ and $N = \alpha\hat{\imath}L_S$. The revenue-neutrality constraint for Country D can be rewritten as

$$\Phi \equiv (z - v)p(E, M + H)[M + H] - E - J(\beta) = 0, \tag{9.21}$$

where J denotes the cost of border enforcement and $J'(\beta) < 0$.

Let us consider the case of decreasing β. Total differentiation of (9.5), (9.6), (9.21), (9.20), and (9.11) results in the following:

$$\begin{bmatrix} \lambda'\bar{K}p_2z - 1 & \lambda'\bar{K} & \lambda'p_1z\bar{K} & -(\lambda'\bar{K}p_2z - 1)\beta L_S & -\lambda \\ 1 & \lambda^{*'}\bar{K}^* & 0 & 0 & \lambda^* \\ \partial\Phi/\partial M & 0 & \partial\Phi/\partial E & -(\partial\Phi/\partial M)\beta L_S & 0 \\ 0 & \beta - \alpha & 0 & 2\mu & 0 \\ \lambda p_2z & \lambda - \lambda^* & \lambda p_1z & -\lambda p_2z\beta L_S & 0 \end{bmatrix} \begin{bmatrix} dM \\ dw^* \\ dE \\ d\hat{\imath} \\ dK_M \end{bmatrix}$$

$$= \begin{bmatrix} -(\lambda'\bar{K}p^2z - 1)(1 - \hat{\imath})L_S \\ 0 \\ J' - (\partial\Phi/\partial M)(1 - \hat{\imath})L_S \\ -(w^* - w^{**}) \\ 0 \end{bmatrix} d\beta. \tag{9.22}$$

As $\partial\Phi/\partial M = \partial\Psi/\partial M = \partial\Phi/\partial H = \partial\Psi/\partial H$, we can conclude that the determinant of the LHS matrix of (9.22), Δ'', is positive in sign under the assumption that $\beta > \alpha$.

By simple calculation, we have

$$dw^*/d\beta = (\Delta'')^{-1}\{(\lambda'p^2z\bar{K} - 1)(1 - \hat{\imath})\lambda zL_S\Theta - (\beta - \alpha)(w^* - w^{**})\lambda L_S\Theta \\ +2\mu\lambda p_1z(\lambda - \lambda^*)[J' - (\partial\Phi/\partial M)(1 - \hat{\imath})L_S]\}. \tag{9.23}$$

Here we consider the case that Country D adopts border control policy between Country G. Keeping the financial balance, the new border control policy introduced by Country D will reduce the effort of internal enforcement. That implies policy conversion without additional public spending. Under the assumptions that $\beta > \alpha$ and $\lambda'\bar{K}p_2z < 1$, we can conclude the sign of (9.23) is negative. The latter condition implies that direct effect on the labor-capital ratio of Country D caused by immigration from Country I dominates indirect effect caused via reduced probability of detection and the wage rate of domestic workers. The wage rate of Country I will increase, which also implies that $dr^*/d\beta > 0$, $dY^*/d\beta > 0$, and $dW^*/d\beta < 0$.

Concerning Country D, similar to (9.18), we have $dw/d\beta < 0$, $dr/d\beta > 0$, $dY/d\beta > 0$, and $dW/d\beta < 0$. We need to remark that these results do not depend on the level of border enforcement by Country D.

Now we establish the following proposition..

Proposition 9.2 *Suppose that Country D started to convert immigration policies from internal enforcement to border enforcement while satisfying the revenue-neutrality constraint. Thus, if its border control is still weaker than that of Country I and the direct effect of immigration on the labor-capital ratio dominates the indirect effect, stricter border control for illegal immigrants from Country G will enhance the wage rates and national welfare of both Countries D and I.*

We need to remark that if Country D intends to enhance domestic workers' wage rate or national welfare, then introducing border enforcement between Country G and restricting the inflow of illegal immigrants that partially substitutes for the previous internal enforcement policy will cause a positive effect under certain conditions due to this stronger control. These political targets can be attained by maintaining financial balance; additionally, not only Country D can enjoy positive results but also the members of the same economic bloc of developed countries, Country I. On the other hand, if Country D does not introduce border control and continues to depend on the border control policy by Country I, accumulated stricter restriction will harm the economic welfare of Country D after a while.

9.4   Concluding Remarks

We have studied the effects caused by the introduction of stricter restriction policies on the economy of two developed countries. We have found that to enhance the wage rate of domestic workers and national welfare, under certain conditions, the final destination developed country should introduce border control to the free labor inflow from the gateway medium developed country. To satisfy revenue neutrality condition, this policy should be partially substituted for the previous internal enforcement policy. On the other hand, political cooperation between two developed countries by introduction of stricter border control at the gateway developed country is not sustainable.

This study still has several topics for further extension. First, we need to formalize welfare function to consider the possible case that the final destination country, Country D, maximizes economic welfare ignoring revenue-neutrality constraint. Second, we can also consider the cooperation of two developed countries taking into account aggregate welfare maximization. Third, we need to consider international capital movement, the direction of which is opposite to international migration. Finally, we may need to consider that many illegal migrants lose their lives at the height of their journeys as often reported in the press. However small the probability of death is, the expected gain of migration should be considered negative. We need to remark that our standard approach to migration, especially illegal migrants, cannot fully explain the range of observed behavior.

Acknowledgment I am grateful to Murray C. Kemp, Ngo Van Long, Binh Tran-Nam, Nicola D. Coniglio, and an anonymous reviewer for their helpful comments. This work was supported by Grants-in-Aid for Scientific Research (no. 16 K03676). All remaining errors are my own.

References

Bond, E. W., & Chen, T. J. (1987). The welfare effects of illegal immigration. *Journal of International Economics, 23*, 315–328.

Coniglio, N. D., & Kondoh, K. (2015). International immigration with heterogeneous immigration policies. *International Economics, 142*, 15–31.

Ethier, W. J. (1986). Illegal immigration: The host country problem. *American Economic Review, 76*, 56–71.

Giordani, P. E., & Ruta, M. (2013). Coordination failures in immigration policy. *Journal of International Economics, 89*, 55–67.

Kemp, M. C. (1993). The welfare gains from international migration. *Keio Economic Studies, 30*, 1–5.

Kondoh, K. (2000). Legal migration and illegal migration: The effectiveness of qualitative and quantitative restriction policies. *Journal of International Trade and Economic Development, 9*, 227–245.

Kondoh, K. (2014). Emigration, immigration and skill formation: The case of a midstream country. *International Journal of Population Research, 2014*, 858460. https://doi.org/10.1155/2014/858460.

Witte, G. (2015, May 18). Europe Plans Military Response to Migrant Crisis, *Washington Post*. Accessed 20 Nov 2017. https://www.washingtonpost.com/world/europe/eu-approbes-plan-for-military-effort-to-foil-human-smuggling-networks/2015/05/18/fd95da52-fd6a-11e4-8c77-bf274685e1df_story.html?utm_term=.c627095873a8

Wong, K. Y. (1995). *International trade in goods and factor mobility*. Cambridge, MA: MIT Press.

Yoshida, C. (1993). The global welfare of illegal immigration. *Indian Economic Review, 28*, 111–115.

Chapter 10
On the Incentive for a Self-Interested Policymaker to Mimic the Behavior of a Social-Welfare Maximizer

Masayuki Hayashibara, Takao Ohkawa, Ryoichi Nomura, and Makoto Okamura

Abstract We consider a government consisting of two policy implementation departments, each of which is self-interested. We examine whether each of these departments disguise itself as a social-welfare maximizer in the sense that it adopts welfare maximization as its "surface" objective to determine the policy variable, although its "true" objective is self-interest maximization under a tariff/subsidy scheme. We also examine whether an increase in the number of departments disguising themselves as welfare maximizers improves welfare. When the cost difference between home and foreign firms is at the intermediate level, the subsidy department does not disguise itself as a benevolent policymaker, whereas the tariff department may do so. In addition, the welfare level in the partial disguise case is lower than that in the no disguise case.

Keywords Surface objective · True objective · Tariff and subsidy scheme · Partial disguise · Benevolent policymaker

10.1 Introduction

Many studies of trade policies assume that a benevolent policymaker sets its trade policy variables (tariff and/or subsidy) to maximize social welfare. In Brander and Spencer (1985), and Eaton and Grossman (1986), for instance, the exporting

M. Hayashibara (✉)
Faculty of Economics, Otemon Gakuin University, Ibaraki, Japan
e-mail: 14145_8z9@biglobe.jp

T. Ohkawa · R. Nomura
Faculty of Economics, Ritsumeikan University, Kusatsu, Japan
e-mail: tot06878@ec.ritsumei.ac.jp; rnt21840@fc.ritsumei.ac.jp

M. Okamura
Faculty of Economics, Gakushuin University, Tokyo, Japan
e-mail: andrew-uf@galaxy.plala.or.jp

© Springer Nature Singapore Pte Ltd. 2018   155
B. Tran-Nam et al. (eds.), *Recent Developments in Normative Trade Theory and Welfare Economics*, New Frontiers in Regional Science: Asian Perspectives 26,
https://doi.org/10.1007/978-981-10-8615-1_10

country's government behaves as a welfare maximizer and sets its export subsidy rate to maximize social welfare. In trade policy with lobbying activities, a government is often assumed to have a biased objective different from welfare maximization, and it thus sets its policy variable to maximize this biased aim (e.g., Baldwin, 1987). In the literature on tariff policy, some researchers such as Johnson (1951–1952), Collie (1991), and Larue and Gervais (2002) dealt with a tariff revenue maximizer that sets its tariff rate to maximize its tariff revenue.

These studies share a common feature about trade policy implementation, namely, that a policymaker determining the rate of a policy variable is assumed to have a surface objective that coincides with its true objective. A surface objective is defined herein as the objective that a policymaker uses when it sets its policy variable, whereas a true objective is what the policymaker actually seeks to achieve. In many models, it is assumed that policymakers choose action to maximize their true objective.

However, Clark and Collie (2008) showed that, for strategic reasons, it may be in a decision-maker's interest to embrace an objective that differs from the true objective. They reconsidered the third country model of Bertrand duopoly in differentiated goods proposed by Eaton and Grossman (1986) and found that both (welfare-maximizing) governments may have an interest in delegating the setting of export tax to an agency that maximizes revenue.[1] From Clark and Collie's (2008) results, we point out the possibility that a policymaker whose true objective is welfare maximization may instead adopt tax revenue maximization as its surface objective. In other words, a benevolent policymaker may disguise itself as a self-interested policymaker to maximize public interest.

As mentioned above, in the trade policy literature, some researchers have examined trade policy from an alternative viewpoint, namely, that presented by Brennan and Buchanan (1977) that a government is self-interested.[2] From this alternative viewpoint, we can consider the following question: Might a selfish policymaker disguise itself as a benevolent policymaker to maximize its self-interest? Our research tries to answer this question.

To do so, we consider that a home firm and a foreign firm exist in the home market and that the home government consists of two departments: the subsidy department and the tariff department. The former subsidizes the home firm, whereas the latter imposes a tariff on the foreign firm. The true objective of the former is producer surplus maximization, while that of the latter is tariff revenue maximization. That is, each of them is self-interested. We examine whether each policymaker adopts welfare maximization as its surface objective, which is different from its true one, to maximize its self-interest.

---

[1]In the literature on oligopolies, Fershtman and Judd (1987) showed that a duopolistic firm's surface objective does not coincide with its true one in the sense that each firm owner seeking to maximize the firm's profit presents his or her objective function, which is different from the firm's profit, to his or her manager when the strategic variable (e.g., output) is determined. See also Vickers (1985).

[2]In Brennan and Buchanan (1977), the government can be regarded as a Leviathan (i.e., a tax revenue maximizer). See also Niskanen (1971).

An increase in the number of departments disguising themselves as welfare maximizers may improve welfare. We examine the validity of the above possibility by using a welfare comparison.

We establish the following main results. Suppose that the cost difference between home and foreign firms is at the intermediate level. (1) A partial disguise may prevail. That is, the subsidy department does not disguise itself as a benevolent policymaker, whereas the tariff department may do so. (2) The welfare level in the partial disguise case is lower than that in the no disguise case.

The remainder of this paper is organized as follows. Section 10.2 presents our model. In Sect. 10.3, we establish the main results by solving the above three-stage game. Section 10.4 considers the centralization of the two departments. In Sect.10.5, some concluding remarks are offered.

10.2 The Model

We consider a two-country model in which a home firm, denoted by H, and a foreign firm, denoted by F, engage in Cournot competition in the domestic homogeneous market. The inverse demand function is $p = p(X) = a - X = a - (x_H + x_F)$, where p is the price, a is the demand parameter, X is total output, x_H is home firm H's output, and x_F is firm F's output. We assume that home firm H is less efficient than the foreign one, i.e., firm H's marginal cost c_H is higher than firm F's one c_F. We also assume that $a > c_H$.

The home government consists of two departments (e.g., ministries). One department subsidizes the home firm, whereas the other imposes a tariff on the foreign firm. The former is called the subsidy department S; the latter is called the tariff department T. We assume that each department seeks to maximize its self-interest. That is, the subsidy department's interest is producer surplus maximization, while the tariff department's one is tariff revenue maximization. These are their true objectives.

We construct the following three-stage game. In the first stage, each department simultaneously and independently adopts welfare maximization or self-interest maximization as its surface objective. That is, each department either disguises itself as a benevolent policymaker or does not. In the second stage, each department simultaneously and independently sets its subsidy/tariff levels to follow its surface objective. In the third stage, given these subsidy and tariff levels, each firm engages in the home market in a Cournot fashion.

We solve the above game by backward induction.

10.3   The Analysis

10.3.1   The Third-Stage Subgame

Firm H's profit and firm F's one are given by

$$\pi_H = (p - c_H + s)x_H \tag{10.1a}$$
$$\pi_F = (p - c_F - t)x_F. \tag{10.1b}$$

Hereafter, we normalize $a - c_H$ to 1 and rewrite $c_H - c_F$ as c for simplicity. From (10.1), we derive the equilibrium output as follows:

$$x_H = \frac{1}{3}(a - 2c_H + c_F + 2s + t) = \frac{1}{3}(1 - c + 2s + t) \tag{10.2a}$$

$$x_F = \frac{1}{3}(a + c_H - 2c_F - s - 2t) = \frac{1}{3}(1 + 2c - s - 2t) \tag{10.2b}$$

$$X = x_H + x_F = \frac{1}{3}(2a - c_H - c_F + s - t) = \frac{1}{3}(2 + c + s - t). \tag{10.2c}$$

To ensure x_H and $x_F \geq 0$, we impose

Assumption 10.1
$0 < c < 1$ and $1 + 2c \geq s + 2t$.

From (10.1) and (10.2), we obtain the equilibrium profits:

$$\pi_H = \frac{1}{9}(1 - c + 2s + t)^2 \tag{10.3a}$$

$$\pi_F = \frac{1}{9}(1 + 2c - s + 2t)^2. \tag{10.3b}$$

From (10.2), we straightforwardly obtain the results of the comparative statics.

Lemma 10.1

 (i) $\partial x_H / \partial k > 0$ for $k = (s, t)$.
 (ii) $\partial x_F / \partial k < 0$ for $k = (s, t)$.
 (iii) $\partial X / \partial s > 0$ and $\partial X / \partial t < 0$.

10.3.2   The Second-Stage Subgame

Setup

We define the home country's welfare W as the sum of the consumer surplus CS, the producer surplus PS, and tariff revenue TR, i.e.,

$$W = CS + PS + TR. \tag{10.4}$$

From (10.1), (10.2), and (10.3), the consumer surplus is

$$CS = \int_0^X p(u)du - p(X)X = \frac{1}{2}X^2 = \frac{1}{18}(2 + c + s - t)^2; \tag{10.5}$$

the producer surplus represents home firm H's profit net of subsidy expenditure, i.e.,

$$PS = \pi_H - sx_H = \frac{1}{9}(1 - c - s + t)(1 - c + 2s + t); \tag{10.6}$$

tariff revenue is given by

$$TR = tx_F = \frac{1}{3}t(1 + 2c - s - 2t). \tag{10.7}$$

We consider the following four cases:

(Case *PR*)   Each department adopts self-interest maximization as its surface objective.

(Case *WR*)   S disguises itself as a benevolent policymaker, whereas T adopts tariff revenue maximization as its surface objective.

(Case *PW*)   S adopts producer surplus maximization as its surface objective, while T disguises itself as a benevolent policymaker.

(Case *WW*)   Both departments simulate a benevolent policymaker.

The Second-Stage Equilibrium Outcomes

When S maximizes the producer surplus, the maximization condition is

$$\frac{\partial PS}{\partial s} = 0 \Leftrightarrow 1 - c - 4s + t = 0; \tag{10.8}$$

when it maximizes welfare, that condition is given by

$$\frac{\partial W}{\partial s} = 0 \Leftrightarrow 1 - s - t = 0. \tag{10.9}$$

When T maximizes tariff revenue, the maximization condition is

$$\frac{\partial TR}{\partial t} = 0 \Leftrightarrow 1 + 2c - s - 4t = 0; \tag{10.10}$$

when it maximizes welfare, that condition requires

$$\frac{\partial W}{\partial t} = 0 \Leftrightarrow 1 + c - s - 3t = 0. \tag{10.11}$$

Table 10.1 Equilibrium outcomes in four cases

	Case *PR*	Case *PW*	Case *WR*	Case *WW*
Subsidy	$s^{PR} = \frac{5-2c}{17}$	$s^{PW} = \frac{2(2-c)}{13}$	$s^{WR} = \frac{3-2c}{3}$	$s^{WW} = \frac{2-c}{3}$
Tariff	$t^{PR} = \frac{3(1+3c)}{17}$	$t^{PW} = \frac{3+5c}{13}$	$t^{WR} = \frac{2c}{3}$	$t^{WW} = \frac{c}{2}$

Equations (10.8), (10.9), (10.10), and (10.11) imply the following. The subsidy rate is a strategic complement (strategic substitute) with the tariff rate when S maximizes the producer surplus (welfare). The tariff rate is always a strategic substitute for the subsidy rate. From (10.8), (10.9), (10.10), and (10.11), we can derive the equilibrium pair of (s, t) in each case. Table 10.1 summarizes these outcomes.

We obtain the following result about the subsidy and tariff rankings among the four cases from Table 10.1.

Lemma 10.2
Suppose that Assumption 10.1 holds.

(i) *If $c \in [0, 3/8)$, then $0 < s^{PR} < s^{PW} < s^{WR} < s^{WW}$ and $0 < t^{WW} < t^{WR} < t^{PR} < t^{PW}$.*
(ii) *If $c \in [3/8, 9/11)$, then $0 < s^{PW} \le s^{PR} < s^{WR} < s^{WW}$ and $0 < t^{WW} < t^{WR} < t^{PW} \le t^{PR}$.*
(iii) *If $c \in [9/11, 1)$, then $0 < s^{PW} < s^{PR} < s^{WR} < s^{WW}$ and $0 < t^{WW} < t^{PW} \le t^{WR} < t^{PR}$.*[3]

From Lemma 10.2, we can now establish the following result about the subsidy.

Proposition 10.1 *Irrespective of the surface objective adopted by T, the subsidy rate when S disguises itself as a benevolent policymaker is higher than that when it does not.*

The intuition behind the above result can be explained as follows. Suppose that (10.10) or (10.11) holds, i.e., a positive tariff rate is imposed. Differentiating (10.4) with respect to s yields the effect of a subsidy on welfare:

$$\frac{\partial W}{\partial s} = -p'(X)X\frac{\partial X}{\partial s} + \left[p'(X)x_H\frac{\partial X}{\partial s} + (p(X) - c_H)\frac{\partial x_H}{\partial s}\right] + t\frac{\partial x_F}{\partial s}. \qquad (10.12)$$

The first term on the right-hand side (RHS) of (10.12) represents the effect of a subsidy on the consumer surplus. Lemma 10.1 (iii) shows that this effect is positive. The second term on the RHS of (10.12) is the effect of a subsidy on the producer surplus. The third one is the tariff reduction effect from Lemma 10.1 (ii). A production subsidy directly enhances the home firms' output and indirectly reduces the foreign firms' output through production substitution. Irrespective of the choice of surface objective by T, therefore, the positive effect on the consumer surplus dominates the negative effect on tariff revenue, because the direct output expansion exceeds the indirect output contraction. Thus, the domestic firm is more subsidized

---

[3]See Appendix 10.1 for the proof.

when S adopts welfare maximization as its surface objective than when it adopts producer surplus maximization.

From Lemma 10.2, we can also establish the following:

Proposition 10.2

(i) *Suppose that S disguises itself as a benevolent policymaker. Then, the revenue-maximizing tariff rate t^{WR} is higher than the welfare-maximizing tariff rate t^{WW}.*

(ii) *Suppose that S does not disguise itself as a benevolent policymaker. If the cost difference c is larger (smaller) than 3/8, then the revenue-maximizing tariff rate t^{PR} is higher (lower) than the welfare-maximizing tariff rate t^{PW}.*

Following Collie (1991), we calculate the effect of a tariff on welfare from (10.4):

$$\frac{\partial W}{\partial t} = -p'(X)x_F \frac{\partial X}{\partial t} + (p(X) - c_H)\frac{\partial x_H}{\partial t} + \left[x_F + t\frac{\partial x_F}{\partial t}\right]. \qquad (10.13)$$

The first term on the RHS of (10.13) is the net consumer surplus effect derived from subtracting the increase in the home firms' revenue through a price increase from the aggregate consumer surplus effect. This is a negative effect from Lemma 10.1 (iii). The second term is the rent-shifting effect, which is positive from Lemma 10.1 (i). The third one is the tariff revenue effect, which is null when the tariff department adopts revenue maximization as its surface objective.

Firstly, we present an intuitive explanation of Proposition 10.2 (i). Suppose that S disguises itself as a welfare maximizer. According to Dixit (1988, p. 59), a production subsidy obliges domestic firms to adopt marginal cost pricing when S disguises itself as a welfare-maximizing policymaker. This means that the rent-shifting effect (the second term on the RHS of (10.13)) vanishes. Then, T sets its tariff rate by being concerned about the negative effect due to the price increase (the first term) as well as the tariff revenue effect (the third term) if it disguises itself as a benevolent policymaker. On the contrary, T is solely concerned about the tariff revenue effect if it adopts revenue maximization as its surface objective. In the case where S disguises itself as a benevolent policymaker, therefore, the welfare-maximizing tariff rate is lower than the maximum revenue tariff rate.

Next, we consider the intuition behind Proposition 10.2 (ii). As S does not disguise itself as a benevolent policymaker, it does not set its subsidy to the level at which marginal cost pricing prevails. This means that the rent-shifting effect does not vanish. If the cost disadvantage of the home firm is small (large), then the rent-shifting effect is significant (negligible). When the rent-shifting effect is significant (negligible), this effect tends to dominate (be dominated by) the net consumer surplus effect. Thus, the cost disadvantage of the home firm is small (large), and the optimum tariff rate is higher (lower) than the maximum revenue tariff rate.

In Johnson (1951-1952), both domestic and foreign producers adopt marginal cost pricing because they are assumed to be price-takers. This assumption enables the rent-shifting effect (the second term) to be null. Thus, Proposition 10.2 (i) is similar to that of Johnson (1951–1952). In Collie (1991), and Larue and Gervais

(2002), domestic firms are pricemakers, and no production subsidy is introduced in their models.[4] This fact implies that domestic firms do not adopt marginal cost pricing, meaning that the second term does not vanish. The result depends on the magnitude of the rent-shifting effect (the second term). Therefore, Collie (1991) and Larue and Gervais (2002) derived a result similar to that of Production 9.2 (ii).

10.3.3 The First-Stage Subgame

In the first stage, each department faces the following game: S and T simultaneously and independently choose whether to disguises themselves as a benevolent policymaker. The strategy when either of them disguises themselves as a benevolent policymaker is denoted by W. The strategy when S (T) adopts self-interest maximization as its surface objective is denoted by P (R). Table 10.2 presents the payoff matrix in the subgame.

Substituting the equilibrium pair of (s, t) in Table 10.2 into (10.6) and (10.7) yields the equilibrium outcomes for the producer surplus and tariff revenue. These are shown in Table 10.3.

From Table 10.3, we establish the following:

Proposition 10.3 (i) *S does not disguise itself as a benevolent policymaker at all.* (ii) *If $c \in [3/8, 49/57)$, then T disguises itself as a benevolent policymaker; otherwise, it does not.*[5]

Proposition 10.3 states that although the *full disguise* case, when both departments disguise themselves as benevolent policymakers, does not prevail at all, the *partial disguise* and *no disguise* cases, when either (neither) of them does so, prevail if (unless) the level of the cost difference is intermediate.

Table 10.2 Payoff matrix in the stage subgame

S\T	R	W
P	PS^{PR}, TR^{PR}	PS^{PW}, TR^{PW}
W	PS^{WR}, TR^{WR}	PS^{WW}, TR^{WW}

Table 10.3 Equilibrium outcomes in four cases

	Case PR	Case PW	Case WR	Case WW
PS	$PS^{PR} = \frac{2(5-2c)^2}{289}$	$PS^{PW} = \frac{8(2-c)^2}{169}$	$PS^{WR} = \frac{c(9-5c)}{81}$	$PS^{WW} = 0$
TR	$TR^{PR} = \frac{6(1+3c)^2}{289}$	$TR^{PW} = \frac{(3+5c)(1+6c)}{169}$	$TR^{WR} = \frac{8c^2}{27}$	$TR^{WW} = \frac{c^2}{4}$

---

[4]Larue and Gervais (2002) assumed that domestic firms are price leaders and that foreign firms are on the competitive fringe.

[5]See Appendix 10.2 for the proof.

The intuition behind Proposition 10.3 (i) is as follows. Suppose that S disguises itself as a benevolent policymaker. Then, irrespective of the determination of T's surface objective, the benevolent policymaker is more likely to subsidize the domestic firm than the producer surplus maximizer when S does not disguise itself as a benevolent policymaker, because the welfare maximizer takes account of the increase in the consumer surplus through the price reduction caused by the production subsidy. This price reduction harms the domestic firm's profit, that is, the producer surplus. Thus, S does not disguise itself as a welfare maximizer at all.

The intuition behind Proposition 10.3 (ii) is as follows. First, we consider the case where the cost difference is very large, i.e., $c \approx 1$. Note that the producer surplus (the home firm's profit) is negligible because of its inefficiency in this case. Suppose that T alters from tariff revenue maximization to welfare maximization as its surface objective. This alteration reduces the tariff rate drastically because the home government takes the consumer surplus as well as tariff revenue into account. Although the drastic tariff reduction enhances the foreign firm's output, the scale of its enhancement is not large. Indeed, since S subsidizes to make its inefficient home firm viable, the foreign firm's drastic output expansion makes the firm unprofitable because of the drastic price reduction. Therefore, the alteration decreases tariff revenue. In the case where the cost difference is large, the tariff department in the home government adopts tariff revenue maximization as its surface objective.

Second, we consider the case where the cost difference is at the intermediate level. Suppose that T alters from tariff revenue maximization to welfare maximization as its surface objective. Following this alteration, T takes the consumer and producer surpluses as well as tariff revenue into account, and it becomes concerned about the consumer surplus rather than the producer one, because the ratio of the producer surplus to the total one is not large. That is, a decrease in the tariff rate to seek a price reduction dominates an increase in that to protect the home firm. Therefore, the alteration reduces the tariff rate. This reduction brings about a decrease in the subsidy rate, because S, to maximize the producer surplus, seeks to relax the price reduction. The reductions in both the tariff rate and the subsidy rate give the foreign firm room to expand its output considerably. Therefore, the alteration increases tariff revenue. Thus, T adopts welfare maximization as its surface objective.

Third, we consider the case where the cost difference is very small, i.e., $c \approx 0$. Suppose that T alters from tariff revenue maximization to welfare maximization as its surface objective. Following this alteration, T takes the consumer and producer surpluses as well as tariff revenue into account, and it becomes concerned about the producer surplus rather than the consumer one, because the ratio of the producer surplus to the total one is large. That is, a decrease in the tariff rate to seek a price reduction is dominated by an increase in that to protect the home firm. Therefore, the alteration increases the tariff rate. This increase brings about an increase in the subsidy rate, because S, to maximize the producer surplus, seeks to expand the home firm's output through production substitution. The increases in both the tariff rate and the subsidy rate give the foreign firm room to shrink its output considerably.

Therefore, the alteration decreases tariff revenue. Thus, T adopts tariff revenue maximization as its surface objective.

10.4 Efficiency

In this section, we compare the level of the home country's welfare among the full disguise, partial disguise, and no disguise cases. An increase in the number of departments disguising themselves as welfare maximizers may raise welfare. Hence, we examine the welfare ranking among the above four cases, as shown in Table 10.4.

From Table 10.4, we obtain

Lemma 10.3

(i) *If* $c \in (0, 3/8)$, *then* $W^{PR} < W^{PW} < W^{WR} < W^{WW}$.
(ii) *If* $c \in [3/8, 125/186]$, *then* $W^{PW} \leq W^{PR} < W^{WR} < W^{WW}$.
(iii) *If* $c \in (125/186, 1)$, *then* $W^{PR} < W^{PW} < W^{WR} < W^{WW}$.[6]

From Proposition 10.3 and Lemma 10.3, we establish the following counterintuitive result.

Proposition 10.4 *Suppose that* $c \in [3/8, 125/186)$. *Then, the level of welfare in the no disguise case is not lower than that in the partial disguise case in the sense that although the tariff department solely disguises itself as a benevolent policymaker, the resulting welfare is lower than if it behaved as a revenue maximizer, i.e.,* $W^{PW} \leq W^{PR}$.

Proposition 10.4 states that since T disguises itself as a benevolent policymaker when the cost difference is at the intermediate level, the partial disguise case prevails, meaning that the level in the partial disguise case may be lower than that in the no disguise case.

The interpretation of Proposition 10.4 is as follows. Suppose that the subsidy department in the home country adopts producer surplus maximization as its surface objective and that T alters from tariff revenue maximization to welfare maximization as its surface objective. This alteration induces T to reduce the tariff rate from t^{PR} to t^{PW} when the cost difference is intermediate (see Lemmas 10.2 (ii) and (iii)). Because the subsidy rate is a strategic complement to the tariff rate, S also reduces the subsidy

Table 10.4 Equilibrium welfare level in four cases

	Case PR	Case PW	Case WR	Case WW
CS	$CS^{PR} = \frac{2(6+c)^2}{289}$	$CS^{PW} = \frac{(2c+9)^2}{338}$	$CS^{WR} = \frac{(9-c)^2}{162}$	$CS^{WW} = \frac{1}{2}$
W	$W^{PR} = \frac{4(16c^2+5c+32)}{289}$	$W^{PW} = \frac{80c^2+18c+151}{338}$	$W^{WR} = \frac{13c^2+27}{54}$	$W^{WW} = \frac{c^2+2}{4}$

[6]See Appendix 10.3 for the proof.

rate from s^{PR} to s^{PW}. Considering the initial subsidy rate s^{PR} is below the "optimal" subsidy rate, s^{WW}, this subsidy reduction expands the distortion in the subsidy rate. The welfare reduction effect associated with the subsidy rate change dominates the welfare improvement associated with the tariff rate change. Then, the level of welfare under PW is lower than that under PR.

Note that this paradoxical result does not occur with respect to the subsidy department, that is, $W^{WR} > W^{PR}$. Suppose that T maximizes its tariff revenue. Initially, S maximizes the producer surplus, and it alters to maximize welfare. S increases its subsidy rate from s^{PR} to s^{WR} (see Lemma 10.2). Because the tariff rate is a strategic substitute for the subsidy rate, this alteration induces T to decrease the tariff rate from t^{PR} to t^{WR} (see Lemma 10.2). From this tariff reduction, the tariff rate is adjusted to the optimal rate t^{WW}. Then, welfare improves from the tariff reduction. Thus, the paradoxical result does not appear.

10.5 Concluding Remarks

In many studies of strategic trade policy, a benevolent government aims to maximize the public interest as an objective function when it determines the levels of its policy variables (e.g., a tariff and/or subsidy). In other words, many studies of strategic trade policies assume that the true objective of the government accords with its surface objective, which it uses to implement trade policies. However, Clark and Collie (2008) pointed out that a welfare-maximizing policymaker may maximize its self-interest when implementing a tariff policy. That is, a benevolent policymaker may disguise itself as a selfish policymaker.

Some studies in the trade policy literature assume that a government is a selfish (i.e., self-interested) policymaker. Assuming a selfish policymaker, we raise the following question: Does a selfish policymaker disguise itself as a benevolent policymaker? We consider that home and foreign firms exist in the home market and that the home government consists of two departments: the subsidy department and the tariff department. The former subsidizes the home firm, whereas the latter imposes a tariff on the foreign firm. The true objective of the former is producer surplus maximization, while that of the latter is tariff revenue maximization. That is, each of them is self-interested. We then examine whether each department adopts welfare maximization as its surface objective to maximize its self-interest.

An increase in the number of departments disguising themselves as welfare maximizers may raise welfare. We also examine the validity of the above possibility by using a welfare comparison.

We have established the following main results. Suppose that the cost difference between home and foreign firms is at the intermediate level. (1) A partial disguise may prevail. That is, the subsidy department does not disguise itself as a benevolent policymaker, whereas the tariff department may do so. (2) The welfare level in the partial disguise case is lower than that in the no disguise case.

Acknowledgement This work was supported by Grants-in-Aid for Scientific Research (nos. 26380340, 5K03492, 17K03734, and 17K03735). We thank an anonymous reviewer for helpful comments. All remaining errors are ours.

Appendices

Appendix 10.1: Proof of Lemma 10.2

First, we compare the subsidy rate in the four cases. We compare s^{WR} with s^{WW}, i.e.,

$$s^{WR} - s^{WW} = \left(1 - \frac{2c}{3}\right) - \left(1 - \frac{c}{2}\right) < 0.$$

Next, the comparison between s^{PW} and s^{WR} yields

$$s^{PW} - s^{WR} \propto 6(2 - c) - 13(3 - 2c) = 20c - 27 < 0.$$

Furthermore, by comparing s^{PR} with s^{WR}, we obtain

$$s^{PR} - s^{WR} \propto 3(5 - 2c) - 17(3 - 2c) = 28c - 36 < 0.$$

Subtracting s^{PW} from s^{PR} yields

$$s^{PR} - s^{PW} \propto 13(5 - 2c) - 34(2 - c) = 8c - 3,$$

which means that if $0 < c < 3/8$, then $s^{PR} < s^{PW}$; if $3/8 \leq c < 1$, then $s^{PR} \geq s^{PW}$.

Secondly, we compare the tariff rate among the four cases. Comparing t^{WR} with t^{RW} yields

$$t^{WR} - t^{PW} \propto 26c - 3(3 + 5c) = 11c - 9,$$

which means that if $c < 9/11$, then $t^{WR} < t^{PW}$; if $9/11 \leq c < 1$, then $t^{WR} \geq t^{PW}$.

Next, we compare t^{WR} with t^{PR}:

$$t^{WR} - t^{PR} \propto 34c - 9(1 + 3c) = 7c - 9 < 0.$$

Finally, by subtracting t^{PR} from t^{PW}, we obtain

$$t^{PR} - t^{PW} \propto 39(1 + 3c) - 17(3 + 5c) = 8c - 3,$$

which means that if $0 < c < 3/8$, then $t^{PR} < t^{PW}$; if $3/8 \leq c < 1$, then $t^{PR} \geq t^{PW}$. Note that $t^{WW} < t^{WR}$. Thus, the statements of Lemma 10.2 hold.

Appendix 10.2: Proof of Proposition 10.3

Suppose that the tariff department selects strategy R as its objective. Subtracting PS^{WR} from PS^{PR} yields

$$
\begin{aligned}
PS^{PR} - PS^{WR} &\propto 162(5 - 2c)^2 - 289c(9 - 5c) \\
&= 2093c^2 - 5841c + 4050 \\
&= (7c - 9)(299c - 450) > 0.
\end{aligned}
$$

Suppose that the tariff department selects strategy W as its objective. Then, $PS^{PW} > PS^{WW} = 0$ clearly. Therefore, strategy P is a dominant strategy for the subsidy department.

Suppose that the subsidy department selects strategy P. Comparing TR^{PR} with TR^{PW} yields

$$
\begin{aligned}
TR^{PR} - TR^{PW} &\propto 1014(1 + 3c)^2 - 289(3 + 5c)(1 + 6c) \\
&= 456c^2 - 563c + 147 \\
&= (8c - 3)(57c - 49),
\end{aligned}
$$

which means that if $0 < c < 3/8$ or if $49/57 \leq c < 1$, then $TR^{PR} \geq TR^{PW}$; if $3/8 \leq c < 49/57$, then $TR^{PR} < TR^{PW}$. Thus, we have proven Proposition 10.3.

Appendix 10.3: Proof of Lemma 10.3

First, we compare W^{WR} with W^{WW}:

$$
W^{WR} - W^{WW} \propto 4(13c^2 + 27) - 54(c^2 + 2) = -2c^2 < 0.
$$

Secondly, by comparing W^{PW} with W^{WR}, we obtain

$$
\begin{aligned}
W^{PW} - W^{WR} &\propto 27(80c^2 + 18c + 151) - 169(13c^2 + 27) \\
&= -37c^2 + 486(c - 1) < 0.
\end{aligned}
$$

Thirdly, comparing W^{PR} with W^{WR} yields

$$
\begin{aligned}
W^{PR} - W^{WR} &\propto 216(16c^2 + 5c + 32) - 289(13c^2 + 27) \\
&= -301c^2 + 1080c - 891 \equiv h(c).
\end{aligned}
$$

Since $h'(c) = -602c + 1080 > 0$ for $c \in (0, 1)$ and $h(1) = -112 < 0$, $h(c) < 0$ for $c \in (0, 1)$. This means that $W^{PR} < W^{WR}$. Finally, we compare W^{PR} with W^{PW}:

$$
\begin{aligned}
W^{PR} - W^{PW} &\propto 1352(16c^2 + 5c + 32) - 289(80c^2 + 18c + 151) \\
&= -1488c^2 + 1558c - 375 = -(8c - 3)(186c - 125)
\end{aligned}
$$

which means that if $0 < c < 3/8$ or if $125/186 < c < 1$, then $W^{PR} < W^{PW}$; if $3/8 \leq c \leq 125/186$, then $W^{PR} \geq W^{PW}$. Thus, we have proven Lemma 10.3.

References

Baldwin, R. (1987). Politically realistic objective functions and trade policy. *Economics Letters, 24*, 287–290.

Brander, J. A., & Spencer, B. J. (1985). Export subsidies and international market share rivalry. *Journal of International Economics, 18*, 83–100.

Brennan, G., & Buchanan, J. M. (1977). Towards a tax constitution for Leviathan. *Journal of Public Economics, 8*, 255–273.

Clark, R., & Collie, D. R. (2008). Maximum-revenue versus optimum-welfare export taxes: A delegation game. *Review of International Economics, 16*, 919–929.

Collie, D. R. (1991). Optimum welfare and maximum revenue tariffs under oligopoly. *Scottish Journal of Political Economy, 38*, 398–401.

Dixit, A. (1988). Anti-dumping and countervailing duties under oligopoly. *European Economic Review, 32*, 55–68.

Eaton, J., & Grossman, G. M. (1986). Optimal trade and industrial policy under oligopoly. *The Quarterly Journal of Economics, 101*, 383–406.

Fershtman, C., & Judd, K. L. (1987). Equilibrium incentives in oligopoly. *American Economic Review, 77*, 927–940.

Johnson, H. G. (1951–52). Optimum welfare and maximum revenue tariffs. *Review of Economic Studies, 19*, 28–35.

Larue, B., & Gervais, J.-P. (2002). Welfare-maximizing and revenue-maximizing tariffs with a few domestic firms. *Canadian Journal of Economics, 35*, 786–804.

Niskanen, W. A. (1971). *Bureaucracy and representative government*. Chicago: Aldine Atherton.

Vickers, J. (1985). Delegation and the theory of the firm. *Economic Journal, Supplement 95*, 138–147.

Part IV
Tranfer Policy

Chapter 11
The Rise and Fall of Political Economy

Murray C. Kemp and Geoffrey Fishburn

Abstract The concept of the Self in political economy has not remained a constant but, as we argue, has changed through time. In this chapter, we trace one line of evolution of the concept starting with Adam Smith. As the concept has underpinned normative analysis, we present three such propositions and show how, with the application of the most extended concept to date of the Self, these propositions must now be abandoned.

Keywords Self · Smith · Walras · Gossen · Normative economics · Imperfect competition

11.1 Introduction

The search for the Self has no self-evident beginning and shows no sign of coming to an end. It has been a feature of philosophical thought for many years and, at least since the time of Adam Smith, has been a feature of political economy. In the present chapter, we describe the search for the Self by political economists from Adam Smith to the present day.

11.2 Adam Smith, Political Economy, and the Search for the Self

Adam Smith was initially trained in philosophy at Glasgow University in Scotland and at Oxford University in England. He later returned to Glasgow as Professor of Logic and, after a year, as Professor of Moral Philosophy. He was a lifelong admirer of the

M. C. Kemp (✉)
School of Economics, UNSW Sydney, Sydney, NSW 2052, Australia

G. Fishburn
Independent Researcher, Sydney, Australia

© Springer Nature Singapore Pte Ltd. 2018
B. Tran-Nam et al. (eds.), *Recent Developments in Normative Trade Theory and Welfare Economics*, New Frontiers in Regional Science: Asian Perspectives 26,
https://doi.org/10.1007/978-981-10-8615-1_11

French philosopher Montesquieu and a close friend of the Scottish philosopher David Hume and eventually served as the founding father of political economy. His view of the Self was reflected in two basic assumptions of *The Wealth of Nations* (1776):

(i) Each country has a population completely homogeneous both in preferences and possessions (including information).
(ii) The utility or well-being of each member of a population depends on the activities of that member only.

Léon Walras published the first edition of his *Eléments d'Économie Pure* during the short period 1874–1877, almost 100 years after the appearance of *The Wealth of Nations*. Walras' book was pathbreaking in abandoning Smith's first assumption.[1] Members of a heterogeneous population have more scope for social interaction than do members of a homogeneous population. Moreover, in 1894, Vilfredo Pareto, who had succeeded Walras at l'Academie de Lausanne, suggested that even without Smith's assumption, government policies might be supported by a population if those members who would benefit from the policies could afford to compensate (and were requested to do so) those members who would otherwise have suffered. However Pareto's paper was published in Italian and, like Walras' book, was not widely read by English-speaking economists until after World War 2.

Smith's second assumption had been disputed by Hermann Heinrich Gossen in 1854, 20 years before the appearance of Walras' *Eléments*. Gossen was aware that the well-being of one individual may depend on the activities of other individuals, observing that many potential pleasures "... become actual pleasures *only if* other persons participate in their enjoyment"[2] (Gossen 1983, p. 110). Indeed Gossen was aware that consumption and all other human activities take time which, for each individual, is in limited supply. Now, 163 years after Gossen's words were first printed in German, the *pooling of time* is beginning to play a central role in Gossenian thought. However, in spite of its importance for political economists and philosophers, Gossen's book was largely ignored worldwide by both groups until an English translation finally appeared in 1983.[3]

---

[1] It was also pathbreaking in asking whether a perfectly competitive economy, without Smith's first assumption, might be satisfied by realistically signed prices and other variables. We will return to this question.

[2] The words are Gossen's; the italics have been added by the present authors.

[3] Jevons (1879) and Walras (1885) had warmly praised Gossen's book without fully appreciating the central importance of Gossen's time constraint on consumption and other human activities.

11.3 The Contributions of Walras, Pareto, Arrow, Debreu, and McKenzie

The progress of political economy had been slowed by the mute reception of the work of Walras, Pareto, and Gossen. After World War 2, however, the subject came to life again as more economists learned about Walras and Pareto and the English translations of their work that were under way. In particular, Kenneth Arrow and Gérard Debreu (1954), Lionel McKenzie (1954), and others answered in the affirmative Walras' fundamental question about the existence of a perfectly competitive equilibrium for a single country; and they showed that each equilibrium is Pareto optimal, in the sense that in no other equilibrium could some individuals be better off and none worse off.

A generation of political economists was satisfied with the closed-economy conclusions of Arrow, Debreu, and McKenzie and was happy to simply extend their results, establishing normative propositions concerning the possible benefits flowing to heterogeneous households from trade in goods and services within and between countries. For example, in the years after 1954, the careful normative appraisal of international trade yielded three core propositions none of which had hitherto been known to political economists.[4]

Proposition 11(a) *Each country, whether large or small, is potentially (after Paretian compensation) better off under free trade than in autarky*; see Grandmont and McFadden (1972) and Kemp and Wan Jr. (1972).

Proposition 11(b) *Any two or more countries, all part of an initial tariff-distorted world trading equilibrium, can form a mutually advantageous customs union without harming any excluded country*; see Kemp (1964, p. 176), Kemp and Wan Jr. (1976, 1986), and Kemp and Shimomura (2001).

Proposition 11(c) *Any two or more countries, all part of an initial tariff-distorted world trading equilibrium, can form a mutually advantageous free trade association without harming any excluded country. Corresponding to each free trade association, whether or not it is Pareto-preferred to the initial tariff-distorted trading equilibrium, there is a Pareto-preferred Kemp–Wan customs union*; see Kemp (2007).[5]

These are core propositions in the sense that they are valid for any trading country and for any subset of trading countries. Evidently the Self of political economists had changed since 1776.

---

[4]The reader may recall the large micro-text written by Mas-Colell et al. (1995).

[5]Ohyama (2002) and Panagariya and Krishna (2002) produced a result not unlike Proposition 11(c). However their finding was based on the assumption that each country chooses its new tariff vector so that its vector of imports remains unchanged at its initial level, whereas Proposition 11(c) was established under the weaker Kemp–Wan assumption that only the *aggregate* import vector of the free trade association need be kept at its initial level.

11.4 A More Dynamic Approach

Each of the core propositions was established in the context of finite competitive economies of the Walras (1874), Arrow and Debreu (1954), and McKenzie (1954) type but extended to accommodate a finite number of countries. Each economy of this type will be referred to as a Walras–Arrow–Debreu or McKenzie (WADM) economy. Among the distinguishing features of WADM economies,

(i) all inputs and outputs are defined in terms of their countries of origin and the time zones of these countries;
(ii) everything (population, number of primary factors of production, number of products, time horizon) is finite; and
(iii) all households and firms are price takers.

These features of WADM economies are mutually compatible if all households are unaware of the finiteness of their number at each point of time and/or all households are incompletely rational; see Kemp (2012). But, even if these additional conditions are satisfied, WADM economies have been recently found lacking in important features of the dynamic and endless real world: overlapping and finite generations (OLGs), two-parent families, and intergenerational bequests.

Adopting a model with time viewed as a discrete variable, Kemp and Wolik (1995) were able to show that, if intergenerational bequests are neglected, there exists a perfectly competitive world equilibrium and that Propositions 11(a) and 11 (b) remain valid. Since Proposition 11(c) emerged only in the year 2007, it could not be considered by Kemp and Wolik in 1995. However if Proposition 11(c) had been available in 1995, then Kemp and Wolik would have had no difficulty in showing that it also remained valid, as was later confirmed by Kemp and Fishburn (2013).

However Kemp and Wolik did neglect bequests, dowries, and other types of intergenerational transfer. This was a serious oversight for, in advanced economies, a considerable proportion of private property has been obtained by means of bequests. As first noted by Kotlikoff and Summers (1981), in the USA at the time of writing, two-thirds of private wealth had been obtained by bequests from parents and parents-in-law. Moreover, as Kemp and Fishburn (2013) have emphasized, parents and parents-in-law can hardly fail to recognize that they are in a strategic relationship with each other. Indeed they may find themselves playing a many-person noncoop-erative game in bequests, the inevitable outcome of which is a loss of efficiency, a loss that may be greater under free trade than in autarky and may be incompatible with each of the core propositions.[6]

---

[6]How would Bertrand Russell have received our finding? In his own work, he concluded that "[n]o one has succeeded in inventing a philosophy at once credible and self-consistent"; see Russell (1946; 637).

The Self of political economists has changed again, possibly adversely. Kemp and Fishburn (2013) have noted that the government of each trading country might intervene with legislation requiring that all parents and parents-in-law maintain under free trade their autarkic vectors of bequests. However, few individuals know what their autarkic vectors would have been, and some of those few might have been unwilling to provide precise information to the government.

11.5   Two Final Remarks

Hermann Gossen's book has not been mentioned since Sect. 11.2. The neglect may be partly explained by the fact that the pooling of time has been found to have no bearing on the validity of the *normative* Propositions 11(a), 11(b), and 11(c); for a detailed demonstration, see Kemp (2010). On the other hand, as is now well known from Georgescu–Roegen (1983, 1985) and Steedman (2001), many *descriptive* propositions require some reformulation under Gossenian assumptions.

In Sect. 11.4, we found that the assumption of perfect competition is incompatible with the assumption that most families contain two sets of parents. This suggests that economists should be focusing more on imperfect competition. There has in fact been a recent step in that direction. In September 2001, Kemp and Shimomura (2001, p. 294) published a long-awaited result in the *Japanese Economic Review*:

> Suppose that agents play the Cournot–Nash game before and after trade begins. Then, there is a balanced scheme of income redistribution within each country such that, if agents play the Cournot–Nash game under the scheme of income redistribution, and if the game has a solution, each country gains from trade.

That theorem is essentially correct but incomplete. We can now in 2017 expand the earlier result by incorporating outsourcing, cost sharing by two or more agents, indeed, many of the phenomena that are the foci of attention in "the new trade theory." Readers will understand that the proof of 2001 can be easily adjusted to become the proof of 2017.

Acknowledgment We are grateful to Binh Tran-Nam for his helpful assistance.

References

Arrow, K. J., & Debreu, G. (1954). Existence of an equilibrium for a competitive economy. *Econometrica, 32*, 265–290.

Georgescu–Roegen, N. (1983). *Herman Heinrich Gossen: His life and work in historical perspective*. In H. H. Gossen (1983, pp. xi–cxlv).

Georgescu–Roegen, N. (1985). Time and value in economics and in Gossen's system. *Rivista Internazionale di Scienze Economiche e Comerciali, 32*, 1121–1140.

Gossen, H. H. (1854). *Entwickelung der gesetz des menschlichen verkehrs*. Braunschweig: F. Vieweg und Sohn.

Gossen, H. H. (1983). *The laws of human relations and the rules of human action derived therefrom*. Cambridge, MA: MIT Press. English translation of H. H. Gossen (1854).

Grandmont, J. M., & McFadden, D. (1972). A technical note on classical gains from trade. *Journal of International Economics, 2*, 109–125.

Jevons, W. S. (1879). *The theory of political economy* (2nd ed.). Harmondsworth: Penguin Books.

Kemp, M. C. (1964). *The pure theory of international trade*. Englewood Cliffs: Prentice–Hall.

Kemp, M. C. (2007). Normative comparisons of customs unions and other types of free trade association. *European Journal of Political Economy, 23*, 416–422.

Kemp, M. C. (2010). Normative trade theory under Gossenian assumptions. In J. Vint, J. S. Metcalfe, H. D. Kuz, N. Salvadori, & P. A. Samuelson (Eds.), *Economic theory and economic thought – Essays in honour of Ian Steedman* (pp. 98–115). London: Routledge.

Kemp, M. C. (2012). Normative trade theory. In M. C. Kemp, H. Nakagawa, & T. Uchida (Eds.), *Positive and normative analysis in international economics: Essays in honour of Hiroshi Ohta* (pp. 7–16). Basingstoke: Palgrave Macmillan.

Kemp, M. C., & Fishburn, G. (2013). Normative trade in the context of overlapping generations and inter-generational bequests. *Global Journal of Economics, 2*. https://doi.org/10.1142/S2251361213500043.

Kemp, M. C., & Shimomura, K. (2001). Gains from trade in a Cournot–Nash general equilibrium. *Japanese Economic Review, 52*, 284–302.

Kemp, M. C., & Wan, H. Y., Jr. (1972). The gains from free trade. *International Economic Review, 13*, 509–522.

Kemp, M. C., & Wan, H. Y., Jr. (1976). An elementary proposition concerning the formation of customs unions. *Journal of International Economics, 6*, 95–97.

Kemp, M. C., & Wan, H. Y., Jr. (1986). The comparison of second-best equilibria: The case of customs unions. In D. Bös & C. Seidl (Eds.), *The welfare economics of the second best, supplementum 5 to the Zeitschift für Nationalökonomie* (pp. 161–167). Wein/New York: Springer-Verlag.

Kemp, M. C., & Wolik, N. (1995). The gains from trade in a context of overlapping generations. In M. C. Kemp (Ed.), *The gains from trade and the gains from aid* (pp. 129–146). London: Routledge.

Kotlikoff, L. J., & Summers, L. H. (1981). The role of intergenerational transfers in aggregate capital accumulation. *Journal of Political Economy, 89*, 706–732.

Mas-Colell, A., Whinston, M. D., & Green, J. R. (1995). *Microeconomic theory*. Oxford: Oxford University Press.

McKenzie, L. W. (1954). On equilibrium in Graham's model of world trade and other competitive systems. *Econometrica, 22*, 147–161.

Ohyama, M. (2002). The economic significance of the GATT/WTO rules. In A. D. Woodland (Ed.), *Economic theory and international trade* (pp. 71–85). Cheltenham: Edward Elgar.

Panagariya, A., & Krishna, P. (2002). On necessarily welfare-enhancing free trade areas. *Journal of International Economics, 57*, 353–367.

Pareto, V. (1894). Il massimo di utilità dato dalla libera concorrenza. *Giornale degli Economisti, 9*, 48–66.

Russell, B. (1946). *History of western philosophy*. London: George Allen and Unwin.

Smith, A. (1776). *An inquiry into the nature and causes of the wealth of nations*. London: W. Strahan and T. Cadell.

Steedman, I. (2001). *Consumption takes time: Implications for economic theory*. London: Routledge.

Walras, L. (1874–1877). *Eléments d'économie politique pure, ou théorie de la richesse sociale*. Lausanne: Corbaz.

Walras, L. (1885). Un économiste inconnu, Hermann-Henri Gossen. *Journal des Économistes, 30*, 68–90. and 260–261.

Chapter 12
Domestic Income Transfer in an Open Dual Economy

Makoto Tawada and Ling Qi

Abstract This chapter investigates the welfare effects of an income transfer from urban manufacturing workers to rural agricultural workers in an open dual economy where the urban manufacturing wage is fixed under the minimum wage legislation. We show that the utility of a rural worker may be reduced by the transfer if capital is specific, but such a transfer paradox never appears if capital is mobile between industries. We also derive the result that the transfer causes urban unemployment to decrease in the sector-specific capital case but possibly increase in the mobile capital case.

Keywords Dual open economy · Minimum wage legislation · Transfer paradox · Labor income disparity · Walrasian price adjustment · Harris–Todaro model

12.1 Introduction

Most developing countries are experiencing a wide income gap among regions. It is recognized in particular that the wage of urban areas is much higher than that of rural areas. This is one of the strong engines for a large-scale inflow of rural labor force into an urban area in those countries. In order to improve the living standard of the national people, the government adopts the minimum wage legislation. But it tends to be executed mainly for the urban workers from a practical point of view. Therefore the legislation seems to enhance a regional income gap. The direct method to resolve this deficiency is the income transfer from urban workers to rural workers.

M. Tawada (✉)
Faculty of Economics, Aichi Gakuin University, Nagoya, Aichi, Japan
e-mail: mtawada2@dpc.agu.ac.jp

L. Qi
China Institute for Actuarial Science, Central University of Finance and Economics, Beijing, China

© Springer Nature Singapore Pte Ltd. 2018
B. Tran-Nam et al. (eds.), *Recent Developments in Normative Trade Theory and Welfare Economics*, New Frontiers in Regional Science: Asian Perspectives 26, https://doi.org/10.1007/978-981-10-8615-1_12

In the present chapter, we examine how this transfer works for rural workers as well as urban workers under the existence of the minimum wage legislation.

There exist a vast literature concerning the modern treatment of the international transfers appears after the Keynes and Ohlin dispute in 1929 and the penetrating comment by Samuelson (1947). Among others, a rigorous and comprehensive treatment was explored by Kemp (1995), and a survey of this field was conducted by Brakman and Marrewijk (1998). On the contrary, there are few studies concerning the theoretical treatment of the domestic transfers, particularly focusing developing countries. One exceptional work is Ravallion (1984). He analyzed the domestic transfer in a dual economy of the Harris and Todaro type but assumed that labor is the only primary factor in his model. Therefore the role of capital is disregarded in the analysis. In our present chapter, we show that the role of capital is crucial in the welfare of the regional workers.

In order to deal with this topic, we consider an open dual economy based on Harris and Todaro (1970). So there are two sectors which are a manufacturing sector located in an urban region and an agricultural sector located in a rural region. The minimum wage legislation is applied to the urban manufacturing sector. The production of each sector is operated by the use of labor and capital. We consider two cases. One is where capital is sector specific and the other where capital is mobile between sectors. Then we examine the effect of the domestic income transfer from the urban manufacturing workers to the rural agricultural workers. The analysis is simple but the derived result seems to be interesting. In the specific capital case, there possibly appears the transfer paradox that the rural workers become worse off by the transfer. In the mobile capital case, however, such a paradox never appears. In this sense, capital mobility between sectors plays a crucial role to the emergence of a transfer paradox. Based on these discussions, we also show that the labor income disparity between these two sectors necessarily contracts in all cases. Finally we investigate the effect of the income transfer to urban unemployment and reveal that urban unemployment necessarily reduces by the transfer in the specific capital case, while the transfer possibly enlarges the urban unemployment in the mobile factor case.

The remainder of our chapter is organized as follows. Our basic model is presented in Sect. 12.2. Sections 12.3 and 12.4 deal with the specific capital case and the mobile capital case, respectively. The effect of the transfer to urban unemployment is analyzed in Sect. 12.5, and our conclusion is placed in the last section.

12.2   The Model

We consider a dual open economy of the Harris and Todaro type. There are two industries which are rural agricultural and urban manufacturing industries. In the production of each industry, labor and capital are used as primary inputs.

Let the production functions of the manufacturing and agricultural industries be, respectively,

$$M = F(L_M, K_M), \tag{12.1}$$

and

$$A = G(L_A, K_A) \tag{12.2}$$

where M and A are, respectively, the outputs of the manufacturing and agricultural goods, L_M and L_A are, respectively, the labor inputs in the manufacturing and agricultural industries, and K_M and K_A are, respectively, the capital inputs to the manufacturing and agricultural industries. The production functions $F(\cdot)$ and $G(\cdot)$ are assumed to be linearly homogenous, concave, and twice continuously differentiable with positive first derivatives.

Perfect competition prevails in all industries. The minimum wage legislation is, however, introduced into the urban manufacturing industry, so that the wage is fixed at $\bar{w}$ in the manufacturing industry. Labor is assumed to be mobile between the rural and urban regions according to the difference in the expected wage between two regions.

There are four different income groups which are:

(i) Manufacturing worker group
(ii) Agricultural worker group
(iii) Manufacturing capitalist group
(iv) Agricultural capitalist group

In each group, every individual owns one unit of the respective primary factor, provides it in production inelastically to all prices, and consumes the manufacturing and agricultural goods.

Each individual's demands for the manufacturing and agricultural goods are determined by the individual's utility maximization behavior. The utility function of each individual is assumed to be identical within the same group. We assume that the economy is small and open, and the manufacturing and agricultural goods are tradable.

The profit maximization conditions for each industry are described as

$$F_L = \bar{w}, \tag{12.3}$$
$$F_K = r^M, \tag{12.4}$$
$$pG_L = w^A, \text{ and} \tag{12.5}$$
$$pG_K = r^A, \tag{12.6}$$

where $F_L \equiv \partial F/\partial L_M$, $G_L \equiv \partial G/\partial L_A$, $F_K \equiv \partial F/\partial K_M$, $G_K \equiv \partial G/\partial KL_A$, p is the price ratio of the agricultural good to the manufacturing good, w^A is the wage of the agricultural industry, and r^M and r^A are, respectively, the rental prices of capital in the manufacturing and agricultural industries.

The labor market equilibrium condition is

$$L_M + L_A + L_U = L, \tag{12.7}$$

where L_U is urban unemployment and L is the labor endowment of this economy and supposed to be given and constant.

Let t^{ML}, t^{AL}, t^{MK}, and t^{AK} be, respectively, the per capita income transfer to the manufacturing workers, agricultural workers, manufacturing capitalists, and agricultural capitalists. Then the per capita income of each group (i) to (iv) becomes $\bar{w} + t^{ML} \equiv i^{ML}$, $w^A + t^{AL} \equiv i^{AL}$, $r^M + t^{MK} \equiv i^{MK}$, and $r^A + t^{AK} \equiv i^{AK}$, respectively. Here we assume each worker to be risk neutral, so that all workers move from the lower expected income region to the higher expected income region. Then the arbitrage condition for the labor movement between urban and rural areas can be described as

$$w^A + t^{AL} = \frac{L_M}{L_M + L_U} \left(\bar{w} + t^{ML} \right). \tag{12.8}$$

Throughout of this chapter, we basically consider the transfer scheme from the manufacturing worker group to the agricultural worker group. Let T^{ML} and T^{AL} be the total income transfer received by the manufacturing worker group and agricultural worker group, respectively. Now we suppose the case where $T^{AL} = -T^{ML} \geq 0$ and initially $T^{AL} = T^{ML} = 0$. T^{ML} and T^{AL} should be $t^{ML}L_M$ and $t^{AL}L_A$, respectively. Then, by the use of (12.7), (12.8) can be rewritten as

$$w^A + \frac{T^{AL}}{L^A} = \frac{L_M}{L - L_A} \bar{w} + \frac{T^{ML}}{L - L_A}. \tag{12.9}$$

12.3 Specific Capital Case

In this section we consider the case where capital is specific to the industry and cannot move between industries. In this case K_M and K_A are given and fixed. Then, once T^{ML} and T^{AL} are given, the equilibrium conditions, described by the set of Eqs. (12.3, 12.4, 12.5, 12.6, and 12.7), and (12.9), determine L_M, L_A, L_U, w^A, r^M, and r^A.

In particular, Eqs. (12.3), (12.4), and (12.9) determine L_M, L_A, and w^A. Total differentiation of these equations gives

$$F_{LL}dL_M = 0, \tag{12.10}$$
$$pG_{LL}dL_A = dw^A, \text{ and} \tag{12.11}$$

$$dw^A - \frac{\bar{w}}{L - L_A} dL_M - \left(\frac{T^{AL}}{L_A{}^2} + \frac{L_M \bar{w} + T^{LM}}{(L - L_A)^2} \right) dL_A$$

$$= -\frac{1}{L_A} dT^{AL} + \frac{1}{L - L_A} dT^{ML} \tag{12.12}$$

where $F_{LL} \equiv \partial^2 F / \partial^2 L_M < 0$ and $G_{LL} \equiv \partial^2 G / \partial^2 L_A < 0$.

Equation (12.10) implies $dL_M = 0$. Moreover, $dT^{AL} = - dT^{ML} > 0$, and $T^{AL} = T^{ML} = 0$ by assumption. Thus (12.12) becomes

$$dw^A - \frac{L_M \bar{w}}{(L - L_A)^2} dL_A = -\frac{L}{L_A (L - L_A)} dT^{AL},$$

which can be further expressed as

$$\left[pG_{LL} - \frac{L_M \bar{w}}{(L - L_A)^2} \right] dL_A = -\frac{L}{L_A (L - L_A)} dT^{AL}$$

from (12.11).

So we have

$$\frac{dL_A}{dT^{AL}} = -\frac{\frac{L}{L_A (L - L_A)}}{pG_{LL} - \frac{L_M \bar{w}}{(L - L_A)^2}} > 0, \tag{12.13}$$

and

$$\frac{dw^A}{dT^{AL}} = -\frac{\frac{pG_{LL} L}{L_A (L - L_A)}}{pG_{LL} - \frac{L_M \bar{w}}{(L - L_A)^2}} < 0. \tag{12.14}$$

The transfer effect to the per capita income of a typical agricultural worker is calculated as

$$\begin{aligned}
\frac{di^{AL}}{dT^{AL}} &= \frac{dw^A}{dT^{AL}} + \frac{1}{L_A} - T^{AL} \frac{1}{L_A^2} \frac{dL_A}{dT^{AL}} \\
&= \frac{-\dfrac{pG_{LL} L}{L_A (L - L_A)}}{pG_{LL} - \dfrac{L_M \bar{w}}{(L - L_A)^2}} + \frac{1}{L_A} \\
&= \frac{-pG_{LL} L_A - w_A}{L_A (L - L_A) \left(pG_{LL} - \dfrac{L_M \bar{w}}{(L - L_A)^2} \right)}
\end{aligned} \tag{12.15}$$

from (12.9) and the assumption that initial T^{AL} is nil. This yields

$$\frac{di^{AL}}{dT^{AL}} \overset{>}{\underset{<}{=}} 0 \Leftrightarrow \varepsilon^{AL} \overset{<}{\underset{>}{=}} 1,$$

where $\varepsilon^{AL} \equiv -\frac{L_A}{G_L}\frac{dG_L}{dL_A}$ is the labor elasticity of the marginal labor productivity of the agricultural industry.

Concerning the transfer effect to the per capita income of the manufacturing worker group, it works as a negative impact, implying that the transfer lessens the income of each manufacturing worker. This is because $\bar{w}$ is not affected by the transfer, and the present transfer works negatively to the income of this group.

As for the per capita income of the manufacturing capitalist group, (12.10) and (12.4) imply

$$F_{KL}\frac{dL_M}{dT^{AL}} = \frac{dr^M}{dT^{AL}} = 0.$$

So the transfer does not affect the income of any manufacturing capitalist. On the other hand, the transfer raises the income of any agricultural capitalist since

$$pG_{KL}\frac{dL_A}{dT^{AL}} = \frac{dr^A}{dT^{AL}} > 0,$$

by (12.6).

Under the assumption that the prices of all goods are given and constant, a consumer's utility rises if and only if the consumer's income goes up.

Finally, in view of (12.13), (12.7) and the fact that $dL_M/dT^{AL} = 0$, we can easily see $dL_U/dT^{AL} < 0$. Now we can establish

Theorem 12.1 *Consider a small open country where capital is immobile between industries. Suppose that an income transfer from manufacturing workers to agricultural workers is introduced. Then,*

(i) *The level of unemployment decreases.*
(ii) *A typical manufacturing worker's utility falls.*
(iii) *A typical agricultural worker's utility rises if and only if the labor elasticity of the labor marginal productivity in the agricultural industry is less than one.*
(iv) *A typical manufacturing capitalist's utility is unchanged.*
(v) *A typical agricultural capitalist's utility rises.*

In Theorem 12.1, the most important result is (iii). In a previous study, Ravallion (1984) showed that if the labor elasticity of the marginal labor productivity in the agricultural good is large enough, the income transfer from manufacturing workers to agricultural workers lowers the utility of agricultural workers. This transfer paradox appears even if there is no price effect.[1] The direct effect of the income

---

[1]If the agricultural production function is of the Cobb-Douglas type, then $\varepsilon^{AL} < 1$. Hence, the transfer paradox would not occur in this case.

transfer necessarily raises the agricultural wage. This wage increase, however, attracts the urban workers to the agricultural industry, so that the agricultural wage falls. If this indirect effect is sufficiently large to outweigh the direct effect, the transfer paradox occurs.

Even though there is a possibility of the transfer paradox, we can prove that the labor income disparity between two sectors always contracts. In order to see this, it is sufficient to consider the case where the income of an agricultural worker decreases by the transfer, since the income of a manufacturing worker necessarily decreases by the transfer. On the one hand, since $i^{ML} = \bar{w} - (T^{AL}/L_M)$, we have

$$\frac{di^{ML}}{dT^{AL}} / i^{ML} = -\frac{1}{L_M} \frac{1}{\bar{w}}$$

for $T^{AL} = 0$ initially. Bearing (12.15) in mind, we have

$$\frac{di^{AL}}{dT^{AL}} / i^{AL} = \frac{-pG_{LL}L_A - pG_L}{L_M\bar{w}(pG_{LL}L_A - L_ApG_L/(L - L_A))} < 0$$

by the assumption that $di^{AL}/dT^{AL} < 0$. Then it is obvious that

$$\left| \frac{di^{AL}}{dT^{AL}} / i^{AL} \right|$$

$$-\left| \frac{di^{ML}}{dT^{AL}} / i^{ML} \right|$$

$$= \frac{1}{L_M\bar{w}} \left[\frac{-pG_{LL}L_A - pG_L}{-(pG_{LL}L_A - L_ApG_L/(L - L_A))} - 1 \right] < 0,$$

$$(12.16)$$

because

$$-(pG_{LL}L_A - L_ApG_L/(L - L_A)) > -pG_{LL}L_A > -pG_{LL}L_A - pG_L > 0.$$

The inequality (12.16) means that the labor income disparity between sectors contracts even when the agricultural income decrease by the transfer.

Now we can state

Theorem 12.2 *Consider a small open country where capital is immobile between industries. Suppose a labor income transfer from manufacturing to agricultural workers is instituted. Then the labor income disparity between these two sectors necessarily contracts.*

The possibility of this transfer paradox has nothing to do with the stability of the Walrasian price adjustment since all good prices are given and constant. If labor moves sluggishly between two regions according to the difference of the expected wages of two industries, the labor movement process can be expressed as

$$\dot{L}_A = a\left(w^A + \frac{T^{AL}}{L_A} - \frac{L_M}{L - L_A}\left(\bar{w} + \frac{T^{ML}}{L_M}\right)\right),$$

where a is the adjustment speed and assumed to be a positive parameter. Then the equilibrium is shown to be globally stable for

$$\begin{aligned}
\frac{d\dot{L}_A}{dL_A} &= a\left[\frac{dw^A}{dL_A} - \frac{\bar{w}}{L - L_A}\frac{dL_M}{dL_A} - \left(\frac{T^{AL}}{L_A^2} + \frac{L_A\bar{w} + T^{ML}}{(L - L_A)^2}\right)\right] \\
&= a\left[pG_{LL} - \left(\frac{T^{AL}}{L_A^2} + \frac{L_A\bar{w} + T^{ML}}{(L - L_A)^2}\right)\right] < 0.
\end{aligned}$$

The transfer paradox can possibly appear under these circumstances.

   Although we have considered the case where the transfer is from manufacturing workers to agricultural workers, we can extend the scheme to the case where the transfer is from capitalists as well as manufacturing workers to agricultural workers. Even in this extended case, the primal results such as Theorem 12.1 (i), (ii), and (iii) carry over because the income transfer of the capitalists does not have any influence in the equation system described by (12.3, 12.4, 12.5, 12.6, and 12.7) and (12.9).

12.4   Mobile Capital Case

In this section we examine the case where capital can move freely between industries. Then the equilibrium system can be described by the following set of equations:

$$F_L = \bar{w}, \tag{12.3}$$

$$F_K = r, \tag{12.4'}$$

$$pG_L = w^A, \tag{12.5}$$

$$pG_K = r, \tag{12.6'}$$

$$L_M + L_A + L_U = L, \tag{12.7}$$

$$w^A + \frac{T^{AL}}{L^A} = \frac{L_M}{L - L_A}\bar{w} + \frac{T^{ML}}{L - L_A}, \tag{12.9}$$

$$K_M + K_A = K, \tag{12.17}$$

where K is capital endowment and assumed to be given and constant.
   By (12.4') and (12.6'), we have

$$F_K = pG_K. \tag{12.18}$$

The endogenous variables L_M, L_A, K_A, K_M, and w^A are determined by (12.3), (12.5), (12.17), (12.18), and (12.9) once T^{AL} and T^{ML} are given.

Now we examine how the individual utility of each income group is influenced by the introduction of the transfer, where the capitalist income groups are now combined together as one capitalist income group and each capitalist receives income r.

Let $F(L_M, K_A) = L_M f(k_M)$, where $k_M \equiv K_M/L_M$. Then (12.3) can be expressed as $f(k_M) - k_M f'(k_M) = \bar{w}$, where $f' \equiv df/dk_M$, so that the transfer has no impact on k_M. Since $f'(k_M) = r$, r does not change by the transfer. Therefore, $k_A \equiv K_A/L_A$ does not change because of (12.6') and neither does w^A by (12.5). Thus the transfer raises the per capita income of the agricultural worker group and reduces that of the manufacturing worker group necessarily, implying that the individual utility of the agricultural worker group rises and that of the manufacturing worker group falls. Since r stays constant to a change in the level of transfer, the individual utility of the capitalist income group does not change. Obviously these results hold without the condition that the initial level of the transfer is zero.

Now we can assert

Theorem 12.3 *Consider a small open country where capital is mobile between domestic industries and in which there is an income transfer from manufacturing workers to agricultural workers. If the level of the transfer is raised, then,*

(i) *A typical agricultural worker's utility rises.*
(ii) *A typical manufacturing worker's utility falls.*
(iii) *A typical capitalist's utility does not change.*

The results (i) and (ii) of Theorem 12.3 immediately bring forth

Theorem 12.4 *Consider a small open country where capital is mobile between domestic industries and in which there is an income transfer from manufacturing workers to agricultural workers. Then labor income disparity between these two sectors necessarily contracts.*

Since neither w^A nor r are affected by a change in the level of any transfer, we can extend the above theorem. We show it as the following remark:

Remark 12.1 *Consider a small open country where capital is mobile between domestic industries. For any scheme that income is transferred from some income groups to some other income groups, the individual utility of the donor group falls, that of the recipient group rises and that of the outside group does not change by an increase in the level of the transfer.*

Again all of these results have nothing to do with the stability of any dynamic adjustment process. The key equation to produce these results is (12.3) which characterizes the dual economy of the Harris and Todaro type. Because of (12.3), none of factor prices are impacted from any sort of income transfer.

12.5 Transfer Effect on Urban Unemployment

In a dual economy, much attention is centered to urban unemployment. We focus it in this section. In the analysis of Sect. 12.3, it was already revealed that if capital is industry specific, the agricultural employment increases, and the urban unemployment decreases by a rise in the income transfer from manufacturing workers to rural workers.

So we deal with the mobile capital case. In view of the analysis of Sect. 12.4, we know that the capital–labor ratio of an industry never varies for a change in the income transfer. Keeping these in mind, we differentiate (12.9) totally. Then we have

$$\frac{L_M \bar{w}}{K_M(L - L_A)}\left(\frac{K_A}{L_A} - \frac{K_M}{L - L_A}\right)dL_A = -\frac{L}{L_A(L - L_A)}dT^{AL}, \qquad (12.19)$$

by the use of (12.7), (12.17), and the assumption that $T^{AL} = T^{ML} = 0$ initially and $dT^{AL} + dT^{ML} = 0$.

Therefore we find

$$\frac{dL_A}{dT^{AL}} \begin{array}{c} > \\ < \end{array} 0 \Leftrightarrow \frac{K_A}{L_A} \begin{array}{c} < \\ > \end{array} \frac{K_M}{L_M + L_U},$$

which implies that if and only if the capital–labor ratio of the urban area is greater (smaller) than that of the rural area, the labor employment of the agricultural industry increases (decreases) by the introduction of the transfer. Since $k_M \equiv K_M/L_M$ and $k_A \equiv K_A/L_A$ are constant to the introduction of the transfer and $dK_M = -dK_A$, we easily show that an increase in L_A implies an increase in K_A and decrease in L_M and K_M and vice versa.

Based on these results, we investigate the sign of dL_U/dT^{AL}. By (12.19) and the fact that $L_A K_M dL_M + L_M K_A dL_A = 0$, we obtain

$$\frac{dL_U}{dT^{AL}} = -\left(\frac{dL_M}{dT^{AL}} + \frac{dL_A}{dT^{AL}}\right)$$

$$= \left(1 - \frac{L_M K_A}{L_A K_M}\right)\frac{\dfrac{L}{L_A(L - L_A)}}{\dfrac{L_M \bar{w}}{K_M(L - L_A)}\left(\dfrac{K_A}{L_A} - \dfrac{K_M}{L - L_A}\right)}$$

$$= \frac{L}{L_A \bar{w}}\frac{\dfrac{K_M}{L_M} - \dfrac{K_A}{L_A}}{\dfrac{K_A}{L_A} - \dfrac{K_M}{L - L_A}} < 0,$$

if

$$\frac{K_A}{L_A} < \frac{K_M}{L_M + L_U}. \qquad (12.20)$$

Thus, if the capital–labor ratio of the urban areas is greater than that of the rural area, the introduction of the transfer reduces the urban unemployment. The condition (12.20) is a global stability condition of the following dynamical factor movement process:

$$(D) \quad \begin{cases} \dot{L}_A = \alpha_L \left(w_A - \dfrac{\bar{w} L_M}{L - L_A} \right), \\ \dot{K}_A = \alpha_K (p G_K - F_K), \end{cases}$$

where α_L and α_K are positive and constant parameters concerning adjustment speeds. The proof of the stability is provided in Appendix 12.1.[2]

Now we can summarize results derived in this section as

Theorem 12.5 *Consider the income transfer from manufacturing workers to agricultural workers. Then,*

 (i) *In the specific capital case, a rise in the level of transfer always increases the labor employment in the agricultural industry and decreases the urban unemployment.*
 (ii) *In the mobile capital case, the introduction of the transfer increases (decreases) the labor employment as well as capital employment in the agricultural industry and decreases (increases) the labor employment as well as capital employment in the manufacturing industry if and only if the capital–labor ratio of the urban region is greater (smaller) than that of the rural region.*
 (iii) *In the mobile capital case, the introduction of the transfer reduces the urban unemployment if the capital–labor ratio of the urban area is greater than that of the rural area.*

12.6 Conclusion

We have investigated the welfare effect of a domestic income transfer from urban workers to rural workers in a dual open economy and shown that the transfer possibly lowers the welfare of the rural workers in the case where capital is sector specific, but such a transfer paradox never occurs in the case where capital is perfectly mobile between sectors. This is because in the specific capital case, the rural income goes up by the transfer, and thus labor flows into the rural area and reduces the rural wage. If this latter effect overwhelms the former, the rural workers will be worse off. This paradoxical phenomenon appears when the wage reduction is very sensitive to the labor inflow. In the mobile capital case, labor should move together with capital since the capital–labor ratio of each sector is constant by the

---

[2]In the mobile capital case, the stability was investigated by Khan (1980) and Neary (1981).

fixed urban wage. Thus, the transfer does not influence the rural wage, so that the paradox cannot occur. All these results have nothing to do with the dynamic stability condition of which is often made use. The reason is the open economy assumption which enables the good prices to be constant.

Based on these two distinct outcomes, one policy implication could be proposed that the effect of a domestic transfer to raise the welfare of the rural worker depends on the capital mobility. If only labor flows into the rural region by the transfer, the policy may not be effective. If capital also together with labor flows into the rural region, however, the policy becomes necessarily effective. For the purpose to shrink the wage disparity, however, this transfer policy is effective in both cases. We have also inspected the effect of the transfer to the urban unemployment and derived the result that the transfer always reduces the urban unemployment in the specific capital case, but it does not so in the mobile capital case. The sufficient condition to reduce the urban unemployment is that the urban region is more capital intensive than the rural region.

Finally it should be noted that our transfer scheme is slightly different from that of Ravallion (1984). Ravallion considers the source of income transfer to agricultural workers comes from manufacturing firms, so that the labor cost in production goes up, while the labor income in the manufacturing sector stay constant. Under our assumption, however, the source of income transfer relies on the income of manufacturing workers, which implies that the labor income of manufacturing workers necessarily decreases but the labor cost in manufacturing production is not affected. This difference does not influence our results much. Consider a Ravallion's transfer scheme. Then, in the specific capital case, the income disparity expands if and only if the agricultural wage decreases. In the mobile capital case, we can see easily that the agricultural wage necessarily increases and the rental of capital decreases.

Our present analysis is simple enough to derive clear results, since we assume the economy to be small and open. If the economy is closed, the analysis becomes complicated by the disturbance of the endogenous good prices. Although most developing countries are small and open, the close economy case is more interesting from a theoretical point of view, and it is a future topic to tackle.

Acknowledgment We are grateful to Professors Xiaochun Li and Dongpeng Liu of Nanjing University, Professor Binh Tran-Nam of University of New South Wales, and, in particular, an anonymous reviewer for their valuable comments. We also appreciate Professors Kojun Hamada of Niigata University and Mitsuyoshi Yanagihara of Nagoya University for their useful discussions.

Appendix 12.1

In this appendix we prove that if $T^{AL} = T^{ML} = 0$, the equilibrium is globally stable under factor movement dynamic process (D). Total differentiation of (D) with respect to the endogenous variables yields

$$dL̇_A \equiv dw^A - \frac{\bar{w}(L - L_A)dL_M + \bar{w}L_M dL_A}{(L - L_A)^2},$$

$$dK̇_A = pG_{KK}dK_A + pG_{KL}dL_A - F_{KK}dK_M - F_{KL}dL_M.$$

Therefore Jacobian matrix of (D) is given by

$$J \equiv \begin{bmatrix} pG_{LL} - \dfrac{\bar{w}L_M}{L - L_A} & pG_{LK} - \dfrac{\bar{w}F_{LK}}{(L - L_A)F_{LL}} \\ pG_{KL} & pG_{KK} + F_{KK} - \dfrac{F_{KL}^2}{F_{LL}} \end{bmatrix}$$

since $pG_{LL}dL_A + pG_{KK}dK_A = dw^A$, $F_{LL}dL_M + F_{LK}dK_M = 0$, and $dK_M + dK_L = 0$.

Now, every diagonal element of J is negative. The determinant of J is derived as

$$
\begin{aligned}
|J| &= \left(pG_{LL} - \frac{\bar{w}L_M}{(L - L_A)^2}\right)\left(pG_{KK} + F_{KK} - \frac{F_{KL}^2}{F_{LL}}\right) - pG_{KL}\left(pG_{KL} - \frac{\bar{w}F_{LK}}{(L - L_A)F_{LL}}\right) \\
&= \left(\frac{F_{KL}^2}{F_{LL}} - pG_{KK} - F_{KK}\right)\frac{\bar{w}L_M}{(L - L_A)} + pG_{KL}\frac{\bar{w}F_{LK}}{(L - L_A)F_{LL}} \\
&= \frac{p\bar{w}G_{KL}}{L - L_A}\frac{L_A L_M}{K_A K_M}\left(\frac{K_M}{L - L_A} - \frac{K_A}{L_A}\right),
\end{aligned}
$$

implying that $|J|$ is positive in sign if the urban area is more capital intensive than the rural area.

Applying the stability theorem in Oleck (1963) to these results, we can assert that the equilibrium is globally stable in the case where $T^{AL} = T^{ML} = 0$.

References

Brakman, S., & van Marrewijk, C. (1998). *The economics of international transfers*. Cambridge: Cambridge University Press.

Harris, J. R., & Todaro, M. (1970). Migration, unemployment and development: A two-sector analysis. *American Economic Review, 60*, 126–142.

Kemp, M. C. (1995). *The gains from trade and the gains from aid*. London: Routledge.

Keynes, J. M. (1929). The German transfer problem. *Economic Journal, 39*, 1–7.

Khan, M. A. (1980). Dynamic stability, wage subsidies and the generalized Harris–Todaro model. *Pakistan Development Review, 19*, 1–24.

Neary, J. P. (1981). On the Harris–Todaro model with intersectoral capital mobility. *Economica, 48*, 219–234.

Ohlin, B. (1929). The reparations problem: A discussion; transfer difficulties, real and imagined. *Economic Journal, 39*, 179–183.

Olech, C. (1963). On the global stability of an autonomous system on the plane. In J. P. Lasalle & J. B. Diaz (Eds.), *Contributions to differential equations* (pp. 389–400). New York: Wiley.

Ravallion, M. (1984). How much is a transfer payment worth to a rural worker? *Oxford Economic Papers, 36*, 478–489.

Samuelson, P. A. (1947). *Foundations of economic analysis*. Cambridge: Harvard University Press.

Chapter 13
Foreign Aid: Equilibria in Pure and Mixed Strategies with Kantian and Nashian Donors

Ngo Van Long

Abstract We propose a model of foreign aid in which donor countries belong to two different behavioral types: Kantian countries and Nashian countries. Kantian countries are motivated by moral norms, while Nashian countries act according to the narrow economic conception of rationality. The concept of equilibrium used here is the Kant−Nash equilibrium proposed by Long (2016). Mixed strategies are permitted. It is found that under certain conditions, Kantian donors may randomize between low and high levels of foreign aid, while Nashian donors will choose to free ride. We show that if there is a decline in the number of Kantian donors because some Kantian countries become Nashian, the aggregate foreign aid may fall more than proportionately. This message can also be read differently: if there is an increase in the number of Kantian donors because some Nashian countries wake up to their responsibility and become Kantian, the aggregate aid may rise more than proportionately.

Keywords Foreign aid · Kant−Nash equilibrium · Moral norms · Social norms · Kantian equilibrium

13.1 Introduction

International economists have devoted quite a lot of attention to the transfer problem, which arises from flows of financial resources that are not directly related to international trade or investment (Bhagwati et al. 1983). These flows include negative aid, such as demands for war reparation, as well as positive aid, such as international assistance to developing countries, undertaken by developed economies or international organizations (Kemp et al. 1992; Kemp and Shimomura 2002, 2003). Among the earlier contributions to the foreign aid literature, the work of

N. Van Long (✉)
Department of Economics, McGill University, Montreal, Quebec, Canada
e-mail: ngo.long@mcgill.ca

© Springer Nature Singapore Pte Ltd. 2018
B. Tran-Nam et al. (eds.), *Recent Developments in Normative Trade Theory and Welfare Economics*, New Frontiers in Regional Science: Asian Perspectives 26,
https://doi.org/10.1007/978-981-10-8615-1_13

Murray C. Kemp (1984) has been most influential. Using a static model where donor countries do not coordinate their policies, Kemp (1984) proves a remarkable proposition: the aggregate amount of aid a country receives is independent of small changes in the distribution of wealth among donor countries.

The assumptions underlying Kemp's 1984 model have been relaxed in several directions. For example, Kemp's invariance result is known to rely on the assumption that changes in income distribution are small enough so that the aid provided by each of the donor countries remains positive after the changes. Bergstrom, Blume, and Varian (1986) show how Kemp's result must be modified in the case where some donor countries reach a corner solution. Another assumption of Kemp's model is that the utility function of each donor country depends on only two arguments: their consumption and the aggregate amount of aid the recipient gets. Under that assumption, the aggregate aid is a pure public good. However, several authors (e.g., Andreoni 1990; Andreoni et al. 2008) have argued that donors could benefit from feeling a warm glow from the act of giving, in other words, their altruism may be impure. In response to this, Kemp and Long (2009) include warm glows in a dynamic model of foreign aid, where donor countries are noncooperative. In all these generalizations, the authors keep the main assumption of Kemp's model, namely, each donor country maximizes its utility (which may include the welfare of the recipient as an argument) while taking as given the actions of other donors. I call this behavioral assumption Nashian, as it is the fundamental feature of the noncooperative game theory approach of John Nash (1951). As is well known, because of the incentives to free ride, the provision of foreign aid under Nashian behavior is inefficiently low (Cornes and Sandler 1986).

The present chapter makes two contributions to the foreign aid literature. First, following the lines of thought of Laffont (1975) and Roemer (2010, 2015), I argue that some donors may adopt a different mode of behavior, called Kantian behavior. Recall that Kant puts forward the argument that humans, as rational and moral beings, ought to obey the categorical imperative. According to Kant, "there is only one categorical imperative, and it is this: Act only on the maxim by which you can at the same time will that it should become a universal law" (Kant 1785; as translated by Hill and Zweig 2002, p. 222). Or, to put it simply, each ought to act as they want others to act (Cornes and Sandler 1986, p. 377). Applying this general moral law to the question of foreign aid, I argue that in choosing among the various levels of aid to give, the government of a Kantian donor country would ask itself the following question: what is the level of foreign aid that we would wish countries in similar stage of development as ours to give?

In this chapter, I show that this Kantian type of behavior would lead Kantian donor countries to overcome the prisoner's dilemma problem, provided they restrict their choice to pure strategies. I relate this finding to the work of Kemp and Shimomura (1995a, b, c) which shows that the prisoner's dilemma is a non-problem if players are symmetric and do not think in the Nashian way. While the results are similar, the reasons are different. Kemp and Shimomura argue that symmetric agents would restrict their choice only to those outcomes that are on the diagonal boxes of the payoff matrix of the prisoner's dilemma game, because they are aware that in equilibrium symmetric players would end up on a diagonal box. My reasoning is somewhat different: symmetric players are aware that they are in the same boat, and it is natural for them to cooperate tacitly in such situations, given that they are morally committed to the Kantian ethics.

My second contribution is to investigate foreign aid equilibrium in mixed strategies, in a model where there are donor countries of both types, Kantian and Nashian. I show that when Kantian donors choose among mixed strategies, there may exist a Kant−Nash equilibrium where Kantian donors choose their levels of foreign aid probabilistically. This does not mean that Kantian donors fail to cooperate. I argue that if they could sign a binding agreement on which mixed strategy to play, they would agree on the mixed strategy Kant−Nash equilibrium. An interesting property of Kant−Nash equilibrium in mixed strategies is that when a Kantian is converted into a Nashian, the remaining Kantians may move from a pure strategy equilibrium to a mixed strategy equilibrium, and the aggregate foreign aid may fall more than proportionately.

This chapter is organized as follows. Section 13.2 discusses the emergence of Kantian behavior as an outcome of an evolutionary process and presents various concepts of equilibrium when a subset of agents adheres to the Kantian ethics (or something similar, as taught by most religions and moral philosophies). Section 13.3 presents a model of foreign aid where donors can choose only pure strategies. Section 13.4 allows agents to choose mixed strategies and characterizes the mixed-strategy Kant−Nash equilibrium. Section 13.5 shows how the equilibrium changes if one Kantian country defects and joins the Nashian camp. Section 13.6 discusses the relationship between the Kant−Nash theory and alternative theories that explain prosocial behavior. Section 13.7 concludes.

13.2 Gifts, Aid, Cooperation, and Moral Norms

Gift giving is as old as life itself. In human history, gifts and reciprocity are well recognized forms of cooperation, as evidenced in the xenial relationship in ancient Greek societies, as well as in modern societies that preserve the gift-giving tradition, such as Japan and the Au and Gnau peoples of Papua New Guinea (Heinrich et al. 2001). It is arguable that the Kantian categorical imperative is a fruit of evolution. Natural selection favors societies in which members have developed the habit of, or reverence for, cooperation. Among the primates, humans have a higher propensity to cooperate than other apes (Tomasello 2014a, b, 2016; de Waal 1996; Kitcher 2011). Experimental evidence suggests that chimpanzees and capuchin monkeys also have a well-developed sense of fairness (Proctor et al. 2013; Brosnan and de Waal 2003), which is very much related to cooperation.

In human societies, the propensity for cooperation is a product of evolution that is reinforced by moral education that spreads the *meme* (Dawkins 1989, p. 192). It is well recognized that tastes and morality are products of evolution (Bala and Long 2005; Bowles and Gintis 2011). Along the evolutionary path, norms of behavior are developed. Elster (2017) makes a distinction between moral norms and social norms. While social norms always involve punishment by third parties (Elster 1989), moral norms need not be associated with external punishment.

Without moral norms or social norms, no human society can survive. Adam Smith puts this view most forcefully in his 1790 book, *A Theory of Moral Sentiment*: "Upon the tolerable observance of these duties, depends the very existence of human society, which would crumble into nothing if mankind were not generally impressed with a reverence for those important rules of conduct" (Smith 1790, Part III, Chap. 6, p. 190).

While it is true that for the market mechanism to function efficiently there is no need for the bakers and the grocers to include the welfare of their clients in their utility function, it is also true that the market outcome would be dismal if factories were to dump their toxic waste into waterways and regulators were to look the other way.

Eminent economists such as Smith, Edgeworth, Arrow, and Sen have long recognized the importance of morality in economic behavior. Nevertheless, for a formalization of the role of Kantian ethics in economic behavior, the economic profession owes much to Jean-Jacques Laffont (1975) and John Roemer (2010, 2015). In fact, Laffont is among the first to point out that in many social situations individuals do not act in a Nashian way. In choosing their action (e.g., should I leave this beer can on the beach, or should I dispose of it properly?), a morally motivated person would do what she would wish other people to do. Thus, she would choose an action that would maximize her utility, subject to the constraint that all others would choose the same action. Laffont calls this a macroeconomic constraint. Roemer (2010, 2015) refers to this constraint as a Kantian optimization protocol.

Note that there is a subtle difference between ethical behavior and altruism. Altruism means that you include other people's welfare in your utility function, such that when other people's welfare goes up, you feel happier, and when it goes down, you feel less happy. Morality means that you choose to do the right thing. In principle, morality and altruism are quite distinct concepts, though perhaps in reality there is a positive correlation between people's degree of morality and their degree of altruism. Such a correlation would not be too surprising, because both are related to the cooperative trait, which is arguably favored by evolution.

Laffont's formal model of Kantian behavior assumes that individuals are identical in all respects. He knows that in a more general model where individuals are not identical, his proposed macroeconomic constraint that all individuals take the same action must be replaced by some formalization of the idea that individuals take similar actions. For various formulations of the concept of similar actions, the readers are referred to Roemer (2010, 2015).

The departing point of this chapter is the realization that in the theoretical world of Laffont (1975) and Roemer (2010, 2015), all individuals are Kantians. They are all saints. This chapter follows the lead of Long (2016), who takes a more realistic view of human interactions: In Long (2016), there are Kantians and Nashians, and even though they may all have the same utility function, they choose their actions according to different principles. As in Roemer (2015), we take it that each Kantian would affirm the following: "I hold the norm that says: If I want to deviate from a contemplated action profile (of my community's members), then I may do so only if I would have all others deviate in like manner" (Roemer 2015, p.46). Each Nashian, on the other hand, would choose an action to maximize his utility, taking as given the actions of others. Long (2016) offers two alternative interpretations of the words *all others* in the Kantian norm stated above. In one interpretation, *all others* refer to all other Kantians, and excluding the Nashians. In another interpretation, *all others* refer to all Kantians and Nashians in the community. The equilibrium that corresponds to the first interpretation is called the Kant–Nash equilibrium, while the one that corresponds to the second interpretation may be called the *inclusive* Kant–Nash equilibrium, because Nashians are included in the Kantian thought experiments.

Grafton, Kompas, and Long (2017) propose a further generalization. They introduce the concept of generalized Kant–Nash equilibrium. They envisage that each Kantian has in mind a set of co-movers. She would deviate from a contemplated action profile only if she would wish her co-movers to deviate in a similar manner, but possibly not to the same extent. Grafton et al. (2017, p. 4) wrote: "Thus, in a situation where everyone steals, when a Kantian considers stop stealing, she contemplates the potential consequence of others following suit by slightly reducing their stealing. Is there any moral philosophy to support this? Buddhism encourages a vegetarian diet: humans should avoid the killing of animals, even for food. However, many Buddhists would be happy enough if they could convince some non-vegetarians to refrain from eating meat a few days per month."

It is important to discuss what we mean by equilibrium when there are both Kantians and Nashians. Grafton et al. (2017) argue that a Kant–Nash equilibrium is an equilibrium in the sense of self-fulfilling predictions: "At a Kant–Nash equilibrium, every Kantian knows that all other Kantians do not deviate from the equilibrium. Every Kantian has a correct model of other Kantians who in turn have a correct model of the model of other Kantians, and so on. Conversely, every Nashian knows that Kantians use the Kantian protocol to determine if they would deviate or not, and they know that the Kantians know what they know, and so on." As an example of a Kantian equilibrium, they write: "The third co-author of this paper maintains that if he discovers that an hour ago he accidentally left his wallet at the cashier counter of a rural store in Japan, he can safely predict that when he drives back to the store, the wallet will be handed back to him by the store keeper, who has been waiting for him to return to collect it. It is plausible to argue that a Kantian equilibrium is a self-fulfilling prediction held by all players in a society where the Kantian *meme* has become widespread."

Finally, it is important to note that while the concept of a Kantian equilibrium with heterogeneous agents has been formalized only recently (Roemer 2010, 2015), the idea of Kantian behavior as a possible explanation of tacit cooperation has been around for quite a long time. Arrow (1973) believes that one can appeal to individuals' sense of ethics to attenuate the tragedy of the commons. Around the same time as Laffont (1975), Sen (1977) offers a profound critique of the Nashian assumption of maximization of utility taking as given the action of others. Johansen (1976) disputes the hypothesis that individuals have only self-regarding preferences. Cornes and Sandler (1986, p. 377) refer to Kantian ethics in their discussion of private provision of public goods. Elster (1989) reviews the role of social norms in economic theory. Sethi and Somanathan (1996) model the evolution of social norms in common property resource use. Brekke et al. (2003) discuss moral motivation in economic affairs. Breton et al. (2010) models the role of social norms in the evolution of membership of international environmental agreements. Buchholz et al. (2014) model enforcement of social norms.

13.3 A Model of Foreign Aid with Kantian and Nashian Donors

We now construct a simple model of foreign aid that illustrates the role of tacit Kantian cooperation. We consider a one-shot game, with simultaneous moves. There are m donor countries, of which n are Nashians and k are Kantians. For simplicity, assume that each donor country can choose only between two actions: to donate x_H dollars or x_L dollars to the Third World countries (collectively called the recipient, for short). The values x_H and x_L are exogenously given.

Denote by X the total donation. Assume that all donor countries have the same income, Y, and the same utility function, U, but they belong to two different behavioral types: a donor country is either Kantian or Nashian. Let S_K and S_N denote the set of Kantian countries and the set of Nashian countries, respectively. Without loss of generality, we may assume that the first n countries are Nashian and the remaining $m - n$ countries are Kantian, and write

$S_N = \{1, 2, 3, \ldots, n\}$ and $S_K = \{n + 1, n + 2, n + 3, \ldots, n + k\}$, where $n + k = m$.

Let S denote the union of the sets S_K and S_N. We assume that for any donor country $i \in S$, the utility function is $u_i = U(c_i, X)$ where c_i is the donor country's consumption, and X is the total donation received by the recipient. We assume that the utility function is increasing in consumption and in total donation. Notice that there is no warm glow in this utility function: the donor does not get enjoyment from the act of giving.

The consumption c_i is the difference between the country's income, Y, and its donation, which is either x_H dollars or x_L dollars. By assumption, each of the developed countries must choose between x_H and x_L. It is convenient to define $\Delta = x_H - x_L$ and write country 's donation as $x_i = x_L + \delta_i \Delta$, where δ_i is either zero or 1. Its consumption is $c_i = Y - x_L - \delta_i \Delta$. Denote by X_{-i} the aggregate donation from all countries except country i, we have $X = X_{-i} + (x_L + \delta_i \Delta)$. Donor country i perceives correctly that, given X_{-i}, its utility is entirely determined by its choice of δ_i. If δ_i is 1, we say its donation is large, and if δ_i is zero, we say its donation is small. The utility of donor country i is then $u_i = U(Y - x_L - \delta_i \Delta, X_{-i} + x_L + \delta_i \Delta) \equiv v(\delta_i, X_{-i})$. To emphasize the contrast between utility and moral commitment, we make the following assumption:

Assumption A 13.1 For all nonnegative X_{-i}, the donor country i will have a higher utility if it chooses to be a small donor (i.e., $\delta_i=0$) rather than a big donor (i.e., $\delta_i = 1$). In symbols, $v(0, X_{-i}) > v(1, X_{-i})$ for all $X_{-i} \geq 0$.

Clearly, Assumption A 13.1 implies that it is rational (in the Nash sense) for any country $i \in S$ to choose to be a small donor, regardless of the value X_{-i}. Our next assumption, Assumption A 13.2 below, ensures that the game we describe is a prisoner's dilemma game for any pair of donor countries, $\{i,j\}$. For this purpose, let us define X_{-ij} as the sum of donations from all countries in S except $\{i,j\}$. Then, if i and j choose the same action, i.e., $\delta_i = \delta_j = \delta$, the utility of each of them is $u = U$ $(Y - x_L - \delta\Delta, X_{-ij} + 2x_L + 2\delta\Delta) \equiv w(\delta, X_{-ij})$.

Assumption A 13.2 For all nonnegative X_{-ij}, if countries i and j could sign a binding contract that forces both to take the same action that they agree upon, the only binding contract that would maximize their utility is the one that specifies that $\delta = 1$. In symbols, $w(1, X_{-ij}) > w(0, X_{-ij})$ for all $X_{-ij} \geq 0$.

Assumptions A 13.1 and A 13.2 taken together imply that cooperation (to agree on the high aid level x_H) by any pair of countries would increase their utility, but since it is not possible to sign a binding contract, any country that adopts Nashian behavior would choose to give only x_L.

Remark 13.3.1 Our model is quite general in the sense that there is no need to specify the utility function U. Readers who like concrete examples may consider the following functional form: $U(c_i, X) = c_i + \beta X$ where $1 > \beta > 1/2$. It is easy to verify that this function satisfies Assumptions A 13.1 and A 13.2.

Let us now define the concept of Kant−Nash equilibrium in pure strategies for our foreign aid game where countries can only choose one of the two aid levels x_H and x_L or, equivalently, each must choose its own $\delta_i \in \{0, 1\}$.

Definition D 13.1 (Kant−Nash equilibrium in pure strategies, with only binary choice.) In the binary choice game where all players have the same utility function $U(c, X)$, the same income Y, and the same individual binary strategy space $\{0, 1\}$, an action profile $\left(\delta_1^N, \delta_2^N, \dots, \delta_n^N, \delta^*, \delta^*, \dots, \delta^*\right)$ in the strategy space $\{0, 1\}^m$ is a Kant−Nash equilibrium in pure strategies if the following conditions are satisfied:

(i) For any Nashian player $j \in S_N$, choosing the alternative action $\delta_j \neq \delta_j^N$ in the individual strategy space $\{0, 1\}$ would reduce her utility, given that all others do not deviate.

(ii) All Kantian players use the same strategy δ^*, and each Kantian player finds that if she were to choose the alternative action $\delta \neq \delta^*$ in $\{0, 1\}$, her utility would fall if all other Kantians were to follow suit.

Remark 13.3.2 Part (ii) of Definition D 13.1 reflects the idea that Kantians choose an action according to the categorical imperative: do not do anything that you would not like if everyone in your community (of Kantians) behaved in the same way.

It is easy to verify that the game described above has a unique Kant−Nash equilibrium: all Nashians choose x_L (i.e., they set their $\delta_j = 0$), and all Kantians choose x_H (i.e., each sets her δ_{n+i} at 1). This is because Assumption A 13.1 implies that for each Nashian, $\delta = 0$ is the dominant strategy, while Assumption A 13.2 implies that each Kantian finds that by moving from $\delta = 0$ to $\delta = 1$, her utility will increase if all Kantians move up the same way. Let us state the result as Proposition 13.1.

Proposition 13.1 *Assume donor countries are restricted to pure strategies, and their choice set is $\{x_L, x_H\}$. If Assumptions A 13.1 and A 13.2 are satisfied, all Nashian countries will choose x_L and all Kantian countries will choose x_H.*

Corollary 13.1 If all donor countries are Kantians, the prisoner's dilemma is overcome by tacit cooperation. Each donor country's equilibrium utility level is $u = U(Y - x_H, m x_H)$.

Let us relate our Corollary 13.1 to the argument put forward by Kemp and Shimomura (1995a, b, c). They state that if players are symmetric, then the prisoner's dilemma disappears, because players would foresee that any equilibrium must be on the diagonal boxes, and all of them can see that the individual payoff on the diagonal box that corresponds to full cooperation is higher than that on the other diagonal box. They assert that this is simply the outcome of logical thinking. To quote Kemp and Shimomura (1995a, p. 247): "If each agent is like every other agent, and if all agents know this to be so, then each agent will make its choices on the understanding that all other agents make the same choice. In effect, each agent will choose on behalf of the whole set of agents." Thus, according to Kemp and Shimomura (1995a, b, c), and also Kemp and Long (1992), cooperation is the logical consequence of symmetry. (See Kaneko and Suzumura 1995a, b, for a critique of this view). My argument in this chapter is different: it is based on Kantian ethics. I maintain that if agents hold Kantian norms, then they will cooperate in any symmetric game. Finally, please note that I can slightly relax the assumption that players have identical utility function, without changing the results. What I need is that their payoffs are the same when they take the same action. For example, in the prisoner's dilemma game, one can modify slightly the payoffs in the non-diagonal boxed so that they need not be mirror images of each other, and the essential results remain unchanged.

13.4   Mixed Strategy Equilibrium in a Model of Foreign Aid with Kantian and Nashian Donors

Let us now consider the case where donor countries can choose mixed strategies. Instead of being forced to choose between x_H and x_L, countries are now able to choose a probability distribution over the two pure strategies. To economize on notation, in this section, we set $x_H = 1$ and $x_L = 0$. Furthermore, we assume that initially there are two Nashian countries and three Kantian countries, i.e., $S_N = \{1, 2\}$ and $S_K = \{3, 4, 5\}$. Each country's income is set at $Y = 2$. With these assumptions, the aggregate donation to the Third World countries cannot exceed five.Later, we will investigate the extent to which expected aggregate donation may fall, when one Kantian country, say country 3, becomes Nashian.

Under the above simplification, the utility function of each potential donor country, $U(c, X)$ is defined over the set $\{(c, X) : c \in \{1, 2\}, X \in \{0, 1, 2, 3, 4, 5\}\}$. Then our assumptions A 13.1 and A 13.2 on utility implies the following utility ranking of feasible bundles:

Property A 13.3 (Utility Ranking)
$U(2, 5) > U(2, 4) > U(1, 5) > U(2, 3) > U(1, 4) > U(2, 2) > U(1, 3) > U(2, 1) > U(1, 2) > U(2, 0) > U(1, 1) > U(1, 0)$.

Remark 13.4.1 We do not need to specify an explicit functional form for $U(c, X)$ that represents the above ordinal ranking of the various feasible bundles (c, X) . However, readers who prefer a concrete representation may use the following function: $U(c, X) = T(F(c, X))$ where $T(.)$ is any monotone increasing transformation, and where $F(c, X) = \pi + (c + \beta X)\sigma$, with $1 > \beta > 1/2$, where $\sigma > 0$ and π is an arbitrary constant.

Clearly, given the above ranking of feasible bundles, the Nashian countries find that their dominant strategy is to donate nothing. Thus $\delta_1^N = \delta_2^N = 0$. It remains to investigate the choice of the Kantian countries. Knowing that the Nashian countries donate nothing, each Kantian country j faces the following possible bundles for (c_j, X):

$$\{(2, 2), (1, 3), (2, 1), (1, 2), (2, 0), (1, 1)\}$$

Without loss of generality, we can adopt the following normalization: $U(1, 3) = 1$, $U(2, 0) = 0$. Then we can write $U(2, 2) = a$, $U(1, 3) = 1$, $U(2, 1) = b$, $U(1, 2) = f$, $U(2, 0) = 0$, $U(1, 1) = g$, and, due to Property A 13.3, it follows that $a > 1 > b > f > 0 > g$. Suppose for the moment that the Kantian country 3 chooses $\delta_3 = 1$. Then, conditional on $\delta_3 = 1$, the other donor countries, 4 and 5, face the following payoff matrix, called Matrix A:

$$A \equiv \begin{pmatrix} (1, 1) & (f, a) \\ (a, f) & (b, b) \end{pmatrix}.$$

The upper diagonal entry $(1, 1)$ in Matrix A represents the utility of countries 4 and 5 when they both choose to donate one unit of output each, given that $\delta_3 = 1$, so that the total donation is 3 and their consumption is 1 (Recall that $U(1, 3) = 1$). The lower diagonal entry (b, b) represents the utility of countries 4 and 5 when they both choose to donate zero unit of output each, given that $\delta_3 = 1$, so that the total donation is 1, and their consumption is 0. (Recall that $U(2, 1) = b$.) The entry (f, a) is the payoff pair when country 4 (the Row Player) chooses to donate one unit of output while country 5 (the Column Player) chooses to donate nothing: the aggregate donation is then $X = 2$, and we know that $U(1, 2) = f$ and $U(2, 2) = a > 1 > f$. Finally, the entry (a, f) is the mirror image of the entry (f, a). Since $a > 1$ and $b > f$, the above matrix is the prisoner's dilemma game for countries 4 and 5. If they behave in the usual Nashian way, they would choose to donate nothing, because it is the dominant strategy. However, since we assume they are Kantian, we will show that they will not choose this strategy. Instead, they will choose a mixed strategy. Before characterizing their Kantian mixed strategy equilibrium, we must consider the payoff matrix for countries 4 and 5 if country 3 chooses to donate nothing. This matrix is called Matrix B:

$$B \equiv \begin{pmatrix} (f,f) & (g,b) \\ (b,g) & (0,0) \end{pmatrix}.$$

Again, if countries 4 and 5 were Nashian, when they face this matrix, their dominant strategy is to donate nothing, and they will end up with the payoff pair $(0,0)$. Being Kantians, however, they each must choose a probability p_j ($j = 4, \ 5$) with which they donate one unit of output (and they donate nothing with probability $1 - p_j$). When they make this choice, they do not know what is the probability with which country 3 chooses to donate one unit of output. Conditional on being faced with Matrix A, the expected utility of country 4 is $V_4(p_4, p_5 \parallel A) = p_4 p_5 + a(1 - p_4) p_5 + f p_4 (1 - p_5) + b(1 - p_4)(1 - p_5)$. And, conditional on being faced with Matrix B, its expected utility is $V_4(p_4, p_5 \parallel B) = f p_4 p_5 + b(1 - p_4) p_5 + g p_4 (1 - p_5) + 0(1 - p_4)(1 - p_5)$. Since country 3 chooses to donate one unit of output with probability p_3, and zero unit of output with probability $1 - p_3$, the expected utility of country 4 is

$$W_4(p_4, p_5, p_3) = p_3 V_4(p_4, p_5 \parallel A) + (1 - p_3) V_4(p_4, p_5 \parallel B)$$

As we have argued, when Kantian countries are symmetric, each Kantian country j would choose a probability p that would maximize its own utility, if other Kantian countries were to choose the same p. Thus they tacitly agree to choose p to maximize

$$W(p) \equiv p^3 + ap^2(1 - p) + f\left[2p^2(1 - p)\right] + b\left[2p(1 - p)^2\right] + gp(1 - p)^2$$

To formalize our discussion, we state the following Definition D 13.2 and Proposition 13.2.

Definition D 13.2 (Kant–Nash equilibrium in mixed strategies.) Consider the binary choice game where all players have the same utility function $U(c, X)$, the same income Y, and the same individual binary pure strategy space $\{0, 1\}$. Assume there are two Nashian countries and three Kantian countries. The vector $\left(p_1^N, p_2^N, p^*, p^*, p^*\right)$ is a Kant–Nash equilibrium in mixed strategies if the following conditions are satisfied:

(i) For any Nashian player $j \in S_N$, choosing any alternative probability $p_j \neq p_j^N$ would reduce her utility, given that all others do not deviate.

(ii) All Kantian players use the same probability p^*, and each Kantian player finds that if she were to choose the alternative probability $p \neq p^*$, her utility would fall if all other Kantians were to follow suit.

We can now state Proposition 13.2, the main result of this section. (A proof is available upon request.)

Proposition 13.2 *Assume donor countries can choose mixed strategies, and that Assumptions A 13.1 and A 13.2 are satisfied, which implies that Property A 13.3 is satisfied. Let $S_N = \{1,2\}$ and $S_K = \{3,4,5\}$. In equilibrium, the two Nashian countries will donate nothing, and all three Kantian countries will choose p^* given by:*

(i) *If $a + 2f \leq 3$, then $p^* = 1$. That is, all Kantian countries choose the highest permissible donation, $x_H = 1$, with probability 1.*

(ii) *If $a + 2f > 3$, then Kantian countries will choose a non-degenerate mixed strategy $0 < p^* < 1$, where*

$$p^* = \frac{2\mu + \sqrt{4\mu^2 + 12(2b + g)[(a + 2f) - 1 - (2b + g)]}}{6[(a + 2f) - 1 - (2b + g)]}$$

and $\mu \equiv (a + 2f) - 2(2b + g)$.

Remark 13.4.2 The condition $a + 2f > 3$ means that even for Kantian countries, on average, it pays to deviate from full donation some of the time. Consider the Matrix A. If all three Kantian countries donate, their utility will be one each. If one country does not donate while the other two donate, the sum of their utility is $a + 2f$. In fact, in this case, if there were a social planner that must recommend a common probability p to all three Kantian countries, to maximize their expected utility, she would recommend the p^* given in part (ii) of Proposition 13.2.

Let us provide a few numerical examples to illustrate Proposition 13.2.

Numerical Example 13.4.1 (The three Kantian countries donate with probability 1.) Let $a = 1.3$, $b = 0.9$, $f = 0.3$, $g = -0.1$, and then $p^* = 1$.

Numerical Example 13.4.2 (Each Kantian country donates with a probability smaller than 1.) Let $a = 1.3$, $b = 0.9$, $f = 0.7$, $g = -0.1$, and then $p^* = 0.96621$.

13.5 Mixed Strategy Equilibrium: Defection of a Kantian Country to the Nashian Camp

In this section, we maintain the assumptions and notations of Sect. 13.4, with the exception that the original Kantian country 3 now becomes a Nashian. How does this affect the equilibrium strategy of the remaining Kantian countries, countries 5 and 6? We will show below that, under some assumptions, these countries will move from the equilibrium of donating with probability 1 to a non-degenerate mixed strategy equilibrium.

Since country 3 has become Nashian, it will choose the dominant strategy of zero donation. The two remaining Kantian countries then face the Matrix B in Sect. 13.4.

The expected utility of country 4 is $V_4(p_4, p_5 \parallel B) = fp_4p_5 + b(1 - p_4)$ $p_5 + gp_4(1 - p_5) + 0(1 - p_4)(1 - p_5)$. Applying the Kantian ethics, country 4 will seek a value p that maximize $W(p) = V_4(p, p \parallel B) = fp^2 + b(1 - p)p + gp(1 - p) + 0$ $(1 - p)^2$. Country 5 will do likewise. Then we obtain the following result. A proof is available upon request.

Proposition 13.3 Mixed Strategy Kant–Nash equilibrium after defection of a Kantian country. Assume donor countries can choose mixed strategies and that Assumptions A 13.1 and A 13.2 are satisfied, which implies that Property A 13.3 is satisfied. Let $S_N = \{1, 2, 3\}$ and $S_K = \{4, 5\}$ after the defection of country 3 to the Nashian camp. In equilibrium, the Nashian countries will donate nothing and the remaining Kantian countries will choose a common $p^{\#}$ given by

(i) If $b + g \leq 2f$, then $p^{\#} = 1$. That is, both Kantian countries choose the highest permissible donation, $x_H = 1$, with probability 1.
(ii) If $b + g > 2f$, then both Kantian countries will choose a non-degenerate mixed strategy $0 < p^{\#} < 1$, where $p^{\#} = \frac{b+g}{(b+g)+(b+g-2f)}$

Remark 13.5.1 The intuition behind Proposition 13.3 is as follows. Consider the Matrix B. If both Kantian countries donate, each of them will obtain the utility level f. If one country does not donate while the other donates, the sum of their utility is $b + g$. Thus, in the case where $b + g > 2f$ if there were a social planner that must recommend a common probability p to both Kantian countries, to maximize their expected utility, she would recommend the $p^{\#}$ given in part (ii) of Proposition 13.3.

Numerical Example 13.5.1 (Both Kantian countries donate with probability less than 1.) Let $a = 1.3, b = 0.9, f = 0.3, g = -0.1$, and then $b + g > 2f$. Consequently, $p^{\#} = 0.8$.

Numerical Example 13.5.2 (Both Kantian countries donate with a probability 1.) Let $a = 1.3, b = 0.9, f = 0.7, g = -0.1$, and then $b + g < 2f$. Hence $p^{\#} = 1$.

Taking both Numerical Examples 13.4.1 (in Sect. 13.4) and Numerical Example 13.5.1 (this section), we have a striking illustration: when there are three Kantian countries and two Nashian countries, the total donation to Third World countries is $X = 3$, with probability 1. But as soon as one Kantian country is converted to the Nashian faith, the expected size of the total donation is less than two. The fall in the total donation is greater than the fall in the size of the (implicit) Kantian coalition.

13.6 Relationship with Alternative Theories that Explain Prosocial Behavior

Many economists, social scientists, and philosophers have sought to reconcile, on the one hand, the maximization of self-regarding utility based on (narrowly defined) individual rationality, and on the other hand, the concern for moral conduct and distributive justice (Smith 1790; Gossen 1854; Edgeworth 1881; Harsanyi 1955; Rawls 1971; Steiner 2011; Long and Martinet 2016; Tomasello 2014a, b, 2016). The tension between selfish interest and distributive fairness had its origin in the hunter-gatherer mode of social cooperation. Tomasello (2014b, p. 189), referring to the famous stag hunt game, explains the relationship between cooperation and sharing: "In a Stag Hunt situation, if an individual can trust that another individual will be going for the stag, then it is in her interest to go too (assuming that she is confident that the spoils will be shared in a satisfactory way)." He argues that the evolutionary basis for prosocial behavior might be the interdependence of individuals who need one another. Moral norms eventually developed from the realization that cooperation is crucial in economic and social activities. The prisoner's dilemma is no longer a dilemma once the moral norm internalizes the realization that "If we do not hang together we will be hung separately." Moral norms, together with guilt and shame, seem unique to human societies.

This chapter argues that some countries give foreign aid on moral ground. This line of thought, based on Kantian ethics and consequently non-Nash behavior, can be used to explain why we often observe prosocial behavior in the lab as well as in the field. In fact, Nash equilibrium has a very poor track record in explaining empirical data (Goeree and Holt 2001). In this section, we review briefly some alternative theories that can explain the same observation.

An alternative approach is to keep Nashian behavior but modify the utility function, to include other-regarding preferences. Thus, Fehr and Schmidt (1999) assume that subjects have preference for fairness; Bolton and Ockenfels (2000) include preferences for equity, reciprocity, and competition (ERC). Andreoni (1990) includes in the utility function the warm-glow from doing an altruistic act. In fact, non-parental altruism could also have its evolutionary roots in the social cooperation much needed in the hunter-gatherer societies. As Tomasello (2014b, p. 190) explains, "the basic idea is that when individuals must collaborate or die, their partners become very valuable to them, and so, they must care for them." Important experimental works to identify the relative importance of various factors include Charness and Rabin (2002) and Camerer (2003); see also Andreoni et al. (2008). Do Kant–Nash theories explain the data better? Admittedly, economic data are fuzzy and empirical evidence always needs to be interpreted with care. According to Bolle and Ockelfels (1990), moral standards explain observed behaviors better than altruism. Many subjects explain their choice in experiments in terms of wanting to do the right thing (Dawes and Thaler 1988; Charness and Dufwenberg 2006).

Another approach is to drop the assumption of perfect Nash rationality. There are a variety of models of bounded rationality, assuming departure from full rationality, for example, the cognitive hierarchy approach (see Camerer and Fehr 2006, for a review). A related approach is neuroeconomics (see Rubinstein 2008, for a review). It has been suggested that humans are innately wired to care (Tankersley et al. 2007). A challenge is to look at fMRI images of brain activity to determine brain regions or neural circuitry that are involved in prosocial behavior.

13.7   Concluding Remarks

This chapter has proposed a theory of foreign aid where some donor countries are motivated by Kantian ethics, while at the same time, there are also countries that are self-regarding and maximize a self-regarding utility function, taking as given the strategies of other countries. An interesting result of our model is that under some conditions on the payoffs, Kantian countries may play mixed strategies. The equilibrium mixed strategy they choose may vary with the number of Kantian countries. A drop in this number may generate a more than proportional drop in the expected aggregate donation.

A possible extension of the model is to allow richer scope for interactions among players, allowing, for example, punishments for noncooperation. The interaction between Kantians and Nashians can potentially explain many social and economic phenomena. For example, Camerer and Fehr (2006) give examples where the existence of strong reciprocators may induce self-regarding players to behave cooperatively. Another extension would be to study the dynamics of population share of Kantian players. For example, one can think of an intermediate type of players, called conditional Kantians: these players are willing to act as Kantians only if there are enough Kantians around. The transition from conditional Kantian status to full Kantian status would be an interesting subject for future research. Finally, the model could be extended to allow for dynamic games (see Dockner et al. 2000; Long 2010) and for intergenerational transmissions of moral values, as in Long (2017).

Acknowledgment   The author is grateful to his life-long mentor, Professor Murray C. Kemp, for helpful comments and suggestions. He thanks Geir Asheim, Wolfgang Buchholz, Dirk Ruebbelke, Justin Leroux, Anthony Millner, and Binh Tran-Nam for comments and discussions.

References

Andreoni, J. (1990). Impure altruism and donations to public goods: A theory of warm-glow giving. *The Economic Journal, 100*, 464–477.

Andreoni, J., Harbaugh, W. T., & Vesterlund, L. (2008). Altruism in experiments. In S. Durlauf & L. E. Blume (Eds.), *The new Palgrave dictionary in economics* (2nd ed., pp. 105–108). New York: Palgrave Macmillan.

Arrow, K. J. (1973). Social responsibility and economic efficiency. *Public Policy, 21*, 303–317.

Bala, V., & Long, N. V. (2005). International trade and cultural diversity with preference selection. *European Journal of Political Economy, 21*, 143–162.

Bergstrom, T., Blume, L., & Varian, H. (1986). On the private provision of public goods. *Journal of Public Economics, 29*, 25–49.

Bhagwati, J., Brecher, R., & Hatta, T. (1983). The generalized theory of transfers and welfare: Bilateral transfers in a multilateral world. *American Economic Review, 73*, 606–618.

Bolle, F., & Ockelfels, A. (1990). Prisoners dilemma as a game of incomplete information. *Journal of Economic Psychology, 11*, 69–84.

Bolton, G. E., & Ockenfels, A. (2000). ERC: A theory of equity, reciprocity, and competition. *American Economic Review, 90*, 166–192.

Bowles, S., & Gintis, H. (2011). *A cooperative species: Human reciprocity and its evolution.* Princeton: Princeton University Press.

Brekke, K. A., Kverndok, S., & Nyborg, K. (2003). An economic model of moral motivation. *Journal of Public Economics, 87,* 1967–1983.

Breton, M., Sbragia, L., & Zaccour, G. (2010). A dynamic model of international environmental agreements. *Environmental and Resource Economics, 45,* 25–48.

Brosnan, S. F., & de Waal, F. (2003). Monkeys reject unequal pays. *Nature, 425,* 297–299.

Buchholz, W., Falkinger, J., & Ruebbelke, D. (2014). Non-government public norm enforcement in large societies as a two-stage game with voluntary public good provision. *Journal of Public Economic Theory, 16,* 899–916.

Camerer, C. (2003). *Behavioral game theory: Experiments in strategic interaction.* Princeton: Princeton University Press.

Camerer, C., & Fehr, E. (2006). When does economic man dominate social behavior? *Science, 311,* 47–52.

Charness, G., & Dufwenberg, M. (2006). Promises and partnership. *Econometrica, 74,* 1579–1601.

Charness, G., & Rabin, M. (2002). Understanding pro-social behavior with simple tests. *Quarterly Journal of Economics, 117,* 817–869.

Cornes, R., & Sandler, T. (1986). *The theory of externalities, public goods, and Club goods.* Cambridge: Cambridge University Press.

Dawes, R., & Thaler, R. (1988). Anomalies: Cooperation. *Journal of Economic Perspectives, 2,* 187–197.

Dawkins, R. (1989). *The selfish Gene.* Oxford: Oxford University Press.

de Waal, F. (1996). *Good natured: The origins of right and wrong in humans and other animals.* Cambridge: Harvard University Press.

Dockner, E. J., Jorgensen, S., Long, N. V., & Sorger, G. (2000). *Differential games in economics and management science.* Cambridge: Cambridge University Press.

Edgeworth, F. Y. (1881). *Mathematical psychics: An essay on the application of mathematics to the moral sciences.* London: C.K. Paul.

Elster, J. (1989). Social norms and economic theory. *Journal of Economic Perspectives, 3,* 99–117.

Elster, J. (2017). On seeing and being seen. *Social Choice and Welfare* (in press).

Fehr, E., & Schmidt, K. (1999). A theory of fairness, competition, and cooperation. *Quarterly Journal of Economics, 114,* 817–868.

Gocree, J. K., & Holt, C. A. (2001). Ten little treasures of game theory and ten intuitive contradictions. *American Economic Review, 91,* 1402–1422.

Gossen, H. H. (1854). *Der Entwickelung der Gestze des menschlichen Verkerhs, und der daraus Fliessenden Regeln fuer menschliches Handeln,* Braunschweig Vieweg und Sohn. Translated into English by R. C. Blitz. (1983). *The laws of human relations and the rules of human action derived therefrom.* Cambridge, MA: MIT Press.

Grafton, R. Q., Kompas, T., & Long, N. V. (2017). A brave new world? Kantian Nashian interaction and the dynamics of global climate change mitigation. *European Economic Review, 96,* 31–42.

Harsanyi, J. (1955). Cardinal welfare, individual ethics, and interpersonal comparisons of utility. *Journal of Political Economy, 63,* 309–321.

Heinrich, J., Boyd, R., Bowles, S., Camerer, C., Fehr, E., Gintis, H., & McElreath, R. (2001). In search of homo economicus: Behavioral experiments in 15 small-scaled societies. *American Economic Review, 91,* 73–78.

Hill, T. E., Jr., & Zweig, A. (2002). *Groundwork for the metaphysics of morals.* Oxford: Oxford University Press.

Johansen, L. (1976). *The theory of public goods: Misplaced emphasis.* Oslo: Institute of Economics, University of Oslo.

Kaneko, M., & Suzumura, K. (1995a). On symmetric agents: Comments on Kemp and Shimomura. *Japanese Economic Review, 46,* 296–299.

Kaneko, M., & Suzumura, K. (1995b). Further comments. *Japanese Economic Review, 46,* 301.

Kant, I. (1785). *Grundlegung zur Metaphysic der Sitten*. Translated by M. J. Gregor. (1998). *Groundwork for the Metaphysics of Morals*. Cambridge: Cambridge University Press.

Kemp, M. C. (1984). A note in the theory of international transfers. *Economics Letters, 14*, 259–262.

Kemp, M. C., & Long, N. V. (1992). Some properties of egalitarian economies. *Journal of Public Economics, 49*, 383–387.

Kemp, M. C., & Long, N. V. (2009). Foreign aid in the presence of corruption. *Review of International Economics, 17*, 230–243.

Kemp, M. C., & Shimomura, K. (1995a). The apparently innocuous representative agent. *Japanese Economic Review, 46*, 247–256.

Kemp, M. C., & Shimomura, K. (1995b). On the representative agents: Reply to Kaneko and Suzumura. *Japanese Economic Review, 46*, p 300.

Kemp, M. C., & Shimomura, K. (1995c). Why must we always follow Nash? A further reply. *Japanese Economic Review, 46*, p 302.

Kemp, M. C., & Shimomura, K. (2002). A theory of voluntary unrequited international transfers. *Japanese Economic Review, 53*, 290–300.

Kemp, M. C., & Shimomura, K. (2003). A theory of involuntary unrequited international transfers. *Journal of Political Economy, 111*, 686–692.

Kemp, M. C., Long, N. V., & Shimomura, K. (1992). A dynamic formulation of the foreign aid process. In G. Feichtinger (Ed.), *Dynamic economics models and optimal control* (pp. 91–103). Amsterdam: North Holland.

Kitcher, P. (2011). *The ethical project*. Cambridge: Harvard University Press.

Laffont, J.-J. (1975). Macroeconomic constraints, economic efficiency and ethics: An introduction to Kantian economics. *Economica, 42*, 430–437.

Long, N. V. (2010). *A survey of dynamic games in economics*. Singapore: World Scientific.

Long, N. V. (2016). Kant–Nash equilibrium in a quantity setting oligopoly. In P. von Mouch & F. Quartieri (Eds.), *Equilibrium theory for cournot oligopolies and related games: Essays in honour of Koji Okuguchi* (pp. 199–202). Berlin: Springer.

Long, N. V. (2017). *Sustainable fishery with endogenous evolution of Fisherfolk's behavior and biomass dynamics*, Typescript, McGill University.

Long, N. V., & Martinet, V. (2016). How to take rights seriously: A new approach to intertemporal evaluation of social alternatives (Working paper 2016-s-60). CIRANO, Montreal. (Revised and resubmitted to *social choice and welfare*).

Nash, J. (1951). Non-cooperative games. *Annals of Mathematics, 54*, 286–295.

Proctor, D., Williamson, R., de Waal, F., & Brosnan, S. (2013). Chimpanzees play the ultimatum game. *Proceedings of the National Academy of Sciences, 110*, 2070–2075.

Rawls, J. (1971). *A theory of justice*. Cambridge, MA: The Belknap Press of Harvard University Press.

Roemer, J. E. (2010). Kantian equilibrium. *Scandinavian Journal of Economics, 112*(1), 1–24.

Roemer, J. E. (2015). Kantian optimization: A microfoundation for cooperation. *Journal of Public Economics, 127*, 45–57.

Rubinstein, A. (2008). Comments on neuroeconomics. *Economic Philosophy, 24*, 485–494.

Sen, A. (1977). Rational fools: A critique of the behavioral foundation of utility. *Philosophy and Public Affairs, 6*, 317–347.

Sethi, R., & Somanathan, E. (1996). The evolution of social norms in common property resource use. *American Economics Review, 86*, 766–788.

Smith, A. (1790). The theory of moral sentiments. In K. Haakonssen (Ed.), (2002), *Cambridge texts in the history of philosophy* (pp. 1–411). Cambridge: Cambridge University Press.

Steiner, P. (2011). The creator, human conduct and the maximization of utility in Gossen's economic theory. *European Journal of History of Economic Thought, 18*, 353–379.

Tankersley, D., Stowe, C. J., & Huettel, S. (2007). Altruism is associated with an increased neuro response to agency. *Nature Neuroscience, 10*, 150–151.

Tomasello, M. (2014a). *A natural history of human thinking*. Cambridge: Harvard University Press.

Tomasello, M. (2014b). The ultra-social animal. *European Journal of Social Psychology, 44*, 187–194.

Tomasello, M. (2016). *A natural history of human morality*. Cambridge: Harvard University Press.

Part V
Positive Trade Theory

Chapter 14
A Geometric Proof of Complete Specialization in a Three-by-Three Ricardian World Economy

Makoto Tawada and Takeshi Ogawa

Abstract This short chapter provides an illustrative explanation of the Ricardian theory of comparative advantage. Making use of a geometric approach, the proofs of Jones' well-known theorem and its extended version by Shiozawa are reproduced in the three-country and three-good case. For the use of a geometric explanation, we employ the idea of Amano and Ikema on the goods price set which assures complete specialization.

Keywords Ricardian Theory of Comparative Advantage · Complete Specialization · Goods Price Vector · Jones · Shiozawa

14.1 Introduction

Although a number of positive trade theories have appeared in recent decades, the classical Ricardian theory of comparative advantage is still playing a basic and important role in explaining the patterns of trade. Jones (1961) once proposed the condition for the production pattern that the ith country specializes in the ith good, $(i = 1,\ldots,n)$ to be efficient in the world economy with n countries and n goods. Recently Shiozawa (2015) presented the complete version by an extension of Jones' theorem.

In this short chapter, we explain their theorems in a geometrical way in the three-country, three-good case. Thus the present chapter does not contain new ideas but it is hopefully useful for gaining a better understanding of the theorems mentioned above. Such an approach may be potentially useful in extending the Ricardian theory of comparative advantage as discussed below.

M. Tawada (✉)
Faculty of Economics, Aichi Gakuin University, Nagoya, Aichi, Japan
e-mail: mtawada2@dpc.agu.ac.jp

T. Ogawa
Faculty of Economics, Senshu University, Kawasaki-shi, Kanagawa-ken, Japan

© Springer Nature Singapore Pte Ltd. 2018
B. Tran-Nam et al. (eds.), *Recent Developments in Normative Trade Theory and Welfare Economics*, New Frontiers in Regional Science: Asian Perspectives 26, https://doi.org/10.1007/978-981-10-8615-1_14

It is commonly recognized that the Ricardian theory of comparative advantage should be extended to the case where tradable intermediate goods are allowed to exist. Despite this long recognition, virtually no decisive studies have yet appeared subsequent to Jones' influential paper. As discussed by Deardorff (2005), it is not so easy to unambiguously define a country's comparative advantage in an economy with intermediate goods.

As a first step to tackle this topic, it seems to be better to focus an economy with three countries and three goods, because we can approach the problem in a graphical manner like those studies by Amano (1966) and Ikema (1993). Although Ogawa (2012) paid attention to their illustrative techniques, his discussion is centered on the properties of production possibility sets. Our interest is placed directly on the proof of the necessary and sufficient condition for complete specialization. Our analysis might be useful for the investigation of complete specialization in a Ricardian economy with intermediate goods.

The remainder of this chapter is organized as follows: Sect. 14.2 discusses Jones' theorem (1961) in the three-by-three case. Then, in Sect. 14.3, we present a graphical proof of Shiozawa's theorem. The last section presents our conclusion.

14.2   Jones' and Shiozawa's Theorems

We consider a Ricardian world economy where n countries and n goods exist. Each country can produce n goods by the use of labor under constant returns to scale technologies. Each country is endowed with a certain amount of labor. We define l_j^i as the labor input for one unit production of the jth good in the ith country for $i, j = 1, 2, \ldots, n$. We also define the complete specialization as a production pattern such that every country specializes in one good in production and all goods are produced in the world. Moreover, the $i-i$ specialization is defined as the complete specialization such that the ith country specializes in the ith good in production for $i = 1, 2, \ldots, n$. In this economy, any point in the world production possibility frontier (PPF) is efficient in the sense that there is a world goods price vector which can make this point to be a world production equilibrium point. We now define an extreme point of the world PPF as follows.

Definition 14.1
Consider a point in the world PPF. The point is an extreme point if, in the world PPF, there are no other points which differ from that point and whose linear combination can express that point.

If we carefully read Jones' paper (1961, pp.164–166), we notice that Jones proved the following theorem.

Jones' Theorem *Consider a Ricardian economy where n countries and n goods exist. Then the world production point attained by the $i-i$ specialization is efficient, if and only if*

$$\prod_{i=1}^{n} l_i^i \leq \prod_{i=1}^{n} l_{\sigma(i)}^i \tag{14.1}$$

for all permutation functions $\sigma : \{1,\ldots,n\} \rightarrow \{1,\ldots,n\}$.

In order to prove this theorem, Jones employed the Hawkins and Simon condition. In his proof of the "if" part, however, he implicitly assumed that there is at least one efficient world production point attained by the complete specialization. This is because he showed that, for any $\prod_{i=1}^{n} l_{\sigma(i)}^i$ less than $\prod_{i=1}^{n} l_i^i$, the $i - \sigma(i)$ specialization is inefficient. Then he concludes that the $i-i$ specialization must be efficient.

Jones' theorem presupposed the existence of an efficient complete specialization. Shiozawa (2015), however, recently proved Jones' theorem without such a presupposition but under a stronger version. That is, he proved.

Shiozawa's Theorem *In the Ricardian economy with n countries and n goods, the world production point attained by* $i - i$ *specialization is an extreme point in the world production frontier if and only if*

$$\prod_{i=1}^{n} l_i^i < \prod_{i=1}^{n} l_{\sigma(i)}^i \tag{14.2}$$

for all permutation functions $\sigma : \{1,\ldots,n\} \rightarrow \{1,\ldots,n\}$ *except the identity function.*

Although Shiozawa proved his theorem by the application of Helly's theorem, we will prove the theorem in the three-by-three case by a direct method with the use of geometry in the next section.

14.3 A Geometric Proof of Shiozawa's Theorem in the Three-by-Three Case

We prove Shiozawa's theorem in the three-country and three-good case in a geometric way so we assume that $n = 3$. Let p_j stand for the world price of the jth good. We take the first good to be the numeraire so that $p_1 = 1$ always. Suppose that free trade prevails and the competitive world equilibrium price vector is $(1, p_2^*, p_3^*) > 0$. Then the condition that the first country specializes in the first good at the equilibrium is that

$$(p_2^*, p_3^*) \in A_1^1 \equiv \left\{ (p_2, p_3) > 0 \Big| \frac{1}{l_1^1} > \frac{p_2}{l_2^1} \text{ and } \frac{1}{l_1^1} > \frac{p_3}{l_3^1} \right\}. \tag{14.3}$$

Similarly the condition that the second country specializes in the second good is that

$$\left(p_2^*,p_3^*\right) \in A_2^2 \equiv \left\{ (p_2,p_3) > 0 \left| \frac{p_2}{l_2^2} > \frac{1}{l_1^2} \text{ and} \frac{p_2}{l_2^2} > \frac{p_3}{l_3^2} \right. \right\}. \tag{14.4}$$

Finally the condition that the third country specializes in the third good is that

$$\left(p_2^*,p_3^*\right) \in A_3^3 \equiv \left\{ (p_2,p_3) > 0 \left| \frac{p_3}{l_3^3} > \frac{1}{l_1^3} \text{ and} \frac{p_3}{l_3^3} > \frac{p_2}{l_2^3} \right. \right\}. \tag{14.5}$$

Therefore, the condition for the $i-i$ specialization to be attained as a competitive equilibrium is that

$$\left(p_2^*,p_3^*\right) \in A_1^1 \cap A_2^2 \cap A_3^3. \tag{14.6}$$

Such a case is illustrated as in Fig. 14.1, for example. In Fig. 14.1, the region of A_1^1 is the inner area of the rectangular $APBO$ and those of A_2^2 and A_3^3 are, respectively, the right hand side area of the line CQD and the upper area of the line ERF. Thus the shadow area exactly exhibits the intersection $A_1^1 \cap A_2^2 \cap A_3^3$.

First we show

$$\prod_{i=1}^{3} l_i^i < \prod_{i=1}^{3} l_{\sigma(i)}^i, \tag{14.7}$$

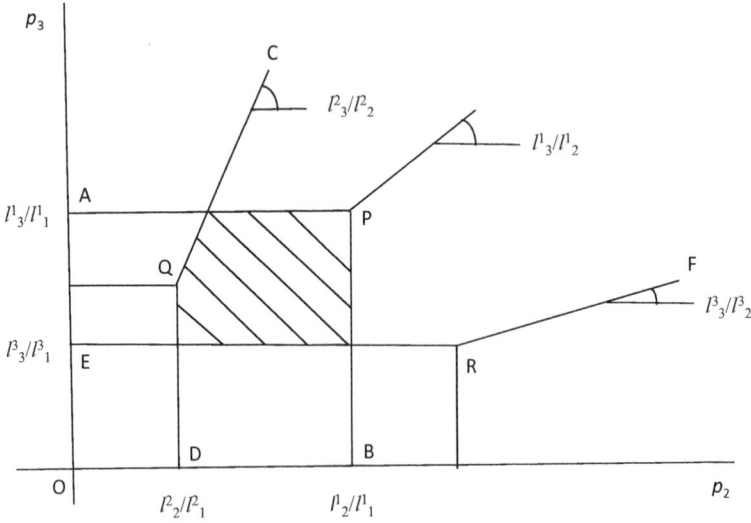

Fig. 14.1 The $i-i$ specialization as a competitive equilibrium

for all permutation function σ except the identity function, if there is $\left(p_2^*, p_3^*\right) > 0$ such that $\left(p_2^*, p_3^*\right) \in A_1^1 \cap A_2^2 \cap A_3^3$. The condition that $\left(p_2^*, p_3^*\right) \in A_1^1 \cap A_2^2 \cap A_3^3$ assures

$$l_2^1/l_1^1 > p_2^*, \tag{14.8a}$$

$$l_3^1/l_1^1 > p_3^*, \tag{14.8b}$$

$$l_2^2/l_1^2 < p_2^*, \tag{14.8c}$$

$$l_3^3/l_1^3 > p_3^*, \tag{14.8d}$$

$$l_3^2/l_2^2 > p_3^*/p_2^*, \text{ and} \tag{14.8e}$$

$$l_3^3/l_2^3 < p_3^*/p_2^*. \tag{14.8f}$$

In view of (14.8a) and (14.8c), we can derive $l_1^1 l_2^2 l_3^3 < l_2^1 l_1^2 l_3^3$. In view of (14.8b) and (14.8d), we can also derive $l_1^1 l_2^2 l_3^3 < l_3^1 l_2^2 l_1^3$. Moreover, (14.8e) and (14.8f) imply that $l_1^1 l_2^2 l_3^3 < l_1^1 l_3^2 l_2^3$. By the use of (14.8a), (14.8d), and (14.8e), we have

$$\frac{l_3^2}{l_2^2} > \frac{p_3^*}{p_2^*} > \frac{l_1^1 l_3^3}{l_2^1 l_1^3},$$ which implies $l_1^1 l_2^2 l_3^3 < l_2^1 l_3^2 l_1^3$. Likewise, making use of (14.8b), (14.8c), and (14.8f) yields $l_1^1 l_2^2 l_3^3 < l_3^1 l_1^2 l_2^3$. Hence we obtain (14.7).

Our next task is to prove the converse that, if (14.7) is true, the $i-i$ specialization point is an extreme point in the world production frontier. For this purpose, it is sufficient to show $A_1^1 \cap A_2^2 \cap A_3^3 \neq \varnothing$ under (14.7).

First we define

$$A_{21}^2 \equiv \left\{ (p_2, p_3) > 0 \middle| \frac{p_2}{l_2^2} > \frac{1}{l_1^2} \right\}, \tag{14.9a}$$

$$A_{23}^2 \equiv \left\{ (p_2, p_3) > 0 \middle| \frac{p_2}{l_2^2} > \frac{p_3}{l_3^2} \right\}, \tag{14.9b}$$

$$A_{31}^3 \equiv \left\{ (p_2, p_3) > 0 \middle| \frac{p_3}{l_3^3} > \frac{1}{l_1^3} \right\}, \text{ and} \tag{14.9c}$$

$$A_{32}^3 \equiv \left\{ (p_2, p_3) > 0 \middle| \frac{p_3}{l_3^3} > \frac{p_2}{l_2^3} \right\}. \tag{14.9d}$$

Then it is obvious that $A_2^2 = A_{21}^2 \cap A_{23}^2$ and $A_3^3 = A_{31}^3 \cap A_{32}^3$. Now we can establish

Lemma 14.1 *Under (14.7) we have the followings:*

(i) $p^1 \in A_{21}^2$ *and* $p^1 \in A_{31}^3$, *when* $p^1 \equiv \left(\dfrac{l_2^1}{l_1^1}, \dfrac{l_3^1}{l_1^1} \right)$.

(ii) $A_{23}^2 \cap A_{32}^3 \neq \varnothing$.

Proof

By the use of (14.7), we have $l_1^1 l_2^2 < l_2^1 l_1^2$ and $l_1^1 l_3^3 < l_3^1 l_1^3$. Thus we have $p^1 \in A_{21}^2$ and $p^1 \in A_{31}^3$. We also have $l_2^2 l_3^3 < l_3^2 l_2^3$ by (14.7), implying (ii).

QED

In view of Lemma 14.1(i), it is obvious that $A_1^1 \cap A_{21}^2 \cap A_{31}^3 \neq \varnothing$. This is illustrated in Fig. 14.2.

Our remaining task is to show $(A_1^1 \cap A_{21}^2 \cap A_{31}^3) \cap (A_{23}^2 \cap A_{32}^3) \neq \varnothing$. There are only two cases for $(A_1^1 \cap A_{21}^2 \cap A_{31}^3) \cap (A_{23}^2 \cap A_{32}^3) = \varnothing$. One is the case where the ray from the origin with the slope l_3^3/l_2^3 is steeper than the ray from the origin and passing through the point $S \equiv (l_2^2/l_1^2, l_3^1/l_1^1)$ in Fig. 14.2. The other is the case where the ray from the origin with the slope l_3^2/l_2^3 is milder than the ray from the origin and passing through the point $T \equiv (l_2^1/l_1^1, l_3^3/l_1^3)$ in Fig. 14.2. The first case is illustrated in Fig. 14.2. As is shown in the figure, $(A_{23}^2 \cap A_{32}^3) \cap (A_1^1 \cap A_{21}^2 \cap A_{31}^3) = \varnothing$ is clear.

Therefore, it is sufficient to show under (14.7) that these cases never appear. The slope of the ray passing through S is expressed as $l_3^1 l_1^2/l_2^2 l_1^1$. We have $l_1^1 l_2^2 l_3^3 < l_3^1 l_1^2 l_2^3$ from (14.7), which yields

$$\frac{l_3^1 l_1^2}{l_2^2 l_1^1} > \frac{l_3^3}{l_2^3} \tag{14.10}$$

So the first case can never occur. In a similar manner we can easily show that the second case can neither occur. Thus we can conclude that

$$A_1^1 \cap A_{21}^2 \cap A_{23}^2 \cap A_{31}^3 \cap A_{32}^3 = A_1^1 \cap A_2^2 \cap A_3^3 \neq \varnothing \tag{14.11}$$

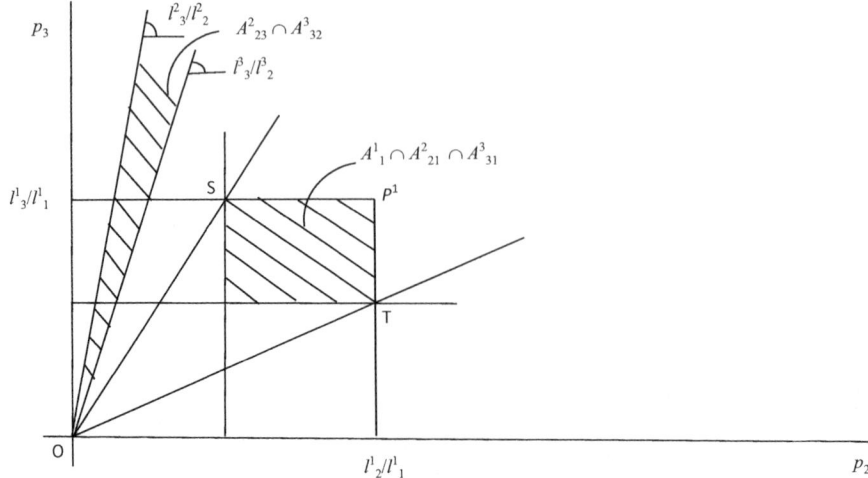

Fig. 14.2 The proof of sufficiency $A_1^1 \cap A_2^2 \cap A_3^3 \neq \varnothing$

14.4 Concluding Remarks

As mentioned in the introduction of this chapter, our analysis does not reveal anything new but provides a graphical explanation of Shiozawa's theorem in a special case of a three-by-three model. In a similar manner we can also prove Jones' theorem without the existence assumption, that is, $\prod_{i=1}^{3} l_i^i \leq \prod_{i=1}^{3} l_{\sigma(i)}^i$, for all permutation functions σ, if and only if $\overline{A_1^1} \cap \overline{A_2^2} \cap \overline{A_3^3} \neq \varnothing$, where $\overline{A_i^i}$ is the closure of A_i^i, for $i = 1, 2, 3$.

An important yet untouched issue of the Ricardian principle of comparative advantage is to develop a theory to consider the case where tradable produced goods can be used as intermediate goods in production. This extension is particularly important since the weight of the intermediate good trade is remarkably growing in the contemporary world trade. Once, however, we allow this possibility, the analysis seems to become extremely difficult. Even in the three-by-three case, we cannot exclude multiple extreme points in the world PPF. One example of that case is shown by Higashida (2005). This suggests that it is difficult to express the principle of comparative advantage by a simple technological condition and that the analysis better starts with the local theory. So the first step to tackle this theme is to consider the three-by-three case and to employ the geometrical approach along the line explored in the present chapter.

Acknowledgment We would like to express our thanks to an anonymous reviewer for very useful comments which have vastly improved our chapter.

References

Amano, A. (1966). Intermediate goods and the theory of comparative advantage: A two-country, three commodity case. *Weltwirtschaftriches Archiv, 96*, 340–345.

Deardorff, A. V. (2005). Ricardian comparative advantage with intermediate inputs. *North American Journal of Economics and Finance, 16*, 11–34.

Higashida, K. (2005). Intermediate goods and the patterns of international division of labor: The many-country and many-good model. In J. Ishikawa & T. Furusawa (Eds.), *Development of international trade theory* (pp. 289–302). Takasaki: Bunshin-do. (in Japanese).

Ikema, M. (1993). Determination of the patterns of international division of labor. *Hitotsubashi Ronso, 110*, 873–894. (in Japanese).

Jones, R.W. (1961), Comparative advantage and the theory of tariffs: A multi-country, multi-commodity model, Review of Economic Studies, 28, pp. 161−175.

Ogawa, T. (2012). Classification of the three-country, three-good Ricardian model. *Economics Bulletin, 32*, 639–647.

Shiozawa, Y. (2015). International trade theory and exotic algebras. *Evolutionary and Institutional Economics Review, 12*, 177–212.

Index

© Springer Nature Singapore Pte Ltd. 2018
B. Tran-Nam et al. (eds.), *Recent Developments in Normative Trade Theory and Welfare Economics*, New Frontiers in Regional Science: Asian Perspectives 26,
https://doi.org/10.1007/978-981-10-8615-1

Printed by Printforce, the Netherlands